INSIDE OUT

A BIBLICAL AND PRACTICAL GUIDE TO SELF-LEADERSHIP

by

BRUCE HILLS

CHI–Books
PO Box 6462
Upper Mt Gravatt, Brisbane
QLD 4122
Australia

www.chibooks.org
publisher@chibooks.org

Inside Out — *A Biblical and Practical Guide to Self-leadership*

Print ISBN: 978-0-6480116-0-6
eBook ISBN: 978-0-6480116-1-3

Printed in Australia, United Kingdom and the United States of America.Distributed in the USA and Internationally by Ingram Book Group and Amazon. Also available from: Bookdeposity.co.uk and others like Koorong.com in Australia.

Distribution of eBook version: Amazon Kindle, Apple iBooks, Koorong.com and others like Barnes & Noble NOOK and KOBO.

Editorial assistance: Anne Hamilton.
Cover design: Dave Stone
Layout: Jonathan Gould

DEDICATION

Heartfelt thanks to my wife, Fiona, who has faithfully and lovingly journeyed with me through life and leadership. I wouldn't be who I am or where I am without her selfless, sacrificial support.

ACKNOWLEDGEMENTS

Special thanks to Karen Pack, who edited the manuscript and made many very helpful recommendations. I am grateful also to Alana Robinson for drawing the diagrams.

WHAT OTHERS ARE SAYING ABOUT THIS BOOK ...

Bruce Hills has been a ministry leader and a personal friend for many years. As a leader he has been tested and shaped in the crucible of numerous leadership roles over many years. Clearly, here is a man who knows what he is talking about! He has written a book of tremendous value for every person in ministry intentional about being the best leader they can be for good and for God. Inside Out is an honest and frank approach to an often missed, yet crucial part of leadership, namely the leaders role and efforts in their own formation. This book offers a comprehensive, deeply grounded yet easy to read multi-dimensional approach to leadership formation and development–a must read for those serious about 'sharpening the saw'! Not only do I gladly endorse this book I would urge ministry leaders of today and tomorrow to embrace this as an essential resource–doing so will greatly benefit the Kingdom and ministry as a whole.

Dr Johan Roux

President, CEO of Tabor College, Adelaide – Australia

Bruce Hills has been demonstrating leadership excellence for decades now in a variety of contexts and situations. This book digs deep, showing that leading ourselves well is the foundation for all credible and impacting leadership. Bruce takes the reader on a journey of transformation that could be truly life changing. Highly recommended.

Mark Conner

Former Senior Minister, CityLife Church, Melbourne – Australia

Inside Out carries a simple yet profound core truth. Lead from the "Inside out rather than top down". I enjoyed every chapter as it hit hard the need to earn leadership respect rather than demand it. I've always loved Bruce's teaching and training insights and style. And this book does not disappoint. It is written in a way that communicates cross-culturally and to the religious or non-religious mindset. This is a very valuable read.

Mal Macleod

Director Equip Ministries International, Senior Pastor, South West Christian Church, Melbourne – Australia

Leadership starts with leading yourself. If you can't lead yourself effectively, the hope of leading others will end in tragedy. Bruce Hills uses *Inside Out* to walk alongside you as a fellow leader, sharing what he has learned about leading himself through both victories and pain. Packed with powerful, practical and Biblical principles, mixed with personal stories and examples, *Inside Out* is an excellent handbook for every aspiring and practicing ministry leader.

I've known Bruce Hills for more than 25 years and I can say with confidence that he has been living these principles throughout his ministry and personal life. It is my privilege and joy to recommend *Inside Out* to you. If you take the time to read and to apply these principles, you will not only become a better leader but you'll also enjoy the journey more.

Jossy Chacko

Founder and President, Empart, Melbourne – Australia

INSIDE OUT

A BIBLICAL AND PRACTICAL GUIDE TO SELF-LEADERSHIP

by

BRUCE HILLS

CHI
BOOKS

By the same author

PRAYING WITH POWER
How to Engage in a Deeper Level of Personal Prayer by Praying the Scriptures

FEARPROOF
How to Overcome the Paralyzing Power of Fear – Exploring the 'do not fear' statements of the Old Testament

You can purchase other titles by Bruce Hills from:
www.amazon.com
www.koorong.com.au
www.bookdepository.co.uk

eBooks also available from Amazon Kindle; Apple iBookstore; Koorong.com and others like Barnes & Noble NOOK and KOBO

CONTENTS

FOREWORD

I have long believed that after faith, leadership is the single most important function in our societies whatever our culture.

Find a good school and it almost invariably has a good leader as the principal and so the maxim holds true for Christian ministries and churches and even nations. But throughout the world leadership is under pressure. At one level it is suddenly made disproportionately more difficult by a social media that strips character to the bone on the slightest anonymous whim and leaves an un-erasable memory of every mistake, whether real or contrived.

In the West, nations that once rushed to honour leaders now reject a "political class" seen as not motivated by a sense of duty and service, but self-interest and power. Disillusionment has destabilised long trusted political systems and in parts of the world has left a legacy of enduring violence. At the same time the worldwide church is reeling under the weight of sexual abuse scandals that increasingly reveal a failure of leadership in both the broken trust of the abusers and the failure of church leadership to deal with it.

Of course for any Christian it should come as no surprise that if leadership is so crucial to the effective work of the church and the peace of man, that Satan would give it a good deal of attention. What a disproportionate effect when his target is a leader.

However any honest assessment of this disillusionment with leadership must also see the failure to find genuineness and integrity in leadership as a consistent theme. It is leadership turning on the fact that it has always been an art not a science, always something that dealt with the spirit not the mind and is therefore difficult to box in the convenient three step methodologies beloved of our busy world.

In over forty-five years of leadership I have seen time and time again the most unlikely leader in the world's terms win the willing co-operation and commitment of his or her team. They might have failed the Hollywood image test disastrously, not been particularly articulate or necessarily as good professionally as another. Yet they were followed and even protected by those they led, because they were genuine. People knew as a result they could be trusted.

If genuineness and trustworthiness are the redeeming currency of leadership, then the challenge by Bruce to build our leadership from the *inside out* is a timely one. For Christians of course it assumes that Christ is at our core as individuals and that leadership fashioned and lived from there will be not only effective but attractive.

Unashamedly applying the positive and negative lessons of more than thirty years in leadership, Bruce describes a Biblically centered approach that not only offers Christians the chance to develop effective and resilient individual leadership, but one by which the art of leadership itself can be redeemed. I strongly recommend it.

Jim Wallace AM

Brigadier (ret), former commander of the Australian SAS, Special Forces and the Army's Mechanised Brigade and more recently Founder of the Australian Christian Lobby

'You are the most difficult person you will lead.'

Bill Hybels, author; founding pastor of Willow Creek Community Church, Chicago[1]

'In reading the lives of great people, I found that the first victory they won was over themselves.'

Harry S Truman, 33rd President, USA[2]

1 http://www.azquotes.com.
2 http://www.quoteparadise.net.

INTRODUCTION

It's not scientifically possible, but wouldn't it be great to travel through time? If you could choose any period of time and any place, where would you go? What year would you return to? Is there some famous historical event you'd like to witness firsthand?

If I could time travel, if only one time, I'd like to travel back to 1983 and talk to the younger version of myself. He was a lot skinnier, much better looking and far less teachable. Still I would like to reason with him and prepare him for the journey of leadership ahead.

What would I say to my younger self? Essentially, I'd say everything I've written in this book. I wish someone had spoken to me about the many issues I'll raise in this book. It would have saved me a lot of heartache, a lot of unnecessary struggles and a lot of painful life lessons. On the other hand, it would have helped me to get my life and leadership together a lot more quickly.

Of course, time travel is *not* possible. As much as I would love to go back in time and counsel myself, it can't happen. But I can pass on what I have learned to guide the tiers of leaders who are following.

Leading from the inside out is another way of saying that we must be leading ourselves, so we can effectively lead others.

That is what this book is all about. It is a Biblical and practical guide for how leaders of all ages can get their life and leadership together. Blending the wise principles of Scripture with examples from Biblical leaders, along with practical experiences from contemporary leaders and my own life, we're going to explore how we lead ourselves.

In Christian leadership, we don't primarily lead from the top down (hierarchical), but from the inside out (incarnational). In other words, the *way* we lead and influence people, in a ministry context, is not *just* by our words, decisions, directives or position, but by the authenticity and example of our lives–who we are *within*.

Confidence and trust in leaders doesn't automatically come by virtue of their position, title or gifting, but from the consistent fruit of their Christlike character, competency in leadership and the follow-ability of their lives. The key to attaining credibility and authority as a leader, therefore, is to lead from the inside out.

Leading from the inside out is another way of saying that we must be leading *ourselves*, so we can effectively lead others. Exercising leadership in and over our own lives is called 'self-leadership'.

Before offering a working definition of self-leadership, I need to make a qualifying statement. I am writing this book to *Christian* leaders who are working in a ministry context. For the sake of clarity, whenever I use the generic term of leader or leadership, I am actually referring to ministry leaders–those actively serving in local churches or parachurch ministries. This distinction is significant because, when it comes to self-leadership, there can be a world of difference between secular leaders and Christian leaders in terms of their motivation, ambition, attitudes, vision, goals or measurement of success.

Working definition of self-leadership

Throughout this book, the term *self-leadership* is based on the following working definition:

> Self-leadership, in a ministry leadership context, is the intentional practice of disciplining, regulating and developing our lives and leadership so that we can effectively lead ourselves and others to fulfill God's ultimate purposes of maturity and mission.

Goal and motivation of self-leadership

The ultimate and ongoing goal of self-leadership is to be Spirit-led. In response to God's call upon our lives to lead, we seek to do whatever is necessary, by God's grace and power, to *be* what he has called us to be and *do* what he's called us to do. This is only possible by yielding and cooperating with the Spirit's work *in* and *through* us. Self-leadership, therefore, is taking disciplined responsibility to surrender to, and align ourselves with, the work of God's Spirit within us.

To achieve this goal, self-leadership requires self-motivation. We do not depend on others to motivate us; we motivate ourselves. However, our motivation is not a ruthless, selfish or ambitious goal to 'climb the (leadership) ladder'. On the contrary, self-leadership is motivated by deep convictions derived from Scripture, a burning passion to serve Jesus, and a compelling desire to be the best leader we can be for Jesus.

Gulf Crisis

A leader can acquire and cultivate skills to competently lead others but, unless there is a correlation between their practice of faith and their practice of leadership, there will be an irreconcilable credibility gap. If there is an incongruence between a leader's character and skills, words and actions, profession and practice, or public and private lives, then people's confidence and trust will inevitably and eventually erode.

Diagram 1. Gulf crisis

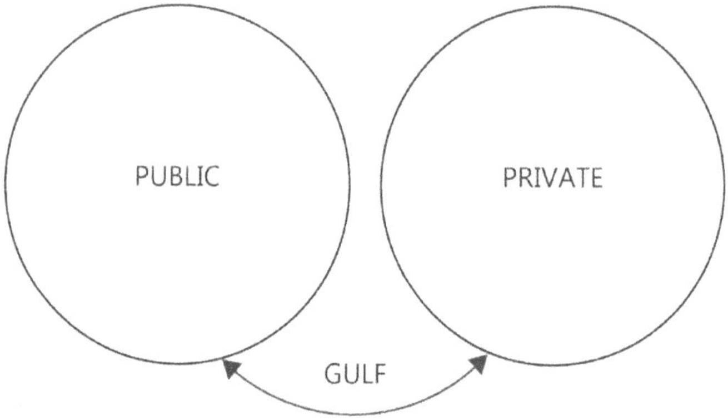

In diagram 1 above, the two circles represent our *public* life and our *private* life. Our *public* life is what everybody sees and perceives–our *public* ministry, visible conduct and the image we portray. Our *private* life is what we are unobserved, at home, in the dark and within. If there is a gulf between what a leader is privately and how they depict themselves publicly, this disparity is often where leaders unravel or fail. It's as if they're living two separate, disconnected lives: one in public, quite another in private. The danger of the 'gulf crisis' is that, when the duplicity and deceit is exposed, people become disillusioned and distrustful of leaders. It can sometimes take a long time for disenchanted people to trust leaders again.

Diagram 2. Eclipse

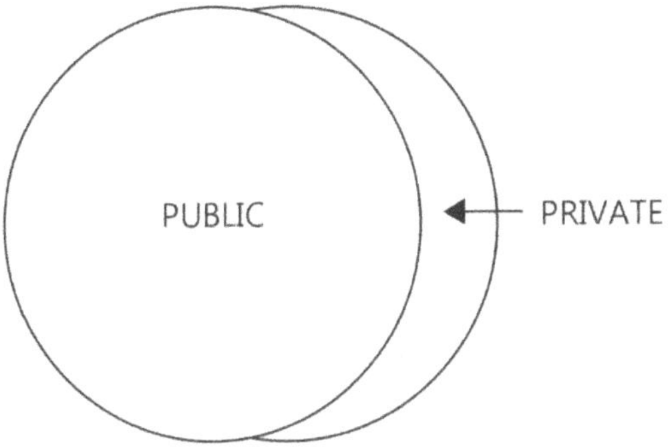

What is needed is an *eclipse* of the two worlds, as diagram 2 illustrates. Our *public* life needs to be an expression and extension of all that we are privately. The degree to which these two worlds eclipse is the degree of our authenticity as leaders, and the degree of our spiritual integrity.

You'll notice, however, in the diagram above, that it's not a perfect eclipse. Why? Because there are no perfect leaders. We *all* have our frailties, predispositions and faults. The lesson from this is to be on guard in those areas of vulnerability and frailty, so that we do not spiral down into the 'gulf' and potentially destroy our leadership.

Jesus–the embodiment of the 'eclipse'

The Lord Jesus perfectly embodies the harmony of his private and public life. He had no grey areas, no inconsistencies and no duplicity. All that he was publicly, he was privately.

After his baptism, he was led by the Spirit into the wilderness to be tested by the devil (Luke 4:1–2). It was in his private

> **Self-leadership gives credibility and legitimacy to our leadership.**

world–when no-one else was watching–that Jesus overcame the tempter and temptation (Luke 4:3–13), so that, when he returned to his public ministry, he did so in the power of the Holy Spirit (Luke 4:14).

The application here is that the Lord is working in our private (inner, unseen) life to mould and form us to be effective in our public (outer, visible) ministry. God uses the ordinary, common irritations of everyday living to expose our weaknesses, transform our character and thus equip us to be effective in leadership.

Why is self-leadership important?

To me, there are four compelling reasons why self-leadership is crucial for effective leadership.

First, as we have seen, self-leadership gives *credibility and legitimacy* to our *leadership position and practice*. Leading from the inside out gives us credibility, believability and follow-ability.

Second, one of the principal ways we lead and influence people is by the *example* of our own life, as shown by the examples of Jesus (John 13:15; Philippians 2:5; 1 Peter 2:21), Paul (1 Corinthians 4:16; 1 Corinthians 11:1; Philippians 3:17), and the Old Testament prophets (James 5:10). Because of his relatively young age and inexperience, Timothy was instructed by Paul to neutralize any devaluing of his leadership by setting '*...an example for the believers in speech, in life, in love, in faith and in purity*' (1 Timothy 4:12; cf. Titus 2:7). Self-leadership sets an example of how to conduct one's Christian life and service.

Third, we can only *reproduce in others* what has been, or is being, produced in us. There's a well-known adage that states,

'You can teach what you know, but you reproduce what you are.' We can't lead others where we've never been before. By proactively leading ourselves, we are better equipped to nurture and develop other leaders.

Fourth, self-leadership is the way by which we take *personal responsibility to grow* as a leader. The sole prerogative for the maturity of our character, the development of our leadership and ministry is entirely our own. Leaders who actively lead themselves take the initiative to develop themselves.

Biblical framework

This exploration of self-leadership will primarily be grounded in Paul's letters to Timothy and Titus, which are commonly called the Pastoral Epistles. Both Timothy and Titus were relatively young, emerging leaders in need of guidance, encouragement and wisdom. Aside from giving them directives on how to handle specific pastoral issues, Paul focused a great deal of his attention on their personal development as godly leaders. It is from these specific instructions this book is formed.

Five basic areas of self-leadership

To dissect the topic of self-leadership, this book will examine five inter-related categories of self-leadership.

1. Self-awareness – having an accurate and honest understanding of ourselves
2. Self-discipline – exercising personal discipline in all areas of our life and leadership
3. Self-control – internally regulating and exercising self-control in our life
4. Self-development – intentionally growing our life and leadership
5. Self-sacrifice – paying whatever price is necessary to fulfill the will of God and be what God has called us to be

These five categories will form the sections of this book, in which each will be explored, unpacked and applied.

Self-development verses spiritual growth

One of the objections I occasionally hear in opposition to the language of self-leadership runs along the lines of, 'God is the one who calls someone to leadership. God is the one who gives the person a gift of leadership. It is God who develops the leader. Therefore, growth comes from God. It is not *self*-leadership; it is *God* who is leading the leader.' I wholeheartedly agree with this line of reasoning. Growth *does* come from God. As leaders, we all operate under the sovereign reign of the Father, the Lordship of Jesus and the empowering of the Holy Spirit. We should lead others as we are being led. We should empower others as we have been empowered. *However*, there are some things that we can do to increase and enhance our gifts, skills and effectiveness as a *response* to God's call and gifts. In doing so, we will be better equipped to serve God in leadership.

When I first started out in ministry, I knew virtually nothing about *how* to prepare a sermon or *how* to communicate. Consequently, a short time later I went to Bible College, I attended preaching seminars, I read a lot of books on the art of preaching, I watched myself on video (as it was then) for self-analysis, and I sought critique from seasoned preachers. In this way, I progressively improved. The development of my preaching gift and skill was *my* initiative and *my* response to the call and gift of God in my life. I worked on *myself* so I could become more effective.

Reflection

After each point in each section I have added one or a number of questions for personal reflection. The purpose of including these questions is for you to take some time to honestly and transparently assess yourself, then, in response, to formulate whatever actions or adjustments may be necessary to grow in that area. If appropriate, you may wish to invite your spouse, close friend, ministry leader or pastor to help you in this process. Please don't just gloss over the questions, but interact with them. In this way, you're more likely to maximize the impact of the point.

In Section Four of this book, which addresses self-development, one of the things I will suggest is to draft a growth plan for your life and leadership. Utilizing the questions in this book will help considerably in formulating a growth plan and to prioritize which areas of your life or leadership need attention. My goal (and prayer) in writing this book is not to add to your knowledge of leadership, but to help in whatever way I can, to *develop* your leadership.

Do your best to be your best

I'll conclude this introduction with a story I first read nearly three decades ago. I read the following excerpt in Gordon MacDonald's book, *Ordering Your Private World*, but it was originally in Polmar and Allen's biography of Admiral Hyman Rickover, the head of the United States Nuclear Navy from 1949-1982. By all accounts, Admiral Rickover (1900-1986) was a controversial man. He personally interviewed and selected every prospective officer to serve on a US nuclear vessel. Interviewees would often leave the Admiral's office 'shaking in fear, anger, or total intimidation.'[1]

Former US President, Jimmy Carter (1924–), the 39th President, once served in the US Navy, and applied to be an officer on a nuclear submarine. To do so, he too had to be interviewed by Rickover, whom he'd never met before. Carter wrote:

1 Gordon MacDonald, *Ordering Your Private* World (Surrey, England: HarperCollins, 1993), 103.

> ...we sat in a large room by ourselves for more than two hours, and he let me choose any subjects I wished to discuss. Very carefully, I chose those about which I knew most at the time–current events, seamanship, music, literature, naval tactics, electronics, gunnery–and he began to ask me a series of questions of increasing difficulty. In each instance, he soon proved that I knew relatively little about the subject I had chosen.
>
> He always looked right into my eyes, and he never smiled. I was saturated with cold sweat.
>
> Finally, he asked a question and I thought I could redeem myself. He asked, "How did you stand in your class at the naval Academy?" Since I had completed my sophomore year at Georgia Tech before entering Annapolis as a plebe, I had done very well, and I swelled my chest with pride and answered, "Sir, I stood fifty-ninth in a class of 820!" I sat back to await the congratulations–which never came. Instead, the question: "Did you do your best?" I started to say, "Yes, sir," but I remembered who this was and recalled several of the many times at the Academy when I could have learned more about our allies, our enemies, weapons, strategy, and so forth. I was just human. I finally gulped and said, "No, sir, I didn't always do my best."
>
> He looked at me for a long time, and then turned his chair around to end the interview. He asked one final question, which I have never been able to forget–or to answer. He said, "Why not?" I sat there for a while, shaken, and then slowly left the room.[2]

That same question, 'Why not', shook me to the core. Let me ask you similar questions as a leader. Have you given Jesus

2 Norman Polmar and Thomas B. Allen, *Rickover: Controversy and Genius* (New York: Simon & Schuster, 1962), 267.

your best? If not, why not? Have you done your best to be the best leader you can be for Jesus? If not, why not?

This book is an opportunity to work on yourself and develop your life and leadership through the exercise of self-leadership. I urge you to give leadership your best to be the best you can be for the Lord.

SECTION ONE

Self-Awareness

'Watch your life and doctrine closely' (1 Timothy 4:16).

'Keep watch over yourselves…' (Acts 20:28).

'Know thyself' (Socrates).

One of the foundational areas of self-leadership is self-awareness. In essence, to be a self-aware leader means that we have an accurate and honest understanding of ourselves. It is important that we, as leaders, *know* ourselves. This is vital for our personal growth and leadership development, and also so that we can help other emerging leaders to know *themselves*. This self-discovery comes through self-reflection.

To help in the process, this section will focus on a number of key areas of self-awareness that Paul indirectly highlighted in his letters to Timothy. They are not in order of priority, but in the order in which they unfold in the two epistles. I've identified 12 (though there may be many more), and put 4 in each chapter of this section for ease of reading.

Chapter One

Self-Awareness (part one)

To help in the process of understanding ourselves more clearly, the three chapters of this opening section will work their way through 12 areas of self-awareness I've gleaned from Paul's letters to Timothy.

A. Know our *CALLING*

'Paul, an ***apostle*** *of Christ Jesus* ***by the command of God*** *our Savior* ***and of Christ Jesus*** *our hope'* (1 Timothy 1:1; cf. 2 Timothy 1:1, emphases mine).

'And of this gospel I was ***appointed*** *a* ***herald*** *and an* ***apostle*** *and a* ***teacher****'* (2 Timothy 1:11, emphases mine).

A first area of self-awareness for us, as leaders, is to be conscious of our calling. God calls all his people to serve him and one another, but he specifically calls some people of his choosing to Christian leadership, gifting them accordingly (Ephesians 4:11; Romans 12:8).

> **The call of God to Christian leadership is grounded in the sovereign will and prerogative of God.**

The call of God to Christian leadership is based on a

number of factors that are all grounded in the sovereign will (providence) and prerogative of God:

- God sovereignly calls the *person* of his choosing (Jeremiah 1:5; Luke 6:12–13)
- God sovereignly appoints the person to the specific *purpose* (role, function) of his choosing (e.g. evangelist, pastor, teacher, missionary) (Ephesians 4:11; Acts 13:1-3)
- God sovereignly positions them in the specific *place* (context) of his choosing. For example, Paul was chosen as an apostle to the Gentiles (Acts 9:15; 26:17–18), whereas Timothy was called to pastor in Ephesus (1 Timothy 1:3)
- God's sovereign calling is generally recognized and affirmed by human instrumentality (Acts 13:2–3; 1 Timothy 4:14; 2 Timothy 1:6).

Writing about his call to Gospel ministry, Paul stated that he was appointed (called) as a *'herald, apostle and teacher'* (1 Timothy 2:7; 2 Timothy 1:11).

Throughout his epistles to Timothy and Titus, Paul exhorted his spiritual sons to fulfill *their* calling to be:

Preachers of God's Word (2 Timothy 4:1):

- By correctly interpreting and applying Scripture (2 Timothy 2:15)
- By focusing especially on Gospel proclamation (2 Timothy 2:8–9)
- By skillfully and patiently encouraging and correcting people (2 Timothy 4:2).

Teachers of sound and uncompromising truth (Titus 1:13; 2:1–13):

- By refuting false doctrines and spurious teaching (1 Timothy 1:3; 2 Timothy 2:14)

- By providing practical instruction for how the various demographics of the church should conduct their lives (1 Timothy 5:1-20; Titus 2:1-10)
- By unapologetically exercising the authority of Scripture (Titus 2:15)
- By showing '*...integrity, seriousness and soundness of speech...*' in teaching (Titus 2:7-8).

Pastors of local congregations committed:

- To appointing and developing leaders (Titus 1:5; 2 Timothy 2:2)
- To lovingly discharging all the duties associated with pastoring (2 Timothy 4:5)
- To teaching, correcting and exhorting their congregations to know how to '*...conduct themselves in God's household*' (1 Timothy 3:14).

Leaders of unquestionable and exemplary character, conduct, relationships (1 Timothy 4:12), sound teaching (Titus 2:7-8) and focus (1 Timothy 1:3; Titus 1:5).

When I was an eleven-year-old boy, I attended a children's camp at Burleigh Heads, Queensland. During one of the after-service prayer meetings, the Holy Spirit touched my life in a powerful and life-changing way. At that moment, I knew in my heart that I was called to ministry. Given my young age, I naturally didn't understand all that was involved or what that meant. At the time, I interpreted the call in the only paradigm of ministry I'd ever seen, which was to pastor and preach. Later on, however, God's specific call on my life began to be clarified and enlarged as the expressions and context of the call continually expanded. I started off in ministry as a youth pastor in one local church, whereas now I lead a missions' agency impacting thousands of people globally.

It's important that we seek to be *aware* of God's call upon our lives, as best we can understand it, then endeavor to function in that call with the enablement of God's grace and gifts.

Self-reflection:

In your own words, how would you define the call of God?

In your own experience, how did you receive the call of God?

In what ways has your call been affirmed by others, especially leaders?

What do you specifically feel the Lord has called you to do?

How fully are you fulfilling your calling?

B. Know our *SPIRITUAL HERITAGE*

'To Timothy ***my true son*** *in the faith...'* (1 Timothy 1:2, emphasis mine).

'I have been reminded of your sincere faith, which first lived in your ***grandmother*** *Lois and in your* ***mother*** *Eunice...'* (2 Timothy 1:5, emphases mine).

'...how from ***infancy*** *you have known the holy Scriptures...'* (2 Timothy 3:15, emphasis mine).

A second area of self-awareness is to identify the people the Lord brought into our lives to shape our early development.

In some cases, like Timothy's, it may be a Christian parent. After his customary introduction, Paul began his second letter to Timothy by reminiscing about the godly heritage of his mother and grandmother (2 Timothy 1:5).

Luke tells us that Timothy was the son of a mixed marriage. His father was Greek and, presumably, an unbeliever, but his mother, Eunice, was Jewish (Acts 16:1). Timothy's grandmother,

Lois, was also a Jewess. All three (Lois, Eunice and Timothy) had become Christians, most likely during Paul's first visit to Lystra (cf. Acts 14:6-7). It appears that both Eunice and Lois had expressed a devout and sincere love for God *before* their conversion to the Lord. It was this genuine religious heritage that cultivated the soil of their hearts to believe and receive the gospel. These godly women had instructed Timothy in the Old Testament so that, Paul observed, from his '*infancy*' he had '*known the holy Scriptures*' (2 Timothy 3:15). Paul wrote of the '*sincere faith*' of all three generations (2 Timothy 1:5).

I was raised in a pastor's home. I wouldn't have recognized it at the time, but my natural father became my *spiritual* father. When the call of God was awakened in my life in the early 1980s, I realized that I had a strong philosophy of ministry already ingrained in my life through him. I couldn't say he discipled me intentionally, but he discipled me indirectly by his example. I saw how he lived. I listened to him pray. I watched his reactions under pressure. I heard his inspired preaching and teaching. I witnessed the impact of the gift of prophecy through his ministry. I lived in an environment of faith. His example laid the foundations of my future ministry and leadership.

Many leaders, however, may not have been raised in a Christian environment, and may not have had a godly heritage. In this case, the Lord provides spiritual mothers or fathers who will nurture their initial formation as leaders and ministers. Timothy's mother and grandmother may have been instrumental in laying the foundation for him to come to faith, but it was the apostle Paul who was instrumental in nurturing his early ministry formation.

On Paul's second missionary journey, the church leaders at Lystra and Iconium commended Timothy (Acts 16:1-3). It seems that Paul embraced him as an apprentice missionary, and adopted him as a spiritual son (1 Timothy 1:2; 2 Timothy 1:2).

Their relationship from this point–including the companionship (Philippians 2:22), letters (1 & 2 Timothy), prayers (2 Timothy 1:3), correction (2 Timothy 1:6), instruction (1 Timothy 4:6), delegated tasks (1 Corinthians 4:16–17; 1 Timothy 1:3) and encouragement–must have had a powerful molding effect on Timothy's life and leadership. It strengthened and sustained him in the developmental years of his ministry.

In every one of our lives there would have been a Paul who saw something in us and fostered it. In some cases, it may not be as intentional as Paul with Timothy, but they may have provided a model that we were able to imitate. They knowingly or unknowingly, intentionally or unintentionally, directly or indirectly shaped our philosophy of ministry and many of our early leadership practices.

In my own experience, it wasn't until some years after acknowledging God's call on my life that another leader–my youth pastor, Gavin–affirmed the call and actively cultivated it. It was through his belief and confidence *in* me, and the opportunities he provided *for* me, that I began the early steps of leadership. I am profoundly grateful to these two great men (my Dad and Gavin) for shaping my early development.

Self-reflection:

Write down the names of at least 2 people who were used by God to directly or indirectly shape your leadership.

Briefly write down in what ways those people nurtured you.

In what ways did your family help or hinder your spiritual development?

Why do you think there are a lack of spiritual fathers and mothers in today's church (cf. 1 Corinthians 4:15)?

Who have you identified as a Timothy that you could disciple?

C. Know our *TASK AT HAND* (current responsibilities)

*'...stay there in **Ephesus so that** you may command certain men not to teach false doctrines any longer...'* (1 Timothy 1:3, emphasis mine).

A third area of self-awareness is to understand our current task, role and ministry context. In Timothy's case, it was to pastor the church at Ephesus (1 Timothy 1:3). The reason Paul appointed him there was to specifically guard against false teachers and false doctrines (1 Timothy 1:3-4), which were causing controversy, confusion and distraction in the Ephesian church (1 Timothy 1:4-7).

> To be effective in leadership we need to clearly know: where we're called to serve; what we're presently called to do; and why we're doing it.

To be effective in leadership, each of us would be encouraged to clearly know:

- *Where* we're called to serve (location)
- *What* we're presently called to do (commission)
- *Why* we're doing it (motivation).

Without the awareness of these three things we may potentially flounder, feel unfulfilled, lose motivation and eventually become disengaged. By way of example, around mid-March 2013, I was running a training seminar at a retreat centre about an hour out of Dhaka, Bangladesh's heavily populated capital. Another Christian ministry was also sharing the venue. After one meal, I met a very gifted and capable couple from the other group who were seeking guidance about their future. As our discussion progressed, it became clear to me that this couple was serving in a ministry that they *could* do because of their skills and experience, but didn't feel *called* to do. As a consequence, they were extremely frustrated, even though their ministry was keeping them occupied and was worthwhile. I suggested they not just do what they *can* do, but focus on what they were *commissioned* to do. When I asked them what was in their heart–what they felt called to do–they lit up and became very animated as they articulated their passion. As they talked, it became obvious to the three of us that they needed to transition their ministry to concentrate on their calling. Our short, but fruitful, conversation ended with this couple being relieved of an unnecessary burden and re-envisioned about their future.

Self-reflection:

Write down your current leadership role.

What does it entail?

With what degree of certainty can you say you're serving in the right area of ministry at this time?

Please write the reasons for your response.

If you're serving in the wrong area of ministry, what steps can you take to change to the right area?

D. Know our *PROPHECIES*

'Timothy, my son, I give you this instruction in keeping with the ***prophecies*** *once made about you…'* (1 Timothy 1:18, emphasis mine).

A fourth area of self-awareness is to be mindful of the prophetic utterances which have been spoken over our lives.

From the two epistles to Timothy, we discover that Paul, along with the body of Ephesian elders, publicly affirmed and commissioned (ordained) Timothy for ministry (1 Timothy

4:14; 2 Timothy 1:6). As hands were being laid upon him, visibly signifying his being set apart (sanctified) for ministry, prophetic utterances were spoken over his life.[1] 1 Timothy 4:14 suggests that Timothy actually received a gift–a divinely given capacity and enablement to discharge his call–as the prophetic message was being spoken, accompanied by the laying on of hands. This suggests that prophecies and gifting are strongly linked.

The content of the prophecies is unknown to us but, in 1 Timothy 1:18–19, Paul made a reference to, and application of, them. He urged Timothy to *'follow'* the prophecies so that he would be enabled to *'fight the good fight'*. What did Paul mean by *'following'* the prophecies? The Greek word translated 'following' is *parangelia*, and can be translated as *'command'* (cf. 1 Timothy 1:5). It was used in a military context as the '... usual word for the commands given by the officer to his men... to signify any authoritative order.'[2] The word '...conveys a sense of urgent obligation.'[3] This implies that Timothy was to *follow* the prophecies while discharging his ministry in the same way a soldier obeys his commanding officer while discharging his duty (cf. 2 Timothy 2:3–4).

Timothy was explicitly told to follow the prophecies *'so that'* he *'may fight the good* fight'. The metaphor of *'the good fight'* (cf. 1 Timothy 6:12) speaks of Timothy's ministry defending the revealed truth of Scripture and the authentic gospel against those who Paul had warned were ignorantly distorting the truth (1 Timothy 1:3-7). This *fight* would be like an ongoing campaign of warfare. Therefore, in order for Timothy to endure and prevail in ministry, he was encouraged to adhere to and

1 For other references to the laying on of hands as a sign of the public commissioning of someone for specific service or office, see Numbers 27:18–19; Deuteronomy 34:9; Acts 6:6, Acts 13:3.

2 Leon Morris quoted in David J Williams, *Paul's Metaphor's: Their Context and Character* (Peabody, MASS: Hendrickson, 1999), 242, n. 131.

3 Guthrie, quoted in John R. W. Stott, *The Message of 1 Timothy & Titus,* (Leicester, England: Inter-Varsity, 1996), 56.

apply the prophetic utterances *as he ministered*. Importantly, Paul added that he was to do so while '*...holding on to faith and a good conscience*' (1 Timothy 1:19).

The lesson for contemporary leaders is that *if* we have received prophecies that were pertinent and powerful, we should remember them and apply them as we fulfill our leadership responsibilities.

Through a very painful set of circumstances, I resigned from pastoring my last church in early 2009. I then began itinerant ministry, teaching in Bible Colleges and providing consultancy for churches. Though I was active in ministry, in my heart I knew that the Lord had something else planned for us. Late 2009 I received an email from a friend of mine, who is a senior denominational leader in Malaysia and recognized as a Prophet. In essence, his email read, "Bruce, this Christmas God is going to open a door for you, and this will be his new thing for your life and ministry." At the time, I had no idea what it could possibly be, but, because of his credibility, I took notice.

On Christmas Day itself, my wife and I were meeting with the pastors of the church at which we were based. The pastor, Chris, asked, "Are you coming to church on Sunday?" To be truthful, I wasn't planning to because it was holidays, but because of the prophecy about Christmas, and this being Christmas Day, I thought I better go to church. I answered, "Yes, I am, why?" He responded that he had a guest speaker coming on Sunday, who does work in missions and may be looking for someone to help teach in training seminars from time to time.

The following Sunday I met John Elliott who, at the time, was the International Director of World Outreach International, a non-denominational missions' agency working among least-reached people groups. I ended up having lunch with John and his wife, Mary, along with our pastors. In the course of the conversation, John said, "Bruce, we're looking for someone to head up all of our leadership development seminars globally. Would you be interested in a role like that?" That conversation over lunch was the catalyst for me joining World Outreach in 2010 and serving in it ever since.

Remember what the Lord has prophetically said in the past.

My Malaysian friend's prophecy was a profoundly significant message that I had to follow. If I hadn't 'followed' the prophecy and gone to church that day, I *may* have missed the moment.

Remember what the Lord has prophetically said in the past.

Self-reflection:

Write the prophecies that you have received over your life and ministry.

In what ways were they an encouragement at the time?

How have they been a stabilizing, encouraging and empowering strength as you have conducted your ministry, especially in adverse times?

In what ways have you 'followed' the prophetic words?

Chapter Two

Self-Awareness (part two)

E. Know our (potential) *DISTRACTIONS*

'***Have nothing to do with** godless myths and old wives' tales…*' (1 Timothy 4:7; cf. 2 Timothy 2:23, emphasis mine).

'*But you, man of God, **flee** from all this…*' (1 Timothy 6:11, emphasis mine).

'***Flee** the evil desires of youth…*' (2 Timothy 2:22, emphasis mine).

A fifth area of self-awareness is to be vigilant and watchful of *distractions*, which are things that can divert us from pursuing our ministry.

Early in his first letter, Paul had instructed Timothy to '*… command certain men not to teach false doctrines…nor to devote themselves to myths and endless genealogies*', which, he wrote, promote '*controversies*' and '*meaningless talk*' (1 Timothy 1:7). But in 1 Timothy 4:7, Paul warned Timothy about being caught up with similar arguments and debates *himself*

Be vigilant and watchful of distractions, things that can divert us from pursuing our ministry.

(cf. 1 Timothy 6:20). Earlier Paul had written about the false teachers who were *'conceited...quarrelsome'* and considered godliness as *'...a means to financial gain'* (1 Timothy 6:3-5). This seems to have prompted him to write of the dangers and allurement of chasing money above the greater gain of *'godliness with contentment'*. Then he instructed Timothy, whom he called a *'...man of God'*, to *'flee from all this...'* (1 Timothy 6:11). Further, in 2 Timothy 2:22, Paul exhorted Timothy to also flee *'...the evil desires of youth'* which, John Stott adds, '...is not to be understood exclusively as a reference to sexual lust, but to self-assertion...self-indulgence...self-ambition, headstrong obstinacy, arrogance and indeed all the "wayward impulses of youth" (NEB).'[1]

Put simply, Paul was warning Timothy against being distracted from what he was called to do. Paraphrased, it seems Paul was saying, 'Timothy, don't be distracted by controversies, conceit, covetousness or carelessness.'

For us in the contemporary church, it is easy to be distracted by these exact same things, such as:

- *Controversies*. Arguing over meaningless and trivial controversies, conjecture and conspiracy theories which have nothing to do with sound doctrine (Titus 3:9)
- *Conceit*. Being caught up in the self-importance or pride of our position as a leader, rather than recognizing any position we may have as an opportunity to serve and empower others (Matthew 20:25-28)
- *Covetousness*. Pursuing money and financial gain above pursuing God and things of eternal value (Matthew 6:33)
- *Carelessness*. Not giving appropriate thought or care to the way we're living our lives, or not exercising self-control over our passions, drives and desires (1 Timothy 3:2 *'self-controlled'*; cf. Titus 1:8).

1 John R. W. Stott, *The Message of 2 Timothy* (Leicester, England: Inter-Varsity, 1997), 73.

Distractions, however, can come in many different forms. Some of them may be legitimate things, such as pastimes, pursuits, amusements or leisure activities. They may not be evil or sinful, but any one of them can subtly and seductively divert us from the centrality of our leadership unless we are watchfully aware.

Before concluding this point, let's return to the warnings Paul brought to Timothy. In each case, Paul always offered a positive alternative to the negative distraction. It seems Paul was saying, 'Timothy, rather than be distracted by senseless, time-wasting activities, proactively pursue godliness (1 Timothy 4:7) and its fruit (1 Timothy 6:11; 2 Timothy 2:22).' The following chart displays these two alternatives.

Distraction	*Alternative*
(1 Timothy. 4:7a) *'godless myths... old wives tales'* (controversies)	(1 Timothy 4:7b) *'...rather, train yourself to be godly'*
(1 Timothy 6:11) *'...eager for money'* (covetousness)	(1 Timothy 6:11b) *'...pursue righteousness, godliness, faith, love, endurance and gentleness'*
(2 Timothy 2:22) *'Flee the evil desires of youth...'* (carelessness)	(2 Timothy 2:22) *'...and pursue righteousness, faith, love and peace...'*

What is not immediately obvious is the stark contrast between the two words: 'flee' and 'pursue' in 1 Timothy 6:11 and 2 Timothy 2:22. The Greek word translated 'flee' has also been translated as 'shun', 'seek safety in flight' or 'escape' (Matthew 2:13; Acts 7:29). The word for 'pursue' was used in races, including chariot races, and metaphorically denotes hot pursuit or chasing after (cf. Philippians 3:12-13).[2] It was an active, vigorous word. Timothy was urged to flee from spiritual

2 Williams, 278, n. 33.

> **Every leader has insecurities. We need to be aware of them and not allow them to pollute or pervert our thinking or leadership.**

danger in order to escape it, *but* alternatively to pursue spiritual good in order to attain it.[3]

As contemporary leaders we should, therefore, be acutely aware of the many possible distractions in our lives. Instead of succumbing to them, let's intentionally and decisively pursue a godly life and a godly character.

Self-reflection:

Being honest with yourself, what can you identify as the biggest potential distractions in your life and leadership?

What practical preventative measures can you put in place to prevent yourself being distracted?

F. Know our *INSECURITIES*

'Don't let anyone look down on you ***because you are young****...'* (1 Timothy 4:12, emphasis mine).

A sixth area of self-awareness is that of our insecurities. Every leader has insecurities. Even seasoned, veteran and experienced leaders sometimes struggle with them. I have them. But we must not be misguided or mastered by our insecurities. Instead, we need to be *aware* of them so that we can keep them at bay and not allow them to pollute or pervert our thinking or leadership.

There is convincing evidence in Paul's letters that Timothy *felt* inadequate and, arguably, *insecure* about assuming the heavy

3 Stott, *The Message of 2 Timothy*, 75.

responsibility of the Ephesian church.[4] He was comparatively young and inexperienced. It is estimated that Timothy was most likely in his 30s, possibly as old as 40, when Paul wrote these words. In the culture of his day he would still have been regarded as a 'youth' (cf. 2 Timothy 2:22).

But Paul did not allow Timothy's insecurities to influence his leadership. Whether people in Ephesus actually thought Timothy was too young to lead, or whether Timothy *thought* that people thought he was too young, is unknown. Paul didn't give any place to either way of thinking. In 1 Timothy 4:11-16, Paul instructed Timothy to do five things to silence the inner voice of insecurity, and to silence the potential voices of criticism of his inexperience. Some of these will be covered more extensively in the remainder of the section, but are listed here as a reference:

- Timothy was to *'**set an example**'* to neutralize any devaluing of his leadership. His example was to embrace all aspects of his private and public life by including his *'...speech, life, love, faith and purity'* (1 Timothy 4:12; cf. Titus 2:7; 1 Peter 5:3; Hebrews 13:7). Setting an example requires conscious and conscientious attention.
- Timothy was to **devote himself to the public declaration, explanation and exhortation of the Word of God** (1 Timothy 4:13 *'public reading of Scripture...preaching and...teaching.'*) As a young leader, very few things build credibility and rapport more than the life-giving ministry of preaching and teaching the Word. Toward the end of his second letter, Paul actually *'charged'* Timothy to *'preach the Word...with great patience and careful instruction'* (2 Timothy 4:2). Preaching and teaching the

4 Paul instructed the Corinthians to ensure Timothy had *'nothing to fear'* if he visited, and to be sent *'on his way in peace'* (1 Corinthians 16:10). Added to this is Paul's encouragement about not being timid (2 Timothy 1:7), nor to *'be ashamed to testify'* about the Lord (2 Timothy 1:8), but to *'endure hardship like a good soldier of Jesus Christ'* (2 Timothy 2:3).

uncompromising truth of Scripture is one of the ways a leaders exercise their authority.

- Timothy must **exercise his gift** and not be negligent of its use (1 Timothy 4:14).
- Timothy must **show his progress** (1 Timothy 4:15) by wholeheartedly and diligently being an example (1 Timothy 4:12), preaching (1 Timothy 4:13) and exercising his gift (1 Timothy 4:14).
- Timothy must **persevere** in the development of his 'life and doctrine', which could be paraphrased as persistently working toward soundness in maturity and ministry.

These five actions (setting an example, declaring God's Word, exercising our gifts, showing our progress and perseverance) are all ways by which we address the unfounded and often irrational insecurities that plague our thoughts. May we be aware of our insecurities so that we can diminish and, potentially, extinguish their influence in our lives and leadership.

Self-reflection:

Please write down your insecurities truthfully and transparently,

How do these insecurities affect you? Be specific.

How would the five actions listed above help you to diminish the voice and feelings of insecurity that you battle with?

What other actions could you employ to deal with your insecurities?

G. Know our *GIFTING*

*'Do not neglect your **gift**...'* (1 Timothy 4:14, emphasis mine).

*'...fan into flame the **gift of God**, which is in you...'* (2 Timothy 1:6, emphasis mine).

A seventh area of a leader's self-awareness is that of their gifting. The notion of gifting is strongly linked to that of calling. A leader's gifting is a God-given enablement and capacity of God's grace to fulfill and function in their call.

As we saw in the previous point, Paul urged Timothy not to *'neglect'* his *'gift'* (1 Timothy 4:14) which he later called the *'gift of God'* (2 Timothy 1:6). Paul's words stress '...first of all that Timothy must regard his "gift" as carrying with it the responsibility to put it to proper use; he must live up to his God-given potential and exercise the authority that goes with the gift.'[5]

While the text does not specifically identify Timothy's particular gift, Paul normally uses the word *gift* when referring to the various gifts of God given to people to serve in the body (Romans 12:4-8; 1 Corinthians 12:7-11; Ephesians 4:9-16; cf. 1 Peter 4:10).[6] God, by his Spirit, graciously endows and empowers each member of Christ's body with gifts (Ephesians 4:7; 1 Corinthians 12:7). Because of the strong link between the gifts and the Holy Spirit, gifts have been seen as 'Spirit-given abilities for Christian service.'[7]

Timothy was reminded of his ordination when the body of elders laid their hands on him, presumably to commission him for Christian ministry (1 Timothy 4:14). Through an accompanying prophetic message, Timothy was equipped with an unspecified gift that must have affirmed and confirmed his sense of call. Importantly, this gift was not to be dormant or static in Timothy's life. Accordingly Paul challenged him not to *'neglect'* it. Using the imagery and metaphor of a fireplace, Paul reminded Timothy to *'fan'* the gift *'into flame'* (2 Timothy 1:6). Fire has a natural tendency to go out unless it is fanned

5 Philip H. Towner, *The Letters to Timothy and Titus,* The New International Commentary of the New Testament (Grand Rapids, MI: Eerdmans, 2006), 321.
6 The word 'gift' translates the Greek word *'charisma'* of which the plural is *'charismata'*.
7 Aubrey Malphurs, *Being Leaders* (Grand Rapids, MI: Baker, 2003), 77.

> **Leaders must proactively develop and nurture the gift(s) sovereignly given by God.**

and fuelled. The lesson here is that leaders must proactively develop and nurture the gift(s) sovereignly given by God for their Christian service. Exercising self-leadership in respect of our gifts requires both the awareness of them *and* the active exercise of them.

Self-reflection:

List the gifts the Lord has placed on your life.

In what ways have you neglected your gifts?

How have you been exercising your gifts?

What do you need to do to 'fan into flame' the gifts the Lord has entrusted to you?

H. Know our *DOCTRINE* (or what we believe)

'Watch your life and ***doctrine*** *closely...'* (1 Timothy 4:16, emphasis mine).

An eighth area of self-awareness is that of our doctrine. The word translated *doctrine* in the verse above (1 Timothy 4:16) is a translation of the Greek word *didaskalia*, which can also be rendered as *teaching* (cf. 1 Timothy 4:6; 6:3; Titus 2:1, 7; Romans 12:7; Ephesians 4:14),[8] and refers to the 'content or the activity of teaching'.[9]

So, for the purpose of clarity, by using the word *doctrine* I am not calling for leaders to be able to recite the Nicene Creed or any particular denominational statement of faith. What I am

8 For other references to the use of *didaskalia* see 1 Timothy 1:10; 1 Timothy 4:13; 1 Timothy 5:17; 1 Timothy 6:1; 2 Timothy 3:10, 2 Timothy 3:16; 2 Timothy 4:3.

9 Towner, 327.

urging is for leaders: to *know* what they're talking about in the substance of their teaching; to take *care* in their preparation so that their teaching is based on a proper interpretation of Scripture; and to *apply* their teaching to the context in which they lead and minister.

Paul sometimes prefaced the word teaching (doctrine) with the adjectives *'sound'* (1 Timothy 1:10; 2 Timothy 4:3; Titus 2:1), *'godly'* (1 Timothy 6:3) or *'good'* (1 Timothy 4:6). Towner comments that '...the word group is medical language that means "healthy"...' and '...in these letters...describes the quality of what is said or taught. Thus "sound teaching" is a way of describing the approved apostolic teaching which is positively health-producing.'[10]

This may seem like an obvious question, but *why* is it so important for us to bring sound teaching? The background for Paul's call to Timothy and Titus to teach *sound*, health-producing doctrine was the unscrupulous, false teachers who were teaching *unsound*, potentially health-destroying doctrine. The very growth, maturity and health of the Ephesian (1 Timothy 1:3) and Cretan (Titus 1:5) churches was at stake.

Paul urged Timothy and Titus to teach on a diverse range of subjects, such as:

- Practice of prayer (1 Timothy 2:1-8)
- Propriety and place of women in public meetings (1 Timothy 2:9-15)
- Qualities of leaders serving in the local church (1 Timothy 3:1-13; Titus 1:6-9)
- Dangers of heretical teaching in the *'last days'* (1 Timothy 4:1-5)
- How widows should conduct themselves (1 Timothy 5:3-16)

10 ibid, 130.

- Respect for, and public discipline of, elders (1 Timothy 5:17-20)
- Rich people being focused on eternal riches (1 Timothy 6:17-19)
- How the different demographics were to live, such as older men (Titus 2:2), older women (Titus 2:3-5), and young men (Titus 2:6)
- How slaves were to act in their attitude toward their masters (Titus 2:9-10)
- The way Christians were to engage with civic authorities and the broader community (Titus 3:1-2).

We conclude that the people's whole spiritual, relational, doctrinal, social, municipal, vocational and eternal health was dependent upon Timothy and Titus bringing sound teaching. To Timothy, Paul wrote that if he taught '*these things*' he would be a '*good minister of Christ Jesus*' (1 Timothy 4:16).

In regard to *how* the teaching was to be presented, Paul instructed Titus to seek to convince the people through authoritative encouragement (Titus 2:15). But he also urged him not to be afraid of people's scorn or derision, but to also '*rebuke with all authority*' (Titus 2:15).

But 1 Timothy 4:16 doesn't conclude with, '*Watch your life and doctrine closely.*' Paul goes on to instruct Timothy to '*...persevere in them.*' Timothy was told to persevere at the development of his life (his character and conduct) and his teaching (its content and delivery). If Timothy persisted in giving equal and intentional attention to both, he would '*ensure salvation*' (1 Timothy 4:16 NASB) both for himself and his hearers. This does not imply that our salvation is not secure in Christ or is achieved by self-effort. We are saved by grace through faith (Ephesians 2:8; 2 Timothy 1:9), and it is sealed (guaranteed) by the indwelling presence of the Holy Spirit (Ephesians 4:30; 2 Corinthians 1:22). Now that we are saved by grace through faith, it is by our sound teaching that we are enabled:

- to live a life which evidences the fruit of salvation
- to mature in our salvation (Ephesians 4:14; cf. Philippians 2:12)
- to patiently wait for the consummation (fulfillment) of our salvation (Titus 2:11-14).

It's essential that we know how to apply our teaching to the daily realities of the lives of the people we are leading.

Therefore, by way of application, it's imperative that we know what we believe about the core, essential truths of Scripture, because what we believe will determine what we preach and teach, our ministry practices and our philosophy of ministry. Also, it's essential that we know how to apply our teaching to the daily realities of the lives of the people we are leading. We are required to give persistent and diligent attention (perseverance) to the authenticity and conduct of our lives, *and* to the preparation and application of our teaching. If we do, we'll be making an eternal impact upon our own lives and on those we are leading.

Self-reflection:

Why do you believe it is important for a leader to be sound in their Biblical teaching?

In practical terms, what could you do to improve your working knowledge of Scripture?

What practical areas do you need to teach on in your current ministry context?

Chapter Three

Self-Awareness (part three)

I. Know our *WEAKNESSES*

'...use a little wine because of your ***stomach*** *and your* ***frequent illness****'* (1 Timothy 5:23, emphases mine).

'For God has not given us a spirit of ***timidity****...'* (2 Timothy 1:7, emphasis mine).

A ninth area of self-awareness is that of a leader's weaknesses or, in different words, vulnerabilities or limitations.

Timothy was frequently ill and had some kind of recurring stomach problem (1 Timothy 5:23), possibly a persistent gastric complaint. This was a *physical* limitation on his leadership. Because of his timid nature (2 Timothy 1:6-7), some believe that Timothy's condition may have been aggravated by anxiety. Whether Timothy's ailments were because of his disposition or a legitimate condition, Paul's encouragement to him was to take *preventative* action by medicinally drinking a *'little wine'*. Hopefully, this remedy would alleviate the cause and consequences of his illness and enable him to lead and minister in health.

Also, it has been surmised that Timothy's nature was somewhat timid and fearful. This, too, was a limitation to the discharge of his ministry. Paul had to challenge him to stoke the inward fire of his gifting in an effort to get him to function in the fullness of his calling (2 Timothy 1:6). Quite pointedly, Paul did not allow Timothy to be incapacitated by his natural disposition, but reminded him that timidity (fear) was not part of the divine nature (2 Timothy 1:7). God's Holy Spirit does not produce fear, and God is not afraid of anything or anyone.

Every leader has limitations, though it is possible to increase one's leadership ability through experience and personal development.

It is possible that Timothy's hesitancy and reticence was due to a feeling that he lacked sufficient love, inward strength and the mental discipline (or self-control) to be a great leader. So Paul confidently wrote that God's indwelling Spirit can actually equip and energize him with *'power, love and...self-discipline'* (2 Timothy 1:7). The divine nature, available through the Spirit's presence, can empower Timothy to overcome the disempowerment produced by fear. The Spirit would enable him to do what God had called and gifted him to do.

While knowing our strengths is vital for the ongoing development of our life and leadership, it is also imperative that leaders monitor areas of actual, or potential, *weakness*. Even though every Christian leader has *'eternal life'* (John 3:16; 1 John 5:11), we have been created mortal, flesh and blood human beings. Therefore, *every* leader, like Timothy, has limitations, though it is possible to increase one's leadership ability through experience and personal development.

Being self-aware of one's limitations is to honestly recognize and be aware of them. But far from passively surrendering to these limitations, the leader must adopt one of two responses both exemplified by Timothy, either *preventative* or *proactive*. Paul's advice to Timothy over his stomach complaint was to take *preventative* action (i.e. medicinal use of wine). However, in regard to his fearful nature, he was challenged to *proactively* overcome his natural tendency by relying on the Spirit's power within his life. One of the primary reasons for knowing our weaknesses is to be on our guard. The key lesson for contemporary leaders is to know which of these two responses is appropriate for their weaknesses.

Some years ago, I came precariously close to burnout. Some qualified counselors, who specialize in clergy burnout, subsequently informed me that I was hanging over the precipice, and that if I hadn't taken some time-out, I would have plunged into the dark crevasse of burnout. In hindsight, I can now see many of the signs and symptoms of burnout, but, at the time, I had no capacity for recognizing them. I was spiritually robust, in good health, family life was settled and happy; but I failed to appreciate that my emotional reservoirs were virtually empty. Since that time, however, if I ever recognize any of the early warning signs of burnout, I very quickly take preventative measures. It has been 7 years since the initial meltdown, and I don't yet have the same capacity for work or concentration that I once had, but I now *preventatively* manage myself.

Also, as a child, I developed a minor speech impediment in the form of a stammer. Most times, it is not very pronounced and few people would even notice. But there are times, particularly if I am stressed, anxious, tired or jet-lagged, that it is uncomfortably obvious. Sometimes I cannot say a whole sentence without stumbling over some consonants. As a preacher, it has been deeply embarrassing. Preaching is my craft, yet, on the occasion the stammer is particularly bad, I just want to walk off the platform and go and hide under a bed. It is humiliating. My wife has been incredibly supportive and is the only person who knows the inner torment I feel after an especially bad experience. But I don't allow my impediment to go unaddressed. I have taken, and do take, *proactive* steps. For example, I saw a speech therapist for many years. She provided verbal exercises I do to loosen my tongue. I now also ensure I have had adequate sleep and rest before speaking. In addition, I rehearse the sermon out loud to identify any words or places where I may stumble. In this way, I have been enabled to dramatically improve my fluency.

Self-reflection:

What are your biggest weaknesses, vulnerabilities or limitations?

What can you preventatively do to limit their effect?

What can you proactively do to overcome them?

J. Know our *TEMPERAMENT*

'For God did not give us a spirit of ***timidity****...'* (2 Timothy 1:7, emphasis mine).

'***Do not be ashamed*** *to testify about our Lord...'* (2 Timothy 1:8, emphasis mine).

'***Endure hardship*** *like a good soldier of Jesus Christ...'* (2 Timothy 2:3, emphasis mine).

Every leader has a different disposition. There is no optimal or correct personality type for a leader.

A tenth area of self-awareness is that of our temperament and personality.

As indicated in previous points, there is a strong case for concluding that Timothy was timid, possibly shy and cautious, by nature. Nevertheless, Paul urged him not to use his natural disposition as an excuse for holding back on exercising his ministry, but to depend upon the Spirit's power to compensate for his own sense of inadequacy (2 Timothy 1:6–7).

Every leader has a different disposition. There is no optimal or correct personality type for a leader. God chooses all types of people to be his leaders. However, in order for us to skillfully and effectively lead others, we need to understand our nature so we can tailor our leadership style appropriately.

The church I pastored in Brisbane from 2000–2009 was a large church by Australian standards, so I got to mix with so-called 'high flyers'. With few exceptions, I always found them to be down-to-earth, sincere and well-grounded. By nature, I am a shy, mildly introverted person, but most of my contemporaries were loud, funny, larger-than-life extroverts. Initially, I was intimidated, but I had to learn to just be *me*, and be comfortable and confident with how God has made me. Don't feel pressure to be somebody you're not. Be who you are! Oscar Wilde (1854–1900), Irish writer and poet, famously wrote, 'Be yourself; everyone else is already taken'.[1]

After the near burnout experience I had in 2008, I saw the counselors I wrote about earlier. To help them assess and assist me, they asked me to complete a wad of personality and psychological assessments. When the results came back, they sat with the printout in front of them looking at me with perplexed and amused looks on their faces. I asked, "What's so funny? Is there *really* something wrong with me?" They laughed and said, "The results of the 'Bruce' in these assessments are nothing like the 'Bruce' sitting in front of us. On paper you're shy, reclusive and disengaged. According to these results, you have the personality that best suits an auditor or an accountant." To me, that wasn't a complement! "But", they continued, "the 'Bruce' in front of us is warm, friendly and engaging." They were

1 https://www.goodreads.com/quotes.

having trouble reconciling the two Bruces. My response was along the lines of, "Well, those results show my *natural* nature. If I was left to myself, that's what I would be. But those results don't measure the *divine* nature (the life of Jesus) or work of the Spirit in my life."

There are numerous surveys, tests and questionnaires available that guide leaders into an understanding of their temperament and personality type.[2] But I would sound a note of caution in regard to these tests. These tools can accurately portray one's natural disposition and personality type, but they don't allow or measure the work of the Spirit within a leader's life. The calling and gifting of God can sometimes appear to be contrary to a leader's nature. The life of Christ and active presence of the Holy Spirit within us are transforming us day by day (2 Corinthians 4:16). Every leader is a work in progress. We are unfinished lives. Therefore, please don't feel defined or pigeon-holed by the results of the surveys or questionnaires, because the Holy Spirit is at work within you.

Nonetheless, these tools can still be helpful in understanding our temperament and personality in order to determine our leadership style, how best we work on a team and how we can make decisions more effectively.

Self-reflection:

How would you describe your temperament and personality type?

In what ways have you had to modify your natural personality to be a leader? Review any personality tests, questionnaires or surveys you have done to see what you can discover about yourself.

---

2 For example, Malphurs, 173-224, and Myers-Briggs Type Indicator (MBTI) and DISC behaviour assessment.

K. Know our (current) *MODELS OF MINISTRY AND LEADERSHIP*

'What you ***heard from me****, keep as the* ***pattern*** *of sound teaching...'* (2 Timothy 1:13, emphases mine).

'You, however, know all about my ***teaching****, my* ***way of life****, my* ***purpose****,* ***faith****,* ***patience****,* ***love****,* ***endurance****,* ***persecutions****,* ***sufferings****...'* (2 Timothy 3:10-11a, emphases mine).

An eleventh area of self-awareness is that of recognizing the people who are currently influencing and shaping our ongoing maturity, leadership development, thinking, practices, methodologies, styles, structures or mission emphasis.

For Timothy, Paul not only nurtured his early formation in leadership, but provided an ongoing model. Paul advised Timothy to use his teaching as the *'...pattern of sound teaching'* (2 Timothy 1:13), and as a basis for training the next generation of leaders (2 Timothy 2:2). Later in the letter, Paul instructed Timothy to remember the comprehensive nature of his example (*'life, purpose, faith, patience, love, endurance, persecutions, sufferings'*) as something to help him endure in times of persecution or adversity (2 Timothy 3:10-13). Timothy was then urged to use the foundations of what he'd learned from Paul (2 Timothy 3:14), and the Scriptures he learnt as a child (2 Timothy 3:15; cf. 2 Timothy 1:5), as the basis for being *'thoroughly equipped'* for everything God had planned for him (2 Timothy 3:17). Only then would he be able to fulfill Paul's charge to *'preach the Word'* in all circumstances (2 Timothy 4:1-2), stay focused, *'endure hardship'*, preach the Gospel and *'discharge all the duties'* of his ministry (2 Timothy 4:5). In short, Paul was Timothy's

As our leadership develops, we will need other influences to help guide and shape us.

model in his teaching, lifestyle, character, endurance, suffering, leadership and ministry.

Earlier in this section, in point B, we noted that we need to know our *fathers and mothers in the faith*–the people who nurtured our early development in ministry. As our leadership develops, we will need other influences to help guide and shape us as we mature and our ministry context changes.

Since I first started in Christian leadership, I have had many models (influences) at different stages of my growth as a leader. I'll highlight just a few. First, in my early ministry, I was deeply influenced by the model of my Dad. He led predominantly by example. His primary styles of preaching were narrative and expository. He operated in the gift of prophecy most Sunday mornings and always allowed the worship to flow, especially if the Spirit was moving in the congregation. He pastored the people compassionately and prayerfully.

However, I started in leadership as a youth pastor (1983-1993). Even though my Dad was an excellent model for *pastoral* ministry, I needed models to help me with *youth* ministry. At the time (early 1980s), there were very few youth pastors on church teams; in fact, 'team ministry' was a relatively new concept in the Australian church. In our state fellowship of churches, there was one full-time youth pastor, Mal Fletcher, who reached out to me. He radically influenced my life and leadership during my time in youth ministry.

Another major, *ministry-altering* influence was when I embarked on a Post-graduate degree at Ridley College, an Anglican-based, evangelical college in Melbourne. Up to this point, my training had been exclusively in a Pentecostal environment. Ridley's emphasis on proper exegesis of Scripture (rather than proof-texting), building a case for your supposition (rather than dogmatic assertion) and grounding teaching in practical theology (rather than over-spiritualizing everything) *profoundly* transformed my preaching ministry.

I moved to Brisbane late in 1999 to assume the leadership of a large suburban church. I was soon to realize that my *ministry* skills were well developed, but my *leadership* skills were not as well developed for the task at hand. The models of ministry and leadership I had up to that point were not going to be sufficient to transition a large, troubled church into a strong, missional church. This is where Bill Hybels and the Willow Creek Association (WCA) were instrumental. I have only had the honor of meeting Bill Hybels once, though I doubt he'd remember me given the number of people he meets. He probably doesn't realize the ways in which his preaching, teaching, training, seminars and writing helped to develop my church leadership. I am sincerely grateful to Bill and the WCA.

These are only a few examples of people who were models during particular seasons of my formation and the maturity of my life and ministry. Some of those I have not mentioned I have never met, but I have read their work, listened to their preaching or studied their methods.

To be healthily self-aware, I would encourage you to know who is currently influencing your life at this point of your leadership journey.

Self-reflection:

List the current models of leadership (church, ministry) that are presently influencing your thinking.

In what specific ways are they helping?

We need to know the source of our strength for effective and enduring leadership.

List the current leaders or individuals who are having an influence upon you.

In what specific ways are they influencing you?

L. Know our *SOURCE OF STRENGTH FOR MINISTRY*

'*...**be strong** in the grace that is in Christ Jesus*' (2 Timothy 2:1, emphasis mine).

'***Endure hardship** like a good soldier of Jesus Christ...*' (2 Timothy 2:3, emphasis mine).

'*But the **Lord** stood at my side and gave me strength...*' (2 Timothy 4:17, emphasis mine).

A twelfth and final area of self-awareness is to know the source of our strength for effective and enduring leadership. Paul clearly articulated *the* source of strength in 2 Timothy 2:1 when he wrote to Timothy: '*You then, my son, be strong in the grace that is in Christ Jesus.*'

In this previous chapter, Paul had referred to Timothy's timid nature (2 Timothy 1:6-7) and also the large-scale falling away of believers from faith in the Roman province of Asia, with the exception of Onesiphorus (2 Timothy 2:15-18). With this background in mind, the words, '*You then, my son...*' were a challenge to Timothy to stand against the prevailing mood. To me, Paul said, "It doesn't matter what other people may be thinking, saying or doing...never mind how weak or shy you may feel...*you* are to be strong! Live your life and conduct your ministry from a position of strength."

The words '*be strong...*' speak of a choice, an attitude, and a mindset. Importantly, Paul was not speaking of Timothy's *natural* strength or self-effort, nor was he referring to sheer, rugged hard-headedness, toughing it out, or being gritty or determined (although those qualities are sometimes needed).

On the contrary, he told Timothy where to draw his strength for ministry from: '*...be strong* ***in the grace that is in Christ Jesus***' (emphasis mine).

But what does Paul mean by '*...in the grace that is in Christ Jesus*'? Paul had mentioned grace in the previous chapter. In 2 Timothy 1:9 he wrote of how this grace '*...saved and called us to a holy life.*' He then pointed out that our salvation and calling were '*not because of anything we have done but because of his own purpose and grace.*' The last sentence of verse 9 and into verse 10 teaches that the grace he's referring to was part of God's pre-determined plan for our lives. Then he goes on to say that this grace (2 Timothy 1:10) '*...has destroyed death and has brought life and immortality to light through the gospel.*'

Putting all these references to grace together, we see that:

- We are saved and called by grace, not through self-effort
- This grace was part of God's pre-determined plan of salvation in Christ
- This grace has destroyed the power of death and brought us eternal life.

All of this grace, wrote Paul, is available in Christ Jesus. Jesus is the *source* of the grace that brings strength for ministry, and is available, accessible and inexhaustible. All the strength we will ever need to sustain us in ministry is available through the grace that is in Jesus.

Before making application of this verse to our lives and leadership, let's briefly examine two Old Testaments references to demonstrate *how* we can access this grace.

A first reference is that of David and his men returning to find their home city of Ziklag pillaged and destroyed by fire (1 Samuel 30:1–3). To their horror, they also discovered that their wives and children, including David's, had been forcibly taken into captivity by the Amalekites (1 Samuel 30:5). Consequently, '*...David and his men wept aloud until they had no strength to weep*' (1 Samuel 30:4). It seems that David's men turned the brunt of their grief and anger toward David, who became '*... greatly distressed because the men were talking of stoning him; each one was bitter in spirit because of his sons and daughters*' (1 Samuel 30:6).

David was a strong, tough and determined man, but he had reached his emotional capacity. He was emotionally exhausted and '*greatly distressed*' (1 Samuel 30:4, 6); he simply couldn't take any more. '*But David found strength in the Lord his God*' (1 Samuel 30:6). David learned to reach beyond himself to derive strength directly from God himself.

Likewise, every leader must learn to lay hold of God for themselves, through Christ Jesus. The practical lesson is not to battle on with our own internal resources, but draw and derive the strength we need directly from Jesus.

A second, and somewhat negative, reference is Asa, who was the King of Judah for 41 years. For 36 years of his rule he was a great and godly king. In the early part of his reign he experienced an incredible divine intervention when God miraculously answered his prayer and decimated the vastly superior Cushites (2 Chronicles 14:9-15). As he was returning to Jerusalem from the battle, the prophet Azariah met him and said, '*The Lord is with you when you are with him. If you seek him, he will be found by you, but if you forsake him, he will forsake you*' (2 Chronicles 15:2). He subsequently sought the Lord and had peace for 25 years.

But in the 36th year of Asa's reign, Baasha, king of Israel, postured threateningly by fortifying Ramah with the purpose of blockading Judah (2 Chronicles 16:1). Astonishingly, Asa did not seek help from the Lord as he did when facing the Cushites. Instead, he took silver and gold from the Temple and

Palace treasuries to solicit help from Ben-Hadad, King of Aram (2 Chronicles 16:2). His intention was to provide incentive and inducement for Ben-Hadad to break his treaty with Israel (2 Chronicles 16:3). Ben-Hadad was sufficiently persuaded, so he attacked Israel (2 Chronicles 16:4). Consequently, Baasha (King of Israel) withdraw from fortifying Ramah (2 Chronicles 16:5). The threat was gone. Judah was safe. Asa's plan had worked. But the Lord was not happy with what Asa had done.

Consequently, God sent the prophet Hanani to confront Asa with a clear message:

> *'Because you relied on the king of Aram and not on the Lord your God, the army of the king of Aram has escaped from your hand. Were not the Cushites and Libyans a mighty army with great numbers of chariots and horsemen? Yet when you relied on the Lord, he delivered them into your hand. For the eyes of the Lord range throughout the earth to strengthen those whose hearts are fully committed to him'* (2 Chronicles 16:7-9).

Asa relied on the king of Aram, rather than the Lord his God (2 Chronicles 16:7). He had forgotten the lessons of the past (2 Chronicles 16:8). Asa's heart was no longer fully committed to God (2 Chronicles 16:9). This is despite the promise embedded in verse 9 that '*...the eyes of the Lord range throughout the earth to strengthen those whose hearts are fully committed to him.*' This verse suggests that God is actively searching for people whom he can strengthen. The strength that is implied here covers the entire range of human needs–intervention, provision, protection, direction, fortification or restoration. The one criterion God looks for, though, is that the person's heart is fully committed to him.

An application for contemporary leaders is that we must rely on God wholly, solely and constantly. We always need to keep dependent upon him. We must consciously remember what he has done in the past. Most importantly, we need to ensure that our heart is fully committed.

To wrap up this point, whenever we feel weary or drained by the pressures of leadership, we need to draw and derive our strength from Jesus, who is the source of our strength. As we keep our hearts fully committed to him, his grace will sustain and empower us. If we want to have a long and effective ministry, we need to be strong with the grace Jesus provides, not in our own strength.

Self-reflection:

What is the biggest lesson for you from the example of David at Ziklag?

What is the biggest lesson for you from the example of King Asa?

In practical terms, how have you (or will you) derive strength directly from Jesus?

ONE LAST QUESTION

To conclude this opening section, the one big question in self-reflection is:

'What is it about *me* that keeps me from becoming the best me that God intended me to be?'

SECTION TWO

Self-Discipline

A second characteristic of self-leadership is to be *self-disciplined*. As we'll discover, personal discipline should not be confined to the areas of our leadership, but, in practice, should relate to all areas of our public *and* personal life.

The chapters in this section will articulate representative areas for the personal discipline of a Christian leader.

- Self-discipline in *staying focused on our God-given vision*
- Self-discipline in our *time-management*
- Self-discipline in our *financial stewardship*
- Self-discipline in our *spiritual practices*

Chapter Four

Be Disciplined in Pursuing Our God-given Vision

The story is told of a Canadian minister who used to enjoy hunting for relaxation. His youth pastor understood that he needed some space from the rigors of ministry, but began to wonder why the Pastor enjoyed stalking through the Canadian wilderness so much. One day, he plucked up the courage to ask, "Pastor, I'd like to come with you the next time you go hunting?" The minister looked at him bewildered, not really knowing how to respond. He couldn't deny that the youth pastor had been very accommodating and gracious in allowing him to go, so he reluctantly responded, "Sure, that'd be great. You can come next time."

Sometime later, they set off for the pastor's favorite hunting spot. After they had set up camp and built a fire, the pastor, keen as he was to begin hunting, unpacked his guns and dressed himself in appropriate camouflage. Before setting out on an initial reconnaissance trip, he made sure his youth pastor was settled with a mug of coffee and felt secure. He took the precaution of leaving him with a gun in the unlikely event that a grizzly bear or mountain lion ventured near the camp, but he knew that attacks were extremely rare. The last thing he said to him was, "Now, please don't use the gun unless it's an absolute emergency." The youth pastor looked up at his pastor with complete innocence, his facial expression effectively saying, "I wouldn't know how to use it anyway!"

With growing excitement, the pastor set off along well-trodden paths that he knew very well. He crossed meandering creeks by carefully jumping from rock to rock. He scaled steep inclines, then cautiously descended the other side as stealthily as possible. He didn't want to make any noise that would alert an unsuspecting animal. His ears were attentive to any unusual sound, and his eyes scanned the terrain for any hint of movement. He was on the hunt. The pressures of ministry were behind him. He felt alive. Man verses wild.

Several hours later, to his horror, he heard the unmistakable sound of a shot being fired. Knowing his own weapons, he recognized the distinctive single blast as coming from the gun he'd left with his youth pastor. He spun around and ran as fast as he could, scampering over the terrain he had just covered. His legs and lungs longed for rest, but the uncertainty of what may have happened to his youth pastor drove him beyond his physical limits.

Eventually, he breathlessly arrived back at his campsite. To his surprise, he saw the youth pastor pointing his gun at a man standing against a tree, whose hands were raised in surrender. By now the exhausted preacher had his hands on his knees to regain his breath. Between breathes, he asked his youth pastor, "What happened? Why has this man got his hands in the air?" Without taking his eyes off the man in his sights, the youth pastor responded, "I shot a moose and this man is trying to steal my moose." Then the man whose hands were held in the air spoke very quietly and reassuringly to the youth pastor, "Mate, you can keep the moose. Just let me get my saddle off it."

The moral of the story is: you have to know what you're aiming at! That's what this chapter is all about–how a leader can keep focused on their God-given vision. We need to know what we're aiming for.

The God-given capacity of vision is one of the qualities that distinguishes effective leaders.

Paul saw it necessary to refocus Timothy on the important personal tasks of his leadership: '*...set an example... devote yourself to reading Scripture, preaching... teaching. Do not neglect your gift...Watch your life and doctrine closely...*' (1 Timothy 4:12-16). A summary of Paul's words to Timothy could well be, 'Stay focused!'

It is easy for a leader to become diverted from their primary tasks or sense of purpose. Often non-urgent and relatively unimportant issues distract a leader's time and attention. It takes great discipline to retain or regain focus.

One particular area that requires a leader's complete focus is the pursuit of their God-given vision. The God-given capacity of vision is one of the qualities that distinguishes effective leaders. So, how does a leader maintain their discipline in pursuing their God-given vision? Before answering that, we'll begin by clarifying *vision*, as it is used in the contemporary Christian church.

Defining vision

To understand *vision*, let's look at some definitions by popular Christian authors:

- In his ground-breaking book, *Lead On,* John Haggai defined vision as '...a clear picture of what the leader sees his group being or doing.'[1]

1 John Haggai, *Lead* On (Waco, TX: Word, 1987), 12.

- Church researcher, George Barna, wrote an influential book in the early 1990s entitled, *The Power of Vision*, in which he proposed that: 'Vision for ministry is a clear mental image of a preferable future imparted by God to His chosen servants and is based upon an accurate understanding of God, self and circumstances.'[2]

Vision is a combination of a deep dissatisfaction with what is and a clear grasp of what could be.

- Aubrey Malphurs proposes that vision is a '...clear, challenging picture of the future of the church, as leaders believe that it can and must be.'[3] He went on to write that vision must paint '...a compelling picture of what the direction will look like. It communicates not *what is* but *what could be*. It answers the question, "What will it look like around here when our people become passionate and get excited about making and maturing believers?"'[4]
- In similar fashion to Malphurs' definition, John Stott reportedly said that 'vision is a combination of a deep dissatisfaction with what is and a clear grasp of what could be.'[5]

Biblical Reflection

To put the contemporary notion of vision into a Biblical framework, we'll focus on Nehemiah's leadership. The background of this book was that Judah was in exile in Babylon (Nehemiah 1:2). Nehemiah was the cup-bearer to the Persian King, Artaxerxes (Nehemiah 1:11). His brother had recently returned from Jerusalem, so Nehemiah enquired about the state of the city and the remnant of people still living there.

2 George Barna, *The Power of Vision* (Ventura, CA: Regal, 1992), 28.
3 Malphurs, 60.
4 ibid, 60.
5 https://www.bibleinoneyear.org/bioy/commentary/2155.

The brother's answer was alarming–Jerusalem's walls had been broken down, its gates burned with fire, and the people were feeling exposed and humiliated (Nehemiah 1:3). This news deeply affected Nehemiah and, in response, he '*...wept... mourned...fasted and prayed*' (Nehemiah 1:4).

Sometime later, the King noticed that Nehemiah's countenance was sad and asked, 'Why?' Nehemiah transparently responded that he couldn't be happy while his father's city was in ruins. Then he boldly made the request to be sent back to Jerusalem with royal sanction to rebuild it. In Nehemiah's own words, '*...because the gracious hand of my God was upon me, the king granted my requests*' (Nehemiah 2:8).

Based on Nehemiah's example, we discover a number of insights into the nature of God-given vision.

A. Vision is what God places in a leader's heart

Three days after his arrival, Nehemiah set out one night with a few men to survey the extent of the damage. Nehemiah wrote: '*I had not told anyone what my* ***God had put in my heart*** *to do for Jerusalem*' (Nehemiah 2:12, emphasis mine). Obviously, God must have heard and answered Nehemiah's prayer for Jerusalem. At some point not identified in the text, God put a vision in Nehemiah's heart to rebuild the walls of Jerusalem. This vision would define and distinguish his future leadership, and give him and his followers focus, clarity and purpose.

This is a definition of vision in Scripture's own words: **what God places in a leader's heart**. The question every leader must ask themselves is, 'What has God placed in *my* heart?'

B. Vision is a revelation

Nehemiah received vision as a revelation from God. It was a divine disclosure giving insight into God's plans for Nehemiah's life and leadership. What we learn through this is that God is a god of plans and purposes (Jeremiah 29:11), and that he reveals his plans and purposes to leaders.

Theologically, we believe that God knows all things past, present and future. He has a conscious and simultaneous knowledge of everything that *has* taken place, everything that *is* taking place and everything that *will* take place. This is called God's *omniscience*, which is his attribute of all-knowledge or knowing everything that can be known or will be known. Vision, then, is when God takes a fragment of his foreknowledge–his before-the-event knowledge of the future–and reveals it to a leader.

Vision is a revelation from the Lord of his purposes in and through a particular ministry, group or church. Within the Lord's universal purposes for his Church, written and unfolded in Scripture, vision is a divine disclosure of God's unique plans, purposes and objectives specifically designed and shaped for a local body of believers or a Christian ministry.

The Scripture is filled with people who received God-given vision. God gave Noah the vision of an ark and he built it. God gave Abraham the vision of a city and he searched for it. God gave Moses the vision of a promised land and he led the people to its borders. God gave the apostle Paul a vision to evangelize the Gentiles, and he covered the Roman world with the message of Jesus Christ and him crucified.

C. Vision is what a leader 'sees' beyond their natural sight.

Let's return to Nehemiah's night-time reconnaissance survey of Jerusalem. In a physical, material and visible sense, what Nehemiah inspected in Jerusalem that night must have been a mess. While Nehemiah visibly saw the devastated state of Jerusalem, he also saw something which was invisible to the human eye–he saw what God had placed in his heart. Vision, therefore, could be considered as what we see with our eyes closed, because what we see with our eyes closed is often more important than what we see with our eyes open.

We need to focus on what God has placed in our heart and not on the visible evidence that says something to the contrary.

A classic example of this is found in Romans 4 where Paul had been writing about how God '*...gives life to the dead and calls things that are not as though they were*' (Romans 4:17). Continuing his theme on Abraham's faith (Romans 4:18-25), Paul mentioned that Abraham '*...faced the fact that his body was as good as dead...and that Sarah's womb was also dead*' (Romans 4:19). In the face of the stubborn, biological and empirical facts of his sterility and Sarah's infertility, Abraham did not allow his faith to diminish or vacillate. Despite the factual evidence to the contrary, Abraham was '*...fully persuaded that God had the power to do what he had promised*' (Romans 4:21). In other words, Abraham did not focus on what his eyes could see, which was the visible fact that he and his wife were incapable of procreating; instead, he focused on the invisible reality of God's faithfulness to fulfill the promise of a son (Hebrews 11:11).

Abraham's example teaches us that we need to focus on what God has placed in our heart and not on the visible evidence that says something to the contrary. God is faithful to what he has promised and is powerful to do what he has promised. It is our prerogative to stay in a posture of faith and wait with confident expectation for God to do the impossible.

Defining and distinguishing God-given vision

Based on Nehemiah's example, we've noted that vision is what God puts in the heart of a leader by revelation (divine disclosure), which gives the leader an insight into God's unique plans and purposes for the church (or ministry) he or she is leading. Vision is to see something that is not yet visible as it will be.

Why is vision important?

> **Vision breeds passion about God's purposes in the leader and their followers.**

Vision gives a leader navigation into the future by helping leaders to set the right course. Vision equips a leader to know where they're leading the church, its people and leaders. Vision produces a leader's energy to enact change, initiate strategic actions and solve problems. Vision builds unity and momentum in the church as people work and pray towards goals. Vision helps a leader to prioritize their use of time (as we'll see in the next chapter). Vision guides a leader in her or his decision-making processes. Vision necessitates a leader to find the right person for the right role. Vision breeds passion about God's purposes in the leader and their followers. Vision provides a compelling motivation for why leaders do what they do in leadership. 'Vision translates into purpose', which gives the leader a captivating sense of what they're on the earth to do.[6]

Leaders would be encouraged to regularly conduct an honest appraisal of their focus by asking three critical questions:

- Am I doing what I am supposed to be doing with my time, tasks, gifts and skills?
- Am I leading others in a direction that is consistent with Scripture and my God-given vision?
- Am I leading with single-mindedness, resolve and undistracted clarity?

6 Andy Stanley, *Visioneering: God's Blueprint for Developing and maintaining Vision* (Colorado Springs, CO: Multnomah, 2003), 12.

If the answer is 'yes', maintain the focus. If 'no', we need to refocus and get back to pursuing and fulfilling the God-given vision.

Pursuing vision

The major question of this chapter is: how can a leader maintain their discipline in pursuing their God-given vision? The following pages contain a number of principles for how we can do so.

A. Ask God to give you a vision

At this point, you may be asking whether you even have a vision or not. If you can't say with any certainty, or you're new to leadership, then ask God to give you a vision.

So, how does a leader receive vision from God?

As we have seen with Nehemiah, vision comes by revelation. Essentially, this means that vision comes from having an encounter with the Holy Spirit. The Spirit reveals God's plans and purposes by moving upon a leader's life and conceiving divine vision within their heart. After conception, the vision grows within a leader's life.

This conception of vision takes place in either one of two ways. First, it may come by *the sovereign initiative of God*. God sometimes providentially initiates and reveals his plans and purposes to a leader of his choosing, at the time of his choosing, for the purpose of his choosing. Throughout Scripture, it is noted that on many occasions the person of God's choosing wasn't necessarily looking for God, but God sovereignly sought and called them. A prime example of this is the choice and calling of Saul of Tarsus to be an apostle to the Gentiles. Saul certainly wasn't looking for God–he actually thought he was serving God. But God had chosen him (Acts 9:15) and dramatically transformed him on the road to Damascus (Acts 9:1-9).

A second, and most common, way God reveals vision is in response to a leader's specific prayer: 'What do you want me to do? How am I going to do it? Where do you want me to lead these people?'

There is an element of God's sovereignty in the choice, placement and gifting of every leader, but not many leaders receive a dramatic call and envisioning like Saul (Paul). Most leaders do experience a sense of call to serve God in leadership. In response, ministry leaders seek the Lord to discern what he wants them to do through their leadership. Vision is birthed when God responds.

How does the Lord reveal the vision? There is not one common way because everyone is different. Some leaders receive vision in a season of prayer or in a dedicated time of seeking the Lord. Others receive vision at an altar call where they may have responded to a preacher's call to respond to God. For others, the vision may come through a prophetic word from a credible prophetic ministry. Occasionally, some people get a vision from having an encounter with the Lord through a dream, vision or visitation. For others, it may be as simple as seeing a need and feeling the prompting of God to do something about it. The important thing is not *how* God chooses to reveal his vision, but that vision comes from God.

If you don't yet have a vision for your leadership, ask the Lord boldly and expectantly.

B. Ask God to restore your vision

For some of you reading this book, you may be saying to yourself, 'I have lost my vision. Too much has happened. I've been hurt in leadership. I'm discouraged or demoralized because nothing ever seems to happen.' If so, I have great news: God can restore your vision!

One of my close friends, David, has a vivid childhood memory that occurred while on holidays in the Flinders Ranges, northwest of the South Australian capital of Adelaide. He was around 10 years of age and was out exploring the desert environment near his family's campsite. As he walked over the top of a rocky sand dune, he observed some birds of prey circling overhead. Intrigued by the sight, he went to investigate and discovered they were circling above a large goanna in the distance.[7] Goannas are normally lethargic, sluggish creatures, unless they're frightened or hunting food. This one, however, was wagging its large tail wildly and bobbing its head up and down. Attracted by this unusual spectacle, David went over for a closer inspection. As he got nearer, he noticed that the birds were regularly swooping down to attack the big lizard. When he was closer still, he noticed that the goanna had blood all around its eyes.

This is what happens: the birds of prey do not have the power to kill the goanna; it is too large and too strong. So they swoop down and pluck out the reptile's eyes. Sightless, the large lizard then can't find food or water and eventuality, inevitably dies. Once dead, the birds of prey land beside the carcass and eat their fill. Because the goanna lost its sight (vision), it lost its life.

When David conveyed this story, I was immediately struck by the parallels between the birds of prey and Satan's attack on Christian leaders. Like the birds' incapacity to overcome the goanna, our spiritual adversary can't just do whatever he wants to us because we are covered by Jesus' blood and indwelt by God's Holy Spirit. Like the birds targeting the lizard's eyes, the devil will seek to target our vision–our God-given capacity to envision the future. If he can kill the seed, he'll prevent the harvest. Instead of pursuing what God has put in our heart,

7 A goanna is a large, carnivorous, non-venomous, monitor lizard. 25 species are found all across Australia, except in the island state of Tasmania. They have sharp teeth and claws and can grow up to 1.5 meters long.

we'll be caught up in the mundane maintenance of our ministry. Rather than strategically planning for our future, we'll be caught up with the minutiae of the everyday. Rather than believing for greater things with expectant faith, we'll have a cynical acceptance of how things are at the present, and no expectation that the future will be any different than the past.

But, in the same way that Jesus healed the blind eyes of Bartimaeus (Mark 10:52), Jesus can restore our vision with one touch of his Spirit. If you've lost your vision, if you're no longer believing for great and mighty things for the future, if God's promises are dormant within your heart, or if your vision has been suffocated by discouragement, then ask the Lord, by his Spirit, to touch your life right now. Ask him to revive your vision. Ask him to resuscitate your faith, and ask him to help refocus your leadership back to *the* vision he placed in your heart. Seize this moment. Then, be disciplined to pursue the restored vision.

C. Refuse to be distracted

Once you have received a vision, or had your vision restored, another key way to maintain your discipline is to resolutely refuse to be distracted. One thing I have learned is that if the devil can't destroy you, he will seek to distract you. To be disciplined, therefore, you need to guard your mind from distractions, whether they are from a human or satanic source, as we'll now see.

There are a number of examples in Scripture of leaders maintaining their vision despite major diversions.

Firstly, after Nehemiah began the reconstruction of Jerusalem's walls, he received tremendous opposition from Sanballat, Tobiah and Geshem the Arab (Nehemiah 4:1-3; 7-8; 11-12). With great strength and skill of leadership, Nehemiah retained his and his workforce's focus on the reconstruction (Nehemiah

4:13–23). After seeing that Nehemiah was undistracted and undeterred, his enemies schemed to entice him away from the work, presumably to do him harm (Nehemiah 6:1–2). Nehemiah saw through their pretence and sent a messenger to say: *'I am carrying on a great project and cannot go down. Why should the work stop while I leave it and go down to you?'* (Nehemiah 6:3) He kept his focus, diligently persisted with the rebuilding work and was enabled to complete it in 52 days.

Secondly, Jesus exemplified this discipline of focus on a scale no other leader can fully appreciate. After Jesus revealed to his disciples that he must soon suffer, die and be raised to life, Peter took him aside and rebuked him saying, *'Never, Lord! This shall never happen to you'* (Matthew 16:22). Jesus, however, silenced the voice and inspiration of Satan behind Peter's words (Matthew 16:23). He did not allow the well-meaning but misguided words of a friend, or the deceptive, corrupt words of Satan through his friend, to deter him from his mission.

Further, Luke 9:51 records that *'as the time approached for him to be taken up to heaven, Jesus resolutely set out for Jerusalem.'* Jesus knew the horror of what lay ahead in becoming the substitutionary sin-bearer on the cross. Yet with complete single-mindedness of purpose and unshakable resolve, Jesus made his way to Jerusalem to accomplish the Father's redemptive plan.

The lessons for us are to keep doing what we know we should be doing, be discerning of the distracting voices we listen to, and have single-minded resolve to see it through to the end, come what may.

D. Respond strategically

Even though vision comes from God, it needs to be responded to in a strategic way. Strategic planning and actions are a leader's *response* to God-given vision.

I personally believe that strategic planning is the missing link in most churches. Most pastors and leaders have a vision they can articulate with great faith and passion, but it never seems to come to pass. When you ask them *how* they are going to accomplish the vision, they generally don't have stated, specific plans. Sadly, many vision-filled leaders never see the fulfillment of their God-given vision. They're often faith-filled, prayerful and godly women and men, but they've never taken the time, or perhaps lack the skill, to plan and develop people to translate vision into tangible action steps.

A thorough and detailed examination of strategic planning is outside the scope and subject of this book, but this paragraph will seek to give some clarity on the factors involved in strategic planning. *Vision* gives the overall direction and purpose of the church or ministry. *Strategic planning* determines how the church will move forward in specific actions. Strategic planning is organizing the sequential steps, scheduling people and tasks, and developing deadlines, to accomplish the action step. *Goals*, then, become the measureable outcome of each strategy or plan. *Delegation* determines who will fulfill specific tasks and roles in the strategic plan. In simple terms, strategic planning is determining *who* is to do *what* by *when* to accomplish each action toward an agreed objective.

It is leaders who initiate strategic planning, implement the action plans, delegate responsibility, set the time frames, then monitor those who have been delegated with a responsibility or task to ensure it is done effectively and on time. This is a key component of what leaders do, and what will distinguish someone as a leader. It will require a disciplined use of time, a disciplined approach to leading people and disciplined thought processes.

E. Pursue the vision

Another aspect of self-discipline in accomplishing our God-given vision is to actively pursue it. In Philippians 3:12, Paul employed a metaphor taken from the world of athletics and chariot racing to communicate his intense yearning for spiritual growth, development and maturity. He wrote how he was pressing on toward the goal, that being to know Christ. The Greek word translated 'press on' is a vigorous word and can mean 'to pursue or chase' in the sense of 'to follow'. Paul transparently wrote of his burning intention to pursue and apprehend Christ and his purposes with determination, discipline and devotion.

We must not be passively content with having a God-given vision, but proactively pursue the Lord to fulfill all that he's put in our hearts.

Likewise, we must not be passively content with having a God-given vision, but proactively pursue the Lord to fulfill *all* that he's put in our hearts.

Finally

George Bernard Shaw (1856–1950), Irish playwright, socialist, Nobel Prize and Oscar winner, once wrote that: 'Some men see things that *are* and say *why*? I dream things that *never were*, and say *"Why not"?*'[8] In response to God putting a vision in our heart as a leader, can we not loudly declare, 'Why not!' Is anything too hard for the Lord? Is anything impossible for our God? Therefore, we need to discipline ourselves to pursue our God-given vision.

8 http://www.brainyquote.com/quotes/authors.

Self-reflection:

Write down the specific God-given vision you have for your current context of leadership.

Then record what specific actions you are following to see that vision fulfilled.

What do you need to do to more strategically and intentionally pursue the vision God has given you?

How will you help other leaders and parishioners to stay focused on the vision?

Chapter Five

Be Disciplined in Time Management

William Penn (1644–1718) was an English Quaker, best known for founding the American colony of Pennsylvania. He once wrote: 'Time is what we most want, but what we use worst.'[1]

There are two verses in particular that urge us to steward our time well. Ephesians 5:16 exhorts us to: *'Be very careful, then, how you live - not as unwise, but as wise, (16) making the most of every opportunity, because the days are evil.'* In similar language, Colossians 3:5 encourages us to do the same.

These verses should not be interpreted as 'use your time to keep busy', but to use our time 'discerningly', 'wisely, not casually', and '...to free ("redeem") it from unprofitable activities.'[2]

What do these verses mean for us as leaders? Busyness does not make us effective leaders. It is the discerning, wise and planned use of our time that translates into effective leadership.

As leaders, we have busy lives and ministries, and often lament our perceived lack of time. How can we maximize our use of time? How can we balance all our personal and public roles and responsibilities?

1 http://www.brainyquote.com/quotes/authors.
2 Robert Banks, *The Tyranny of Time* (Homebush, NSW: Lancer, 1983), 169–170.

We cannot control how much time we have; we can only control how we use it.

Surprisingly, the answer is *not* time management per se. The term 'time management' is actually a misconception and misnomer. We cannot lengthen or reduce how long an hour, a day or a week is. But, in his ground-breaking and benchmark book, *The Time Trap,* Alec Mackenzie writes that although we '...cannot manage time' as such, we '...can only manage *ourselves* in relation to time. We cannot control how much time we have; we can only control how we use it.'[3] So, when I refer to time management, I am actually referring to self-management. Rather than asking, 'Am I managing my time effectively?' ask 'Am I managing my *life* effectively?'

Time management is *not* so much about our schedule, diary or calendar, but our goals, values and priorities. Our time allocation is a *reflection* of these things. Our priorities determine *how* we spend our time. How we spend our time determines how we're living our lives.

Phrased differently, time management is not simply the organization of our calendar and daily schedule, but the organization of our *inner* life (inside out). Managing our inner life is the true *key* to effective management of our time.

Therefore, I propose the following working definition of time management:

> Time management is managing ourselves, within the time frame granted to us by God, toward Biblical priorities, values and God-given purposes.

3 Alec Mackenzie, *The Time Trap* (New York, NY: Amacon, 1990), 12.

The obvious question, then, becomes, 'How, in practical terms, do we manage ourselves and our time?'

A. Surrender our life to the lordship of Jesus Christ

All effective personal management of our life (and time) begins with one act: that of total surrender to Jesus Christ as the Lord of our lives and therefore the Lord of our time. We must consciously surrender our *all* to him, which includes the surrender of our time to him.

By the yielding of our lives to Jesus at salvation, our lives are no longer our own. They have been bought at a price and now belong to him. We have relinquished our rights to him. Therefore our time is no longer our own to do with as we will. Instead, we should be seeking to live as Jesus wants us to live and do what he wants us to do with our time.

As we'll see, true time management for us as Christian leaders is not how disciplined or regimented we are in using our time, but in whether our time is being used for the right purposes–eternal and kingdom purposes. In this sense, the place where time management truly begins is the place of complete surrender to Jesus and his will for our lives.

A central principle in organizing time is to steward or budget our time.

B. Budget our time

A central principle in organizing time is to *steward* or *budget* our time. Most of us have learned to budget our money by financial priorities:

- Tithes and offerings
- Food

- Household expenses, such as mortgage, rent, board and upkeep
- Utilities, such as power, gas, phone and internet
- Living costs, such as clothes, children's school fees and haircuts.

In doing so, we determine which of our expenses are (a) fixed, and what are (b) discretionary. Our fixed costs are the non-negotiables (what we *have* to pay) such as mortgage, food and utilities; whereas discretionary money (what we'd *like* to do) can be distributed as we see fit. What we do with our discretionary income, however, generally determines if we get ahead financially or not. If it is invested wisely (or used to decrease debt) it will eventually generate net wealth, but if we squander it, we will be living from pay packet to pay packet.

This is a great parallel to our use of time. There are some things we *have* to do with our time and some things we would *like* to do if time allowed. The negotiable and non-negotiable use of time come from our priorities and values. Once we determine *the* important things in our lives, the task of allocating time is straightforward, as the next point will detail.

C. Determine our life and leadership priorities

A next step in managing our time is to determine our life's priorities. We derive these from Scripture, our current context and stage of life, along with what we know to be God's will.

The following are some suggestions of the priorities for our life and leadership:

Personal priorities as a Christian

- To live a godly life that glorifies God
- To become more and more like Jesus
- To spend devotional time with God each day

- To cultivate a happy, fulfilled marriage
- To raise godly children, provide for them and have quality time and relationship with them
- To fulfill our calling and exercise our gifts
- To be a witness by sharing our faith through personal evangelism and exemplary living

Public priorities as a Christian leader / minister

- Time leading people into God's purposes of mission and maturity
- Time fulfilling the specific vision God has placed in our heart
- Time loving, feeding and building the people under our oversight
- Time developing leaders and equipping people for ministry
- Time invested into our personal development

Personal priorities as a human being

- Maintaining personal health and wellbeing
- Fostering healthy friendships and relationships
- Pursuing and practicing leisure activities
- Balancing life, work and leadership
- Stewarding our finances and resources

Our allocation of time is a response to our priorities. We can always find time to do the things we really want to do. Once we've settled on what is really important, we need to apportion our time accordingly. We'll come to some practicalities shortly.

D. Plan our time

Having (a) surrendered our lives to the Lordship of Jesus and God's purpose for our lives, (b) based our allocation of time on the principles of budgeting, (c) determined the priorities of our lives (what is really important to us), and (d) established goals in our leadership (where we're going), we now come to the practical outworking, which is *planning* our time.

As we live according to a plan, and not haphazardly or by whim, we are taking control of our time. Here are some practical suggestions:

Yearly

- Keep a yearly calendar with important events, appointments and deadlines
- Identify key marriage and family celebrations and milestones (e.g. birthdays, anniversaries, holidays) and put them into your calendar before anything else
- Schedule regular time to think and plan
- Keep a 'Master List' of tasks to be done throughout the year (organized by date and priority); keep the list updated as tasks are achieved

Monthly

- Identify the top priorities–both personal and ministry–for the month (e.g. family days, leadership development)
- Estimate how long each one will take to complete
- Determine the time you have available to do your important tasks, then plan blocks of time in your calendar to achieve these priorities
- Organize and schedule your work
- Use the last day of each month to plan and lay out the priorities for next month

Weekly

- Have a written weekly schedule and daily agenda
- Plan marriage or family activities into your schedule

- Plan your weekly schedule based on the rhythms and cycles of your life and leadership

Daily

- Have a written plan for each day
- Be diligent in adhering to your plan for the day
- Maximize the first two hours of the day
- Work on your important tasks first
- Schedule important work in your most productive hours
- Plan tomorrow's work today by organizing the next day at the end of the current day; in this way you'll know what to work on when you arrive

I heard leadership author and speaker, John Maxwell, say that: 'If you fail to plan, you plan to fail.' He also stated that 'Today's actions determine tomorrow's achievements.'[4]

E. Plan each day

Mackenzie wrote that 'planning your day... is the single most important piece in the time management puzzle.'[5] He added later that: 'A daily plan, in writing, is *the* most effective time management strategy, yet not one person in ten does it.'[6]

One of the best ways to plan a daily schedule is to: (a) list everything we're supposed to do, (b) categorize each activity into broader groupings, (c) prioritize each activity within the category, then (d) assign the category to a certain time of day.

To work out the best time of day to do particular tasks, Mackenzie wrote about the 'personal energy cycle' of the day.[7] In the cycle of every day, there will be times when we are fresh,

4 From personal notes taken while listening to Maxwell at the Hillsong Conference, Sydney, 2005.
5 Mackenzie, 28.
6 ibid, 41.
7 ibid, 39.

creative and clear-minded. There may be other times in the day (normally after lunch or late afternoon for me) when we may not be at our peak. Mackenzie suggests we 'plot' our energy cycle by keeping a detailed record of our time usage for 3 days to a week, then, after review and reflection on the results, schedule our 'key tasks for your best working times, and work on these tasks at the same time each day.'[8] The concept is to assign 'blocks of time' for major categories of activities.

For example, I am fresh and mentally alert in the morning, so I have my devotional time of prayer, worship and Scripture as the first block of the day before I begin my actual work. I then tend to do any activity that requires creativity or clear-minded thought, such as study or strategic planning. After lunch, when my creative juices are depleted, I generally focus on organizational or operational tasks, such as email, appointments, phone calls or administrative planning. Often, I have one more energy burst which I usually use to record thoughts, plan the following day and do some writing or preparation. I endeavor to keep evenings free for my wife or relaxation, with the exception of an occasional hour here or there for the unexpected or urgent.

Once you have created your daily plan, please remember to write it down for two reasons: first, it'll give you a plan to adhere to each day; and, second, it'll help you to be far more organized and maximize your use of time.

Conner suggests a helpful way to categorize activities as follows:[9]

Prime time (when we function best) focus on the high priorities, such as:

- Matters that require concentration

---

8 ibid, 39.

9 Mark Conner, *Time Management Tips* (Leadership Now Magazine, July, 2000 edition), 22.

- Preparation
- Strategic planning
- Thinking and reading
- Developing people
- Praying.

Grind time (when we're not at our peak) focus on the low to medium priorities, such as:

- Administration
- Management
- Organizing
- Communication
- Reviewing
- Traveling
- Facilitating.

Unwind time (when we're at home) focus on our personal priorities, such as:

- Quality time with spouse
- Family time
- Relaxation
- Get away from it all
- Hobbies
- Exercise
- Prayer retreats.

Another suggestion, is to assign each activity for the day into one of the four following categories, then carry out the appropriate action:[10]

Importantly, our use of time shouldn't be measured quantitatively but qualitatively.

10 ibid, 21.

Category	*Action*
Do it *now*	Move it to the front of the line
Do it *later*	Move it to the appropriate place
Don't do it	Move it to the waste paper basket
Delegate it	Move it to the appropriate person

Importantly, our use of time shouldn't be measured quantitatively but qualitatively. The effectiveness of the time we use on each priority is not necessarily measured by how long we spend on it, but by the quality of time we spend on it. For example, a busy leader may schedule time for his/her kids, but if they're distracted by other pressures it won't be qualitative time. The whole idea of planning time is to maximize the moment by being fully engaged and involved in the activity qualitatively.

To use our time productively, I would add a few suggestions I've heard from some great leaders:

- Always allow extra time for every task; things always take longer than we think, so add about an extra 50%
- Expect problems–motion causes friction, but stay focused on the actual task
- Expect interruptions, but learn to manage them so they don't derail your priorities
- Be flexible, not rigid or belligerent
- Get ahead when the pressure is off.

Doing the right thing is just as important as doing things right. Until we can say 'no' to the unimportant we will never be able to say 'yes' to the important. Deciding what *not* to do is as important as deciding what *to* do. Dr Howard Hendricks (1924-

2013), long time professor at Dallas Theological Seminary, wrote, 'The secret of concentration is elimination.'[11]

F. Avoid time wasting and time wasters

If we are to use our time effectively, we need to minimize, as best we can, those things or people that distract or consume our time. Here are some examples.[12]

Personal time wasters (caused by me):

- Attempting too much
- Confused about our responsibility or authority
- Daydreaming
- Inadequate planning
- Indecisiveness
- Ineffective delegation
- Inability to say 'no'
- Lack of self-discipline
- Leaving tasks unfinished
- Management by crisis
- Mental worry
- Paper work
- Personal disorganization
- Procrastination
- Socializing or social networking
- Travel
- Unimportant distractions.

---

11 Andy Stanley, *The Next Generation Leader* (Colorado Springs, CO: Multnomah, 2003), 15.

12 Adapted from Mackenzie, 55–188, where in Part Two of his book, he covers '20 Biggest Time Wasters and How to Cure Them'. I have categorised them between 'personal' and 'leadership' time wasters and added a few of my own.

Leadership time wasters (caused by others):

- Crises
- Poor communication
- Drop-in visitors
- Inadequate controls and progress reports
- Inadequate staff
- Incompetent staff
- Incomplete information
- Meetings
- Meetings without an agenda (scheduled or not)
- Poor planning
- Telephone interruptions.

G. Don't procrastinate

An eighth and final practical point in disciplining our time is not to procrastinate. Indecision and inaction are still decisions–decisions to do nothing. Let's do what we need to do within the allocated time. Start the task *now*. Many people never start a task because they think they don't have time to finish it. Just get started. Whenever possible, work on tasks and activities ahead of time or in quiet times. Plan blocks of time to work on the project. Break large tasks into small ones. Get unpleasant duties out of the way as soon as possible. Seek help from other organized people if you can't do it yourself.

> The most important day of our lives is: today (Matthew 6:34)! Therefore, let's make our time matter today

Finally - the most important day of your life

What has been the most important day of your life to date? Many of us may possibly answer, 'It was the day I was saved', or 'It was the day I was married', or 'The day when my first child was born.' All of these are valid answers; but Jesus told us that the most important day of our lives is: *today* (Matthew 6:34)! Therefore, let's make our time matter *today* by disciplining ourselves. It is said of Martin Luther that he only had two days on his calendar: today and *that* day. In a similar vein, Matthew Henry once said, 'It ought to be the business of every day to prepare for our final day.'[13]

Self-reflection:

What is the biggest lesson for you from reading this chapter?

Review your weekly and annual schedule to see if your time allocation reflects your main priorities in life and leadership.

What specific actions will you implement to take control of your time?

In regard to your spouse, family or closest friends, what changes will you make to your use of time to prioritize more time for them?

13 Cited in Rick Warren, *The Purpose Driven Life* (Grand Rapids, MI: Zondervan, 2002), 40.

Chapter Six

Be Disciplined in Financial Stewardship

Another area of a leader's personal discipline is financial stewardship. Our attitude toward, and management of, our finances goes to the very core of our personal discipline. Our attitude to money reveals a lot about the nature of our heart, as we'll soon see. Paul instructed Timothy that a Christian leader must not be a *'...not a lover of money...'* (1 Timothy 3:3) nor pursue *'dishonest gain...'* (1 Timothy 3:8; cf. Titus 1:7).

The word *steward* is not a word we use much in our everyday vocabulary, yet it is a motif used in Scripture to describe how a believer is required to faithfully exercise what has been entrusted to them. Christian stewardship encompasses more than money; it also covers how we use our time, gifts, prowess and skills. Our focus, in this chapter, however, will be on the stewardship of our *finances*.

Biblical concept of *'stewardship'*

Before offering some practical ideas on *how* to responsibly steward our finances as an expression of our self-discipline, let's briefly explore what it means, in Scripture, to be a steward. There are two foundational principles upon which we build a Christian view of stewardship.

Firstly, **God is the *owner* of *all* things** (Genesis 14:19; Psalm 24:1; 50:10; Haggai 2:8). As people, we own *nothing*. As the Creator of the heavens and the earth, and by right of creation, everything belongs to God. That means that everything that exists is God's. 'Ownership is the right of control. Whoever owns anything has the authority over that possession and it is theirs to do what they will with it.'[1]

Secondly, our response to this truth is to recognize that, as believers in Jesus, **we are *stewards* of *entrusted* things**.

In Bible times, just as today, owners would entrust the management of their properties or assets to professional stewards. Obviously the steward had to perform faithfully and proficiently, or he wouldn't last long in his job. A steward was regarded as:

- one charged with the administration of the affairs of another, or of the true owner
- one who managed the property of another
- one who was under the authority of the owner
- one who had to give an account to the owner of the way he has managed the property of the owner.[2]

In our case, God, as the Owner of everything, has placed us in the role of a steward to manage the part of his 'estate' that he's entrusted us with.

Two Scriptures, in particular, help us to understand a Biblical concept of stewardship. First, in 1 Corinthians 4:1-2, Paul wrote, *'So then, men ought to regard us as servants of Christ and as those* ***entrusted*** *with the secret things of God. Now it is required that those who have been* ***given a trust*** *must prove faithful'* (Emphases mine). What we deduce from these verses is that a

1 Conner, *Tithes & Offerings: Christian Stewardship in Old and New* Testaments (Melbourne, VIC: KJC Publications, 1993), 4.
2 ibid, 5.

steward is one who is faithful in fulfilling a trust (responsibility) given to them by God.

A steward is responsible and accountable to God for what has been entrusted to them (Matthew 25:19). There is a day of reckoning.

Second, in Matthew 25:14-30 Jesus taught what is commonly referred to as the *Parable of the Talents*. In the parable, the Lord taught a number of lessons about stewardship:

- All we have has been *entrusted* to us from God (Matthew 25:14)–a Christian, therefore, is a receiver, a trustee and a steward of what God has given them.
- A steward is responsible and accountable to God for what has been entrusted to them (Matthew 25:19). There is a day of reckoning. A steward is not an owner who has *rights*, but one who has *responsibilities*.
- A steward's productivity is measured by their faithfulness (Matthew 25:21). Stewards must be found faithful in the use of whatever has been entrusted to them. That means they must manage what has been entrusted to them, in the most effective way possible, for their master.
- Stewardship requires action (Matthew 25:26-27)–we must *do* something with what has been entrusted to us. The wicked servant knew what he should do, but did nothing. It is negligence to misuse, abuse or lose what has been entrusted to us (Matthew 25:24-30).
- A true and faithful steward will be rewarded (Matthew 25:19-23). *'His master replied, "Well done, good and faithful servant! You have been faithful with a few things; I will put you in charge of many things"'* (Matthew 25:21). Our stewardship has eternal implications.

Definition of stewardship

Based on what we've discovered above, stewardship could be defined as the faithful and responsible use of God-given resources for the accomplishment of God-given goals.

Stewardship begins as an issue of the heart. It is an act of surrender before it is an act of discipline.

Kevin Conner offers a more comprehensive definition:

> Christian stewardship is the practice of systematic and proportionate giving of time, abilities and material possessions, based on the conviction that these are a trust from God to be used in His service for the benefit of His Kingdom. It is a Divine-human partnership, with God as the senior partner. It is a way of living. It is the recognition of God's ownership of one's person, one's powers and one's possessions, and the faithful use of these for the advancement of Christ's Kingdom in this world.[3]

Financial stewardship in practice

If stewardship is a discipline, we must ask ourselves how stewardship works out in the practical realities of our daily lives. The following are some practical and Biblical ideas on how to faithfully exercise financial stewardship as part of our self-discipline.

A. We should give *ourselves* first to the Lord

Stewardship begins as an issue of the heart. It is an act of surrender before it is an act of discipline. In 2 Corinthians 8:5, Paul commended the Macedonians because, *'...they gave **themselves first to the Lord** and then to us...'* (emphasis mine). Despite their *'severe trial'* and *'extreme poverty'* (2 Corinthians 8:2), they gave generously as part of their Christian service (2

3 ibid, 4.

Corinthians 8:4), but their first act of giving was of their *own lives* to the Lord Jesus.

Likewise, if we are to exercise financial stewardship, it begins with the act of surrender of our lives to the person, cause and worship of Jesus, before it begins to affect our actual giving. Our level of surrender to Jesus usually has a big impact on the proportional level of our giving.

B. As a Christian leader, we should lead financially by the example of our own giving

Whether anyone ever knows about the level of our giving or not, there is the spiritual principle of leading by example. As I've underlined throughout this book–we lead from the inside out. There may be times when it is appropriate to publicly disclose what we have given, but our unseen example is setting a spiritual pattern for the giving patterns of those we are leading. In a different context, Jesus taught that, in washing the disciples' feet, his example as the leader should become the baseline for what they, as future leaders, should do in serving others through their leadership (John 13:12-17). His example set the standard for the group. This principle transposes to our giving also.

C. Develop an annual, monthly and weekly personal/family budget[4]

In basic terms, a budget is an annual estimate of our income and expenditure, which we then formulate into a plan for how we'll administer and adjust the funds each week and month to maintain our life and lifestyle. If you're not financially-minded, or perhaps don't know how to prepare a budget, seek help from a financial counselor or from the helpful collection of written material. The key to a budget is to *stick to it*. Importantly, part of our budget should be the proportional (2 Corinthians 9:6; 8:14–

4 For practical suggestions on how to budget see Chapter 18, point 'I' on 'Establishing and sticking to a budget'.

15), regular (1 Corinthians 16:1-2), systematic (2 Corinthians 9:7) giving to God according to our means (2 Corinthians 8:12).

D. Avoid unmanageable debt[5]

According to Proverbs 22:7, debt makes us indebted to the lender. Unmanageable debt incapacitates our ability to use our finances as we desire and it restricts our capacity to give. In the Old Testament, debt was viewed as a curse, a consequence of disobedience and a sign that a person was not living as they should have been (Deuteronomy 15:4-6; 28:1-2; 12-15; 43-45). The key to avoiding unmanageable debt is to *live within our means*. This may mean curbing our spending so that we don't purchase things carelessly or without restraint. If you're currently in debt, do what you can *now* with what you have *now* to repay the debt (Proverbs 3:27-28). Always seek to pay your bills and debts on time (Psalm 37:21; Romans 13:8). Beware of greed (1 Timothy 6:10), coveting (Exodus 20:17) and making plans without due thought, prayer and planning (Luke 14:28-30).

E. Use tithing as the baseline for our giving

The word tithe simply means 'a tenth'. In the Old Testament, both Abraham (Genesis 14:17-20) and Jacob (Genesis 28:22) tithed before it became part of the Law (Leviticus 27:30-33; Proverbs 3:9-10; Malachi 3:6-12). Jesus confirmed tithing, but condemned the Pharisees for giving a tenth while neglecting the *'more important'* character qualities of *'justice, mercy and faithfulness'* (Matthew 23:23). He didn't condemn the Pharisees for tithing, but for their hypocritical attitudes; he condemned them for doing the external duty (tithing) but with a wrong internal heart attitude. This teaches us that we must give with the right motive.

---

5 For practical suggestions on how to reduce our debts see Chapter 18, point 'I' on 'Avoid or minimize debt'.

Then, in the book of Acts and the epistles, giving was taken to a whole new level. We learn that we should give willingly, not under compulsion (2 Corinthians 8:3,12), cheerfully, not grudgingly (2 Corinthians 9:7), generously (2 Corinthians 8:2; 9:13), proportionately (2 Corinthians 9:6; 8:14-15), regularly (1 Corinthians 16:1-2), systematically (2 Corinthians 9:7), lovingly (2 Corinthians 8:24), from a grateful heart (2 Corinthians 8:24), as a ministry to the Lord and his people (2 Corinthians 9:11-13), and according to our ability (2 Corinthians 8:12).

Tithing is not a law in the New Testament, but a recommendation as the baseline for our giving to God.

Putting all this together, it is my contention that tithing is not a law (as such) in the New Testament, but a recommendation as the baseline for our giving to God. My wife and I practice tithing as a recognition of God's provision, but we also give offerings above and beyond our tithe as we're able and as the Lord leads.

F. Give generously and sacrificially to God, his Kingdom and Church

One story that illustrates sacrificial giving is the account of the widow's offering, which is found in Mark 12:41-44 and Luke 21:1-4. In this story, Jesus and his disciples were sitting opposite the place where people were making offerings. He was watching '*...the crowd putting their money into the temple treasury*' (Mark 12:41). (By the way, Jesus is *still* watching both how much we give and our motive in doing so.) He noted that the rich '*threw in large amounts*' of money, but '*a poor widow came and put in two very small copper coins, worth only a fraction of a penny*' (Mark 12:41-42). Her offering impacted Jesus. Something of kingdom significance had taken place.

'Calling the disciples to him, Jesus said, "I tell you the truth, this poor widow has put more money into the treasury than all the others. They all gave out of their wealth; but she, out of her poverty, put in everything–all she had to live on"' (Mark 12:43-44).

True sacrifice leaves an enduring example and legacy. We must ask ourselves, 'What eternal legacy am I leaving?'

At first observation, we would naturally and logically say, "No, she didn't give more than the rich people. She only gave two small coins. The rich put in large amounts of money. How, then, could Jesus say that she had given *more* than the wealthy?" Obviously, God's economy and value system is very different than ours. God doesn't measure as we humanly measure. We measure by how much we *give*; God measures by how much is *left behind*. Or, in different words, God doesn't measure by the *size of the gift*, but by the *level of sacrifice*.

The rich did indeed give a lot, but they also had a lot left. Jesus said, *"...They all gave out of their wealth..."* They gave what was disposable income. They gave what they had calculated was affordable and convenient, but there was no sacrifice involved. This lady, however, gave *"...out of her poverty..."* In fact, Jesus said, she *"...put in* ***everything****–all she had to live on"* (emphasis mine). This was true sacrifice.

The widow's sacrifice also teaches us that *true sacrifice leaves an enduring example and legacy*. Her name is not mentioned. We don't know anything about her except that she was poor, she was a widow and she gave sacrificially. Yet her sacrifice is recorded in two of the Gospels as a permanent memorial in God's eternal Word. She left an enduring example of sacrificial giving. A sobering question we must ask ourselves is, 'What eternal legacy am I leaving?'

One final application of these short thoughts on sacrificial giving is to remember to also give to the *poor and disadvantaged* (Hebrews 13:16; Proverbs 19:17; 21:13; Deuteronomy 15:7; Galatians 2:10).

G. Exercise complete financial integrity (Psalm 41:12; Proverbs 11:3; 20:7)

One of the ways we lead by example is by exercising complete and transparent integrity in the area of our personal finances. When Moses confronted the rebellious faction of Korah, Dathan and Abiram, he was able to say that he '*...had not taken so much as a donkey from them...*' (Numbers 16:15). During Samuel's farewell speech, the people responded that he had '*...not cheated or oppressed*' them, nor had he '*taken anything from anyone's hand*' (1 Samuel 12:4). After being miraculously healed, a very grateful Naaman tried to give Elisha a gift of thanks, but Elisha responded, '*I will not accept a thing*' (2 Kings 5:16). When Joash initiated repairs on the temple, the funds raised were given to supervisors who paid the site workers (2 Kings 12:11), but the priests '*...did not require an accounting from...*' them '*...because they acted with complete honesty*' (2 Kings 12:15).

In contrast to this is the dishonesty of Judas who, '*...as keeper of the money bag...used to help himself to what was put into it*' (John 12:6), and who betrayed Jesus out of greed for 30 pieces of silver (Matthew 26:14-15). Elisha's servant, Gehazi, exploited Naaman by requesting '*...a talent of silver and two sets of clothing*' (2 Kings 5:22) for himself. He reasoned that Elisha had been '*too easy on Naaman...by not accepting*' any of the gifts Naaman wanted to give after being healed of leprosy (2 Kings 5:20). The tragic consequence was that Gehazi and his descendants became leprous once his deception was prophetically exposed by Elisha (2 Kings 5:27). Ananias and his wife, Sapphira, lied about how much they received from the sale of their property when giving an offering for the apostles to distribute. The problem wasn't that they withheld some of the proceeds for themselves, but that they were deceiving people into thinking that they were giving the *whole* of the sale price to God. They both paid a severe penalty for their lies and deceit (Acts 5:1-10). It's understandable, then, why Paul listed one of the qualities of a Christian leader as not pursuing '*dishonest gain...*' (1 Timothy 3:8; cf. Titus 3:7).

Exercising financial integrity means we: pay the right amount of tax (Romans 13:6-7), because there is a huge difference morally and ethically between tax minimization and tax evasion; submit tax returns when required by local legislative authorities; pay bills on time (Romans 13:8); truthfully fill in submissions to banks and other financial institutions about the state and status of our finances; never knowingly give wrong impressions or perceptions about our giving (remember Ananias and Sapphira); manage our finances with unquestioned propriety.

H. Maintain an eternal perspective on giving

Jesus urged his followers not to '*...lay up for yourselves treasures on earth... but lay up for yourselves treasures in heaven...*' (Matthew 6:19-20). What we discover from these verses is that giving has an eternal dimension. The more sacrificially generous we are on earth, the greater the level of our eternal reward and responsibility will be in heaven.

The reason Jesus wanted his disciples to have an eternal perspective on giving is found in the next verse: '*For where your treasure is, there your heart will be also*' (Matthew 6:21). Pastor and author, John Piper (1946-) asked the question, 'Why does Jesus express such a remarkable concern with what we do with our money?' Based on this verse, he answered,

> ...the reason money is so crucial is that what we do with it signals where our heart is. "Where our heart is" means where our worship is. When the heart is set on something, it values it, cherishes it, treasures it. That is what worship means.[6]

Our pursuit of God must far outstrip our pursuit of money.

God's motive in wanting us to steward our resources appropriately is not that he needs our money; on the contrary, the Lord wants our hearts, our worship, and, in a word, our *all*. In this same passage (Matthew 6:19-24), Jesus emphasized the impossibility and incompatibility of serving both God and money (Matthew 6:24). It is possible to serve God *with* money, but not God *and* money. Our pursuit of God must far outstrip our pursuit of money.

In a passage reminiscent of Matthew 6, the Lord told the *Parable of the Shrewd Manager* (Luke 16:1–15). With the concept of stewardship as a backdrop, the sobering application of the parable is found in verses 10–12, where Jesus said:

> *"Whoever can be trusted with very little can also be trusted with much, and whoever is dishonest with very little will also be dishonest with much. So if you have not been trustworthy in handling worldly wealth, who will trust you with true riches? And if you have not been trustworthy with someone else's property, who will give you property of your own?"*

With eternity in mind (true riches), the necessity to discipline ourselves to faithfully and responsibly steward our finances (worldly wealth) is critical.

---

6 John Piper, *What Jesus Demands From The World* (Wheaton, IL: Crossway, 2011), 272.

When my kids were young we used to enjoy playing *Monopoly* as a family. Even though it was only a game, the kids' true nature surfaced. One was completely scrupulous, another cheated whenever possible, and the other one lost his temper when having to pay a sibling some money. It was supposed to be fun! Sometimes, you could accumulate a great deal of wealth in cash and assets. But, outside of the game, I could never take the *Monopoly* money and use it to purchase anything or pay a bill. It was a worthless currency outside of the game.

Similarly, in this life, we may have accumulated or squandered wealth and assets. We can use money to buy and sell, to save or pay bills, to give or keep for ourselves. But in eternity, our money and possessions have no value. We can't take them with us. They are just like *Monopoly* money and properties, even Mayfair and Park Lane. It's only what we have invested for eternity through our regular and sacrificial giving, tithes and offerings that translate into eternal riches (*'treasure in heaven'*). Eternity is a profoundly difficult and mind-numbing concept to understand, which is why it's virtually impossible to comprehend what the nature of the *'treasure in heaven'* really is. It is beyond the scope of the finite mind, except to say that it has a big bearing on our level of reward and responsibility in the age to come. Our giving has an *eternal* dimension.

Let's conclude this chapter on being disciplined in stewarding our finances by quoting British revivalist, preacher, and founder of the Methodists, John Wesley (1703-1791), who once said: 'Make as much as you can, save all you can, give away all you can.'[7]

7 This is the popularized version of a quote from one of Wesley's sermons in which he originally said, "Having, first, gained all you can, and, secondly, saved all you can, then give all you can." Source: https://en.wikiquote.org/wiki/John_Wesley.

Self-reflection:

What principle or thought impacted you the most in this chapter?

Why?

What specific steps or actions will you implement from what you have read?

Chapter Seven

Be Disciplined in Personal Spiritual Practices

The story is told of a young Italian couple, living in a remote village on the picturesque Amalfi Coast. They were having trouble conceiving a child, so they went to see their local priest who, because he was about to be transferred to Rome, promised to light a candle for them.

It was a decade before the priest returned to the village where the young couple lived. As he walked toward his parish church, he came across the young lady he hadn't seen since her tearful request for prayer.

Tentatively, the priest asked her, "My daughter, do you have any children."

"Oh, yes, Father," she replied, "we now have 10 children!"

"That's wonderful," responded the priest, unable to disguise his surprise. Composing himself, he then added, "Congratulations. I'm so happy for you. Where is your husband? I'd like to congratulate him, too?"

With a slightly embarrassed tone, she said, "Sorry, Father, he's not here."

"Where is he, daughter?" asked the inquisitive priest.

> **A leader's devotional life is a fundamental means of growing in intimacy and maturity.**

"He's gone to Rome, Father," came her reply, careful not to say too much.

With a suspicious tone, he probed, "Why has he gone to Rome?"

She couldn't hide the truth any longer, so she conceded, "He's gone to blow out the candle!"

This chapter is about how we can light candles, or, less euphemistically, how we can meaningfully engage with God each day through our daily devotional disciplines.

A leader's devotional life is a fundamental means of growing in intimacy and maturity. A healthy and balanced devotional life is made of up three spiritual practices (though some authors prefer the word 'disciplines'), which are prayer, engaging with Scripture and fellowship with the Holy Spirit. These practices require the leader to exercise daily discipline.

Importantly, it is not discipline *per se* that transforms a leader's spiritual life. Some leaders can be highly disciplined but completely disengaged from God. Rather, it is the vitality and motivation of these practices that produces spiritual growth. We'll now explore each one and provide some practical advice.

A. Prayer

Prayer is the act of conversation and communication with God. The practice of prayer has a number of applications:

Praying. Foremost, the practice of prayer incorporates the *act of praying*. There are many models for developing one's prayer time, such as the Lord's Prayer in Matthew 6:9-13. It is imperative that leaders set aside specific time each day for engagement with God through prayer. Scripture encourages us to *'pray without ceasing'* (1 Thessalonians 5:17), which, in practice, means to seek to maintain a prayerful attitude throughout the day.

Prayer is not a monologue, but a dialogue. Make time to be still in God's presence.

Fasting. Aside from the regular devotion to prayer, a leader would be encouraged to fast. Scripture teaches the value and purpose of fasting on a regular basis.[1] Along with prayer and giving, Jesus portrayed fasting as one of the central Christian duties (Matthew 6:16-18). Strictly speaking, fasting is refraining from food for a spiritual purpose. In broader terms, fasting is abstaining from food partially or totally, for shorter or longer periods, with an expressed spiritual purpose in mind. It is the discipline of self-denial, self-control and self-restraint to accompany prayer to God.

Listening. Prayer involves the discipline of listening. There is an American First Nation proverb that reportedly says: 'Listen, or your tongue will keep you deaf.' Prayer is not a monologue, but a dialogue. Communication and conversation involve more than mere talk. They require active listening–the giving of one's undivided attention. The quality of our listening determines the quality of our relationship, whether it be marital, interpersonal or with the Lord himself. Leaders should take and make time to be still in God's presence to listen to and for his voice (John 10:27).

B. Engaging with Scripture

The Bible is the Word of God. It is the written revelation *of* God and *from* God (2 Timothy 3:16; 2 Peter 1:21). It is God's Word

1 See Esther 4:3, 16; Nehemiah 1:4; 2 Chronicles 20:3; Acts 13:1-2; 14:23.

to us. It is God speaking to us. Therefore, a second spiritual practice is to engage with Scripture. Please notice, I did not just say *reading* the Scripture, though this is imperative, as we'll soon see. I very intentionally have used the words 'engaging with Scripture' because simply reading the Bible does not necessarily mean we have interacted with the Scripture. Engaging with Scripture has a number of practical applications:

Reading the Word of God. Like prayer, it almost goes without saying, but engaging with Scripture involves the actual *reading* of God's Word. There are a number of ways to approach Bible reading: daily Bible reading guide; devotional book; systematic; or chronological reading. The important thing is not the method, but the motivation; that is, to hear from God through his Word.

Journaling. Bible Journaling is the practice of reading a designated passage of Scripture (normally from a bible reading guide), then devotionally recording what phrase, verse or thought was meaningful, and what we felt God was saying through the passage.

The acrostic SOAP is a helpful step-by-step process to follow in learning how to journal: [2]

S = Scripture

O = Observation

A = Application

P = Prayer

Meditating. In Scripture, the word *meditation* can mean 'ponder, muse, mutter or practice.' In practical terms, this may mean reading and rereading the same passage many times over with the clear intention of '...thinking about, reflecting

2 The practice of journaling is explained and articulated in my book, *Praying with Power* (Brisbane, QLD: CHI-Books, 2013), 31-34.

upon, considering, taking to heart, reading slowly and carefully, prayerfully taking in, and humbly receiving in mind, heart and will that which God has revealed' in his Word.[3]

The purpose of meditating on Scripture is twofold:

- to gain *insight* (illumination / revelation) into the meaning concealed within the verses (Psalm 48:9; 77:12)
- to draw *application*–what we must do to *apply* this portion of God's Word to our life (Joshua 1:8).

Meditation is an 'inward digesting' of the Word of God brought about by the Holy Spirit.[4]

Memorizing. Memorizing Scripture is committing key Scriptures to memory so that our heart and mind are full of God's Word (Psalm 119:11; 1 John 2:14b).

Applying. Applying the Scriptures is a means of putting God's Word into practice. James wrote in his epistle that believers are not just to 'hear' or 'know' the Word of God, but actually '*do what it says*' (James 1:22). The author of Hebrews urged his readers to imitate mature Christians who constantly 'use' the Word of God as a way to spiritually discern good from evil (Hebrews 5:14). Toward the end of the Sermon on the Mount, Jesus told a parable comparing two builders–one wise, the other foolish (Matthew 7:24-27). The application of the parable was that, as Jesus' listeners put his words into practice, they were reinforcing and fortifying the foundation of their lives, particularly in trying times. The lesson for leaders is to *apply* the Word of God.

C. Fellowship with the Holy Spirit

The practice of fellowship with the Holy Spirit requires developing a genuine relationship with the *person* of the

3 Peter Toon, *Meditating as a Christian* (London, England: Collins, 1991), 19.
4 ibid, 29.

Holy Spirit. Fellowship has a strong notion of community in Scripture. Leaders would, therefore, be encouraged to commune with the Spirit as a (divine) person. Fellowship with the Spirit is to foster a conscious awareness of his presence and work in our life. This flows out of a daily dependence.

Pray every day, engage with Scripture every day and fellowship with the Holy Spirit every day.

Summary of the spiritual disciplines

In short, pray every day, engage with Scripture every day and fellowship with the Holy Spirit every day. Make time and a place to be with the Lord each day. These daily spiritual practices will sustain our spiritual life and inwardly strengthen us for the work of ministry leadership, *but* it requires personal discipline.

Self-reflection:

Please record the one dominant thought that struck you from this chapter.

What particular practice (or discipline) do you need to give attention?

What specific steps or actions have you identified to enhance your devotional life?

SECTION THREE

Self-Control

A third expression of self-leadership is for the leader to be self-regulated. In other words, the leader must be able to internally regulate, and exercise self-control (self-mastery), over their lives. The late Myles Monroe (1954–2014) wrote of a leader's self-discipline being 'self-imposed standards and restrictions' so they are 'self-policing.'[1]

The chapters in this section will each explore a separate area where self-control is needed in a leader's life, as follows:

- Self-control of our temper
- Self-control in responding to criticism
- Self-control of our tongue (words)
- Self-control of our self-talk
- Self-control of our thought-life
- Self-control of our sexual desires
- Self-control in being above reproach
- Self-control in managing stress.

One of the principal ways leaders self-regulate their lives is through the exercise of self-control. The language of self-control is strongly embedded in Paul's pastoral letters. In the list

1 Myles Monroe, *The Spirit of Leadership* (New Kensington, PA: Whitaker, 2005), 267.

of qualifications for church 'overseers' and 'deacons', Paul writes of leaders being *'temperate'* (1 Timothy 3:2, 11; cf. Titus 2:2) and *'self-controlled'* (1 Timothy 3:2; Titus 1:8). Temperate derives from the Greek word *nephalios* meaning 'sober' in the sense of 'balanced, sober-thinking' whereas 'self-controlled', which comes from the Greek word *sphron*, has a range of meanings including 'disciplined, moderation, sobriety'– depending on the context.[2] Through these words, Paul was calling for leaders to exercise 'control over one's behavior and the impulses and emotions beneath it.'[3] In all areas of their life, a leader is required to be self-regulated by being moderate, sober-minded and self-controlled.

Self-control is one of the *'fruit of the Holy Spirit'* (Galatians 5:22-23). As such, it is a product of the Spirit's indwelling presence (2 Timothy 1:7) transforming believers to be *'conformed to the likeness'* of Christ (Romans 8:29). The essential nature of the fruit is the *reproduction* of the life of Christ in us.

Therefore, self-control could be defined as having one's life under the control of the Holy Spirit. In the context of the Spirit's fruit, self-control is actually brought about by the Spirit's power enabling the leader to exercise restraint, discipline and control *in* and *over* their lives. By the Spirit's power, self-control is the divine capacity to have one's life in check.

The New Testament, in particular, directs Christians to be self-controlled in a number of key areas. In Paul's list of character qualifications for leaders, for example, he lists exercising moderation in drinking alcohol (1 Timothy 3:3; cf. 3:8; Titus 1:7) and watching our attitude to money (1 Timothy 3:3, 8; cf. Titus 1:7).[4] In this section, we're going to highlight a number of representative areas in which a leader must be self-controlled.

---

2 Towner, 50.
3 ibid, 50.
4 Moderation suggests the idea of being balanced, measured, appropriate and under control, in stark contrast to being excessive, indulgent, inappropriate or out of control.

Chapter Eight

Self-Control of Our Temper

I can embarrassingly recall three times when I have lost my temper as a leader. One occurrence stands out vividly. It happened back when I was a youth pastor in the early 1990s. We'd taken all our young adults for a weekend away at a campsite about two hours northeast of Melbourne. The camp had twenty bungalow-style units spread over the site, each with eight beds.

In the middle of the night, a number of the mischievous young men broke into the camp administration office, and turned on the internal PA system, which broadcasts into every unit. For some absurd reason, they began to scream a horrific, blood-curdling scream, as if someone was being murdered. Then they began to speak with deep, sinister voices you'd hear in a horror movie. It woke me (and almost everyone else). Though startled, I knew almost immediately what was happening, so I quickly put on some pants and ran as fast as I could to where they were. I caught them red-handed.

While I am usually measured and careful in my choice and use of words, I am particularly grumpy if I get woken in the night. This night, there was no restraint, just pure unrestrained grumpiness. I don't remember exactly what I said verbatim, but I do remember yelling words like 'idiots, immature, thoughtless' and some other descriptive Christian expletives. At the end of my rant I said, 'Now pack up your things and go home!' It was only after they all sheepishly left the room to go pack their bags to drive home that I realized the PA was still on! Everyone in every cabin had heard my eloquent castigation.

Next morning, I felt bad that everyone at the camp, including the guest speaker, had heard me lose my temper. Far from being disillusioned by my outburst, the young people actually applauded and thanked me. They'd never seen (or heard) that side of me before. Even though I went up in people's estimation, in hindsight I probably should have reacted in a more moderate way. That is what this chapter is all about–the self-control of a leader's temper.

In Paul's lists of character qualities, he writes that a leader must not be '*...violent but gentle, not quarrelsome...*' (1 Timothy 3:3), nor '*...quick-tempered...*' (Titus 3:7). A leader needs to be in control of their temper and emotional state at all times.

Leaders who lost their temper

There are numerous examples of leaders in Scripture who lost their temper. The consequences were sometimes disastrous as the following list portrays:

- Moses murdered an oppressive Egyptian in the misguided attempt to demonstrate to his people that he was a deliverer, and subsequently spent 40 years in the wilderness on the run (Exodus 2:11-12; Acts 7:25)
- Later, Moses struck the rock out of angry frustration with the Israelites, and forfeited entry into the Promised Land (Numbers 20:11-12)
- Out of blind jealousy, Saul mercilessly executed the priests of Nob for innocently harboring David (1 Samuel 22:6-23)

- Saul also angrily hurled a spear at his son, Jonathan, intending to kill him, when the latter sought to explain David's absence from a feast (1 Samuel 20:33)
- David was on his way to kill Nabal and would have been guilty of shedding blood out of vengeance had not Nabal's clever wife, Abigail, intervened and interceded (1 Samuel 25:13; 32-34)
- Motivated by vengeance, Joab, commander of Judah's army, killed Abner, commander of Israel's army, for killing his brother, Asahel (2 Samuel 3:27). Joab did this despite: Abner having defected to David; Abner's intent to bring Israel's forces under David's rule; and David having sent Abner away in peace (2 Samuel 3:21). David attributed guilt and blame fairly and squarely on Joab and, in what is tantamount to a curse, said, '*...may Joab's house never be without someone who has a running sore or leprosy or who leans on a crutch or who falls by the sword or who lacks food*' (2 Samuel 3:29).

A leader who loses their temper will suffer consequences.

The glaring conclusion of these examples is that a leader who loses their temper will suffer consequences.

How, then, can leaders control their temper? There is a passage in James that is rich with gems for how we can exercise self-control over our temper.

> *'My dear brothers, take note of this: Everyone should be quick to listen, slow to speak and slow to become angry, for a man's anger does not bring about the righteous life that God desires. Therefore, get rid of all moral filth and*

> *the evil that is so prevalent and humbly accept the word planted in you, which can save you'* (James 1:19-21).

Slow to become angry

James does *not* say that we should 'never be angry' or that 'anger is always sin'. However he does say to be '***slow*** *to become angry...'* (emphasis mine). Paul also wrote, *'In your anger do not sin...'* (Ephesians 4:26). These Scriptures indicate that not all anger is wrong or sinful. Neither James nor Paul forbid *all* anger, but specify anger that *is* sin or *leads* to sin. This suggests that there is a distinction between righteous anger and sinful anger.

Righteous anger

'Righteous anger' is an anger that is justified or defensible. There are a number of examples in Scripture of so called 'righteous anger'.

Firstly, *God* himself sometimes got angry. His anger was never impulsive or erratic, but a 'righteous response to specific human failures and sin.'[1] By way of example, despite the Lord's responses to Moses' series of objections and excuses for why he couldn't be the Israelites' deliverer, Moses finally blurted out, *'O, Lord, please send someone else to do it'* (Exodus 4:13). At this, *'...the Lord's anger burned against Moses...'* (Exodus 4:14). God also became angry when his people: unjustifiably complained against him (Numbers 11:1, 33; 12:9); disobeyed him (Numbers 32:10); violated his covenant (Deuteronomy 4:23-26); rejected him in favor of idols (Exodus 32:7-12; Numbers 25:3; Deuteronomy 11:16-17); or practiced injustice (Exodus 22:22-24). God's anger is viewed as 'completely justified and also as of ultimate benefit to people. Compared

1 Lawrence O Richards, *Expository Dictionary of Bible Words* (Grand Rapids, MI: Zondervan, 1990), 48.

to his favor, which lasts a lifetime, God's anger is momentary (Psalm 30:5).'[2]

Secondly, *Jesus* got angry. In John 2:13-17, we read of Jesus driving all the money changers, traders, sheep and cattle from the temple courts and overturning the tables. Zeal for his Father's house kindled his righteous anger. The Temple was supposed to be a place of prayer, not a place of commercial exploitation. On another occasion, recorded in Mark 3:1-5, Jesus was in the synagogue along with a man who had a shriveled hand. The Pharisees were there, too, but as part of a conspiracy to find fault with what Jesus said or did. Jesus asked, *'Which is lawful on the Sabbath: to do good or evil, to save life or to kill?'* Incriminating themselves, they remained silent. Jesus, then, '*... looked around at them in anger and deeply distressed at their stubborn hearts, said to the man, "Stretch out your hand"*' (Mark 3:5).

Thirdly, in the Old Testament, there were leaders who became 'righteously' angry. Descending from Mt Sinai, Moses found the Israelites worshipping and dancing before the golden calf as an object of worship. Consequently '*...his anger burned...*' (Exodus 32:19-20), and he took immediate disciplinary and remedial action. Sometime later, poised to enter the Promised Land, the Israelites were blatantly involved in unashamed and brazen immorality with the Moabites. As punishment, a plague broke out against the people. Motivated by zeal for God's honor, Phinehas, Aaron's grandson, drove a spear though the bodies of a prince in the tribe of Simeon and a Midianite princess, while they were in the act of sex, and halted the judgment (Numbers 25:8). He did so because it was behavior dishonoring the name of God among his people.[3]

---

2 ibid, 49.

3 Under the New Covenant, however, there is never any justification for violence in God's name.

For anger to be 'righteous', it must be rightly motivated and rightly controlled.

In addition, Jonathan was angry with his father, Saul, for his *'shameful treatment'* of David (1 Samuel 20:34).

Drawing application from these examples, we note that for anger to be 'righteous', it must be rightly motivated and rightly controlled. In the cases above, the motives behind their anger were love and zeal for what was right and pure, not hate or uncontrolled temper. For anger to be sinless, it must have God's honor and glory as its object, not personal vindication, pride or revenge. CS Lewis (1898–1963) described righteous anger as 'the fluid love bleeds when you cut it.'[4]

Before returning to the passage in James, there is one other distinction to draw. Even though a leader's anger may be righteous (justified), the *expression* of that anger must also be righteous. There can sometimes be unrighteous reactions to righteous anger. For example, when Simeon and Levi heard that their sister, Dinah, had been raped by Shechem (Genesis 34:2), they were justifiably angry (Genesis 34:7). But their actions of deceit and murder of all the men in Shechem's city (Genesis 34:25-26) were condemned (Genesis 49:6-7). As Richards points out, 'Revenge is ruled out for the believer, not only by the principle of forgiveness (Ephesians 4:32) but also to "leave room for God's wrath" (Romans 12:19). God alone is judge; he alone has the right to repay… The feeling of anger may be justified or unjustified. But the feeling of anger is never justification for sinful actions.'[5]

4 http://www.goodreads.com/quotes.
5 ibid, 50–51.

Back to James

So, James wrote that there is such a thing as righteous anger, but what he prohibits (in James 1:19–21) is the thoughtless, unrestrained temper that often leads to rash, harmful and irretrievable words or actions. Motyer (1924–) comments that '... anger and sin are never far apart... Anger is not a *pure* emotion. It is usually heavily impregnated with sin...'[6] Often, anger is motivated by impure motives like pride, self-importance, self-assertion, intolerance, stubbornness, revenge or bitterness.

It is almost impossible to deal with anger in a moment of high emotion, particularly if it is deep and abiding anger, so James wrote wise words about being '...***slow*** *to become angry...*' (emphasis mine). The normal order is that we lose our temper, say too much or do the wrong thing, then listen to God because we feel bad; but James offers a preventative alternative: listen first! Slow down! Manage your temper in the coolness of thoughtful and prayerful analysis. Why? Because '...an angry spirit is never an attentive or patient one. When anger comes, listening flies out.'[7] In essence, James' remedy runs: 'Listen to the Word; keep a tight rein on your tongue; slow down your anger; think before you speak or act; and endeavor to bring your anger under control before it gets out of control.'

Note carefully his wording to be '*...slow to* ***become*** *angry...*' (emphasis mine). The word '*become*' angry suggests that anger *can* and *must* be controlled. Most times, the expression of our anger is a *choice*. We choose to control or lose our temper. We choose to keep it in check or to unchain it. And we choose to what degree we become angry. For example, I was once visiting some friends who had young kids. The kids were being vigorously told off by my friend's wife for some misdemeanor when the phone suddenly rang. Like a switch being thrown, she answered calmly and, in a warm friendly tone, began to engage

6 Alec Motyer, *The Message of James* (Leicester, England: Inter-Varsity, 1997), 66.
7 ibid, 66.

the person on the other end. It was an instantaneous change that was astonishing to behold. It showed me that anger *can* be controlled *if* we want to control it.

But what is actually wrong with becoming angry? James goes on to write: '*...for man's anger does not bring about the righteous life that God desires*' (James 1:20).

What does James mean by '*...for man's anger does not bring about the righteous life that God desires*'? Our anger is not compatible or consistent with the new life we have in Christ. It's simply not right for a born again believer with God's nature within them to have their temper out of control. Hasty, uncontrolled anger is wrong because it violates the standard of conduct that God demands of his redeemed people.

Let me ask the next logical question: Why doesn't anger bring about the righteous life God seeks to produce in us? Here is a list of Scriptural answers to that question:

- Because an uncontrolled temper or '*fits of rage*' are part of the old sinful nature (Galatians 5:19–20)
- Because anger produces strife (Proverbs 30:33)
- Because anger stirs up more anger (Proverbs 15:1)
- Because anger grieves the Holy Spirit, especially if it is between believers (Ephesians 4:29–32, note v. 30)
- Because, unless we deal with anger, Ephesians 4:27 says that we give the devil a foothold, which means we may have opened ourselves up to demonic activity or influence in our life
- Because anger brings the judgment of God (Matthew 5:22)
- Because anger hurts both ourselves and other people. For example, Cain killed Abel in anger and became a 'marked' man (Genesis 4:8, 15). When Absalom heard that his half-brother, Amnon, had raped his sister, Tamar,

he *'...never said a word to Amnon, either good or bad; he hated Amnon...'* (2 Samuel 13:22). Two years later, however, Absalom had him killed.

So, what does James teach that we should do to manage our temper?

A. Get rid of everything in our life that fuels anger

James writes: *'Therefore,* ***get rid of*** *all moral filth and the evil that is so prevalent...'* (James 1:21, emphasis mine). The *'therefore'* directly ties what he's just been talking about (controlling the temper) to the next sentence (*how* to control the temper). Paul uses similar language in Ephesians 4:31 and Colossians 3:8–10 (cf. Ephesians 4:22–24).

'Get rid of' employs the metaphor of changing our clothes, meaning that we should discard anger as we would old clothes. We take old clothes off and, in most cases, throw them aside. Paul's use of the metaphor (Colossians 3:9–10 and Ephesians 4:22–24), implies we must 'take off' the old man (what, by nature, we were) and "put on" the new (what, by grace, we are in Christ).'[8] In non-metaphorical terms, this means getting rid of our old 'pre-Christian patterns of behavior', including our bad temper.[9] They belong to our old nature. Because we *'...have been born again, not of perishable seed, but of imperishable, through the living and enduring Word of God... And this is the word that was preached to you'* (1 Peter 1:23-25). We must, therefore, *'...rid [ourselves] of all malice and deceit, hypocrisy, envy, and slander of every kind'* (1 Peter 2:1). According to Peter, because we have been born again of incorruptible seed, we have a new nature and, by the Spirit, through his inspired and quickened Word, we are being transformed. Therefore

8 Williams, 93.

9 Douglas Moo, *The Letter of James: An Introduction and Commentary* (Leicester, England, Inter-Varsity, 1993), 80.

We must rid ourselves of things which produce anger, such as un-forgiveness, grudges, resentment, hatred, revenge or bitterness.

we must vigorously, decisively, and ruthlessly put off anger as belonging to our old nature.

Boiling down this teaching to the basics, it seems that James is urging us to deal with the *source* of our temper. The *source* of an uncontrolled temper is the old nature which is influenced by the prevailing culture or environment, whereas the source of a self-controlled temper is the new nature which is influenced by the Word and Spirit of God. We can no longer blame our genetic predisposition, upbringing or cultural environment. We have God's loving nature within us.

What does James specifically tell us to get rid of? He explicitly states that we must rid ourselves of *'...all moral filth and the evil that is so prevalent...'* (James 1:21). *'Moral filth'* refers to everything that taints, soils or devalues our lives. It is anything morally questionable or inappropriate. *'Evil'* is a broad word covering everything that might be wrong in character or conduct. It probably refers to the evils in the prevailing culture. In all likelihood, this is a call to jettison and reject every thought, practice or lifestyle that is inconsistent with God's Word.

In this context, we must rid ourselves of things which produce anger, such as un-forgiveness, grudges, resentment, hatred, revenge or bitterness. Doing so will decontaminate and detoxify ourselves from the *source* of our anger. Anger can destroy us, it can eat away at us and it is not glorifying to God. Therefore, we must discard our old patterns of response.

B. Humbly accept the word of truth

James gives us a second key for how we can control our temper. It's found in the second part of James 1:21. *'Get rid of all moral filth and the evil that is so prevalent and* ***humbly accept the word planted in you****, which can save you'* (emphasis mine). The putting off (or getting rid of / unclothing) must always be accompanied by the receiving (or reclothing) with something. In this case, it is the implanted word.

Before we come to that, please note the required attitude for receiving this word: humility (*'...humbly accept the word planted in you...'*). Humility could well be defined as the absence of pride. We will never be able to receive the Word and, by implication, control our temper until we deal with our pride. Until we read, believe, apply and embrace the Scripture with 'self-subduing gentleness' (humility), we'll never be truly able to control our anger.[10]

In regard to anger, pride has a language and rationale of its own that may be seen in the following statements:

- 'I will not forgive them for what they said or did.'
- 'I may forgive, but I will never forget.'
- 'I'll forgive, but if they ever hurt me again I'll tell them what I think of them.'
- 'Who do they think they are?'
- 'I have a right to be angry and to get even.'
- 'My dignity has been violated.'
- 'I can deal with this myself; I don't need God's help.'
- 'I don't care what God's Word says...I feel this!'

James tells us to *'...humbly* ***accept*** *the word planted in you...'* (emphasis mine). This humility says, 'Yes', to what the Word

10 James B. Adamson, *The Epistle of James: The New International Commentary of the New Testament* (Grand Rapids, MI: Eerdmans, 2000), 81.

teaches and commands without disputing or resisting. Humility recognizes our limitations and imperfections–that we aren't what we should be. So humility says, 'Let the Word have its way in my life.' Humility recognizes the Bible's authority and its guidance for life and wholeheartedly accepts it. It is, therefore, necessary to submit to Scripture's authority, truth and power.

Summary:

Leaders sometimes get angry, but they need to *manage* the expression of their anger through self-control. There is a big difference between righteous, justified and defensible anger, and unrighteous, unjustified and indefensible anger. Using James 1:19–21 as a basis, we noted some of James' practical wisdom in handling anger. The alternative to having an explosive temper is to take control of ourselves by slowing our natural impulses and responding in a more measured tone. James urges us to deal with the internal source or cause of our anger. Other Scriptures remind us that, by the presence of God's Spirit living within us, we have the power to bring any and every emotion under control. James also wrote that only by humbly and obediently embracing the Scriptures can we learn to control our temper.

Self-reflection:

What makes you angry?

What do you need to do to take better control of your expressions of anger?

Can you identify some of the internal sources of your anger?

What has been your biggest lesson from reading this chapter?

Chapter Nine

Self-Control in Responding to Criticism

One of the frustrations of leadership is sometimes being unable to defend yourself against unfounded criticism. Let me give you one example.

The moment Kevin walked into my office, I could tell by his facial expression that he was upset about something. He was one of our loyal and supportive zone leaders. Something, however, was bothering him. His demeanor signaled that he was ready to unload on me. After some awkward and perfunctory pleasantries, he began to tell me why he was there. He'd heard a rumor that I had taken a court order out on a parishioner to stop him coming to church. Before I had a chance to respond, he then proceeded to give me a biblical lecture on why we shouldn't take our brother to court. After about 10 minutes he ran out of steam, sat back and expected me to cower and collapse in repentance at his chastizing.

In truth, we *had* taken the unusual and unprecedented step of taking a court order out on an individual we'll call Thomas, to legally prohibit him coming within 150 meters of my wife, family and the church. What my critic didn't know was the reasons *why* we had felt it was necessary to go to the courts. He didn't understand the facts, was unaware of the background, and had completely misunderstood my motivations.

Criticism is one of the costs of leadership.

I restrained my natural impulse to berate Kevin for his judgmental, ignorant and critical rant. I actually respected him and had been appreciative of his service to the church. So, instead, using measured tones, I systematically told him all the mitigating circumstances in the form of rhetorical questions. I asked him whether he knew: that when Thomas was off his medication he was subject to psychotic episodes; that Thomas had a violent background and was a trained boxer; that Thomas had smashed the car of another pastor with a tree branch without provocation; that Thomas had been sending my wife flowers, chocolates and cards; and that Thomas had come up to me and my family in a food court of a major mall and loudly rebuked us in Jesus' name.

By this stage, Kevin's mouth was open. He'd had no idea. I pressed the point, "Did you know any of this?" He slowly shook his head and quietly responded, "No, I didn't." I explained to him that we cannot make a public statement when it relates to just a few people, because we did not want to embarrass him. But, I went on, we had only taken the action in the courts because my wife and family felt unsafe, and we felt it was the only option open to us. "In that case," he conceded, "I suppose it was appropriate that you took action."

I then asked Kevin how many people he told about his critical perception of my actions. To my dismay, he'd told his connect group and a number of other leaders in the church. I strongly urged him to go to them and, without giving too much away, tell every person he'd criticized me to that we were justified in the action we had taken. He promised he would and left.

After he walked out of my office, I was reminded that criticism is one of the costs of leadership. This chapter will deal with how we can process criticism.

Throughout the Pastoral Epistles (Timothy and Titus), Paul often warned his 'sons in the faith' to avoid arguing with others over controversial topics and to authoritatively deal with divisive people (2 Timothy 2:14, 23; Titus 3:9-10). In 2 Timothy 2:24-26, Paul advised Timothy on how to respond to such people by writing that: '*...the Lord's servant must* ***not quarrel****; instead he must* ***be kind*** *to everyone, able to teach,* ***not resentful****. Those who oppose him he must* ***gently instruct****, in the hope that God will grant them repentance...*' (emphases mine). Timothy was urged to be measured and mature in his responses. Christian leaders should do likewise.

Being a self-regulated leader may sometimes mean exercising restraint over our initial impulses or natural reactions. Based on this passage, leaders should respond with a kind (not argumentative) attitude, gently reasoning the issues through with the antagonist. The goal of this measured approach is that the person would have their eyes open to the truth, come to their senses, repent of their error and escape from unknowingly being an instrument of Satan (2 Timothy 2:26).

Being measured does not imply weakness, indecisiveness or ineptitude. Sometimes, strong action is warranted (Titus 3:10). The important principle here, though, is to control ourselves so that we *respond* rather than *react*.

This is especially true in how a leader responds to criticism. Sadly, sometimes *critical* words are spoken about or to a leader. These words can irritate,

A way to maturely handle criticism is to distinguish between positive and negative criticism.

wound, hurt or, in some cases, deeply affect the leader's life. How, then, can a leader develop a capacity for handling the inevitability of criticism?

A. Distinguish between positive and negative criticism

Someone has quipped, 'Criticism is *constructive* when you give it and *destructive* when you receive it.' Unfortunately, it's not that simple or straightforward. Nonetheless, a first way to maturely handle criticism is to distinguish between positive and negative criticism.

Positive Criticism

Positive criticism comes from rightly motivated and appropriate sources–people who have a right or a responsibility to say things to us. The motive of positive criticism is love, correction, instruction or restoration.

Here are some examples of people who have a right or responsibility to make positive criticism:

- Parents (Ephesians 6:4; Proverbs 6:20)
- Leaders (2 Timothy 3:16; 1 Corinthians 4:14; 2 Timothy 2:14; Titus 3:10)
- Faithful friends (Proverbs 27:6)
- Mature and wise believers (Colossians 3:16; cf. 1 Thessalonians 5:14; 2 Thessalonians 3:15).

Scripture is very clear on the virtues of listening and responding to positive criticism (Psalm 141:5; Proverbs 15:31; Proverbs 12:1).

Negative criticism

Negative criticism comes from malicious, ignorant, unwarranted or unjustified sources. The root of negative criticism is not love but often ignorance, hypocrisy, jealousy, cynicism or mistrust.

Leaders need to be particularly aware of listening to people with a critical spirit.

When criticized, a leader must do an internal audit:

- Is this positive or negative criticism?
- Is it from a positive or negative source?
- Is this something I need to listen to or completely reject?

B. Deal with it internally

A second way to deal with criticism is to process it internally. As well as being initially hurtful, criticism can have a lasting and damaging effect within our lives unless we process it by following these steps:

(a) By checking our motive

When criticized, begin by asking the pertinent question, '*Why*'?

- Why did I make that decision?
- Why did I respond like that?
- Why did I handle that particular circumstance that particular way?

By searching our heart in this way, we're more likely to discover our motive. Our actual motive has a large bearing on the way in which we process the criticism. In some cases, the *why* and *way* we led something may have been unwise or inappropriate, therefore there may need to be some remedial words or actions. If, however, the *why* and *way* we led something were wise and appropriate, then we need to hold our ground and seek to explain our words or actions.

(b) By extracting any elements of truth

Some criticism leveled at us may be legitimate, valid and accurate. Therefore, it would be wise to extract the elements of truth. Sometimes, we need to be honest with ourselves by asking some confronting questions:

- What can I learn from this?
- How could I have done things differently?
- Who do I need to see to put things right?
- Is God trying to show me something through this?
- Is this a process of character development in my life?

Critics may simply be expressing views from a different perspective. We can't take the position that wrong has no rights.

Whenever it is appropriate, acknowledge that our critic was right. Critics are not always heretics, but may simply be expressing views from a different perspective. We can't take the position that wrong has no rights. As someone has well said, 'It is not *who* is right, but *what* is right.' In contrast, another experienced leader once commented that we should 'never accept "constructive criticism" from somebody who has never "constructed" anything.'[1]

(c) By keeping a right spirit toward those who initiate the criticism

Criticism is an inadequate word to describe how Jesus and, to a lesser degree, Stephen, were treated. More accurate terms might be venomous, demonically-inspired or jealous. Nevertheless, their attitude to criticism was exemplary. Dying on the cross, Jesus prayed, *"Father, forgive them, for they don't know what they are doing"* (Luke 23:34). While being stoned, Stephen '*...fell on his knees and cried out, "Lord, do not hold this sin against them"*' (Acts 7:60).

1 Original source unknown.

Leaders, too, must watch their attitudes toward their critics by keeping a right spirit. Here are some practical suggestions for how to do this:

- Pray until the effect of the critic's words lift, then pray for the critic (remember Matthew 5:43–48)
- Don't let their words germinate (take root) in your heart, otherwise they will fester and affect your thinking, relationships and judgment
- Carefully censor your words and thoughts about the person who instituted the criticism, otherwise we're in danger of judging.

(d) By forgiving the person

Leaders need to maintain a forgiving spirit because it is the very spirit of Christ. Jesus warned of the dangers of not forgiving (Matthew 6:14–15). Paul encouraged the Ephesian and Colossian believers to forgive others on the basis of God's unconditional forgiveness of all our sins in Christ (Ephesians 4:32; Colossians 3:13). Forgiveness is relinquishing our right to hurt others for hurting us.

A criticized leader would be cautioned not to take the law into their own hands. This means that we must not pursue revenge, retaliation or payback. We must not slander, defame or make disparaging comments about the critic to others. In 2 Timothy 4:14, we read of Alexander the metalworker doing Paul *'...a great deal of harm.'* Obviously Paul was really hurt, and his work hindered, by Alexander's actions and words. Paul responded by letting the Lord deal with him (*'The Lord will repay him for what he has done.'*) The lesson is that criticized leaders must keep a right spirit and let God deal with our critics. No one gets away with anything in the sight of Almighty God. Justice and vindication are God's prerogative.

This is reminiscent of Paul's words in Romans 12:17-21:

> ***Do not repay evil for evil...*** *Do not take revenge my friends, but* ***leave room for God's wrath****, for it is written: "It is mine to avenge; I will repay," says the Lord. On the contrary: "If your enemy is hungry, feed him; if he is thirsty, give him something to drink. In doing this, you will heap burning coals on his head." Do not be overcome by evil, but overcome evil with good* (emphasis mine; cf. 1 Peter 3:9).

When criticized or hurt by people, stay strong in the Lord. Endure, persevere and stand firm.

(e) By staying on top of our emotional and spiritual state

When criticized or hurt by people, stay strong in the Lord. Endure, persevere and stand firm. Pray and ask God for inner strength (Ephesians 3:16). A deeply discouraged and despondent Elijah found renewal in God's presence on Mount Horeb when threatened with death by Queen Jezebel (1 Kings 19:9-18). Elijah's encounter with God rejuvenated him with strength, guidance and hope for the season ahead.

C. Discern and deal with the true source

A third way to handle criticism is for leaders to discern and deal with its *true* source and motivation. Essentially, there are two *sources* of criticism: human and demonic.

Due to the spiritual nature of a leader's work in Christian ministry, there may be a satanic origin in some criticism. If we discern this is the case, we must not initially react to the person, but resist the devil. For this principle, remember Peter taking Jesus aside and rebuking him for mentioning his death. Jesus, however, '*...turned and said to Peter, "Get behind me, Satan! You are a stumbling block to me..."*' (Matthew 16:23). Jesus wasn't implying that Peter was demon-possessed, but that the inspiration behind his words was satanic. Likewise, leaders must discern criticism when it is from a sinister source and deal with it appropriately.

Importantly, most criticism is not from the devil. Frequently, criticism stems from misunderstanding, misinterpretation or misinformation. In this case, it would be wise to address the issues and not react. Sometimes the best course of action is to respond to criticism as best one can and learn from it. At other times, it is prudent to completely ignore it. A wise sage once said, 'Silence is often misinterpreted, but never misquoted.'

The underlying principle in this point, however, is to *discern* the criticism's true source.

D. Respond don't react

A fourth way to handle criticism is to *respond*, but not *react* to the critic. There is a fundamental difference between responding and reacting. Responding is measured, thoughtful and demonstrates maturity, whereas reacting is emotional, erratic and reveals immaturity. Responding brings the possibility of resolution and reconciliation, whereas reacting often produces deeper resistance and distance.

To respond appropriately, take a day or night to think and pray about the criticism. Process the criticism by using the framework proposed in this chapter: distinguish whether it is positive or negative; process it internally; and discern and deal with the true source. Then determine the best way to approach the person who has leveled the criticism.

Wherever possible and practical, it is always wise to speak face to face, person to person through a phone call or personal visit. Responses via social media, mail or email are not as effective because they often don't reveal the heart, facial expressions, or the tone of voice, and can be open to misinterpretation. Seek to be motivated by love in all you do and say to the person. In the words of the old adage, 'Lock heads but don't lock hearts.' Endeavour to maintain or restore relationship throughout the whole process of working through the criticism. Always be respectful, patient and courteous in your dealings with them. Listen patiently. Respond thoughtfully. If there is an impasse, 'agree to disagree'. Always pray together at the end of the discussion.

Remember to always keep things in perspective. Don't let a critical minority diminish the value or view of the majority that may be completely supportive. Avoid overestimating criticism. Some criticisms sting more than damage. A bee sting is not a snake bite. There is an old, philosophical saying: 'This, too, shall pass'.

Summary

Leadership has both highs and lows. One of the lows is handling the negativities of leadership, in which criticism features prominently. Criticism can be hurtful, so it needs to be internally processed so it has no lasting effect. Keeping a right spirit and a forgiving heart are keys to handling criticism. A measured and thoughtful response to criticism, rather than an erratic and emotional reaction produces a much better result.

Self-reflection:

How do you normally cope with criticism?

What have you learnt from this chapter that you'll apply in the future?

What will you do to become more mature and measured in your responses to criticism?

Chapter Ten

Self-Control of Our Tongue (words)

Have you ever said something you deeply regretted? No sooner have the words left your mouth, than you wish you could retrieve them, rewind the conversation and start over.

This has happened to me as a preacher more times than I care to remember. I've made many bloopers. You can get ten thousand words right, but get just one word wrong and everyone remembers it. Here is my worst ever blooper.

When I was just starting out as a preacher in the mid-1980s, I was rostered to speak one Sunday night. I had this great message (or so I thought at the time) about how the devil progressively got hold of Judas' life. It started out with him stealing, but climaxed with Satan entering him before his betrayal of Jesus. I was trying to show how we must deal with the weaknesses in our lives before they become strongholds.

Because Judas ended up taking his own life, my ultimate goal that night was to pray for people who were suicidal. I built the message up to this important moment. I stepped in front of the pulpit to give effect to what I was about to say. People were listening intently. I invited people to close their eyes and bow their heads in a moment of prayerful reflection. What I meant to say at that moment was, "If you've contemplated suicide, would you please raise your hand so I can pray for you." Unfortunately, that's not what came out. What I actually said was, "If you've *committed* suicide, would you please raise your hand."

> **One of the ways a leader leads is through their words. A leader needs to exercise rigorous self-control over their tongue.**

As you can imagine, everyone dissolved into uncontrollable laughter. I was so embarrassed, I wanted a trap door to open under me so I could disappear, but I just stood there (red faced), laughed at myself, and waited patiently for people to compose themselves. After some minutes, order was eventually restored. I once again asked people to be prayerful. This time, I managed to ask the right question. To my surprise, there were dozens of people who responded to my call for people who wanted prayer.

The point is that once words have been spoken, they are irretrievable. This chapter is about the self-control of a leader's words.

Paul exhorted Timothy to '*...set an example for the believers in **speech**...*' (1 Timothy 4:12, emphasis mine).

Leading by our words

One of the ways a leader leads is through their words. A leader's words carry great weight; therefore, a leader needs to exercise rigorous *self-control* over their tongue (words). Self-control over the tongue comes from *within*–from the inside out.

While the Bible says a lot about words, especially in the Proverbs (Proverbs 13:3; 21:23), there are two passages that stand out in particular: James 3:2-12 and Matthew 12:33-37 (cf. Matthew 15:17-20). Below is a summary of the teaching of

Scripture, in regard to our tongue, with emphasis on Jesus and James.

A. Our words can either be used for good or bad

Scripture teaches that words are very powerful: '*The tongue has the power of life and death*' (Proverbs 18:21). Words can build up or tear down, bless or curse, strengthen or weaken, recharge or drain, help or harm, encourage or criticize, empower or disempower.

James wrote how our tongue, though a relatively small part of our body, has disproportionate power (James 3:5). Moo wrote that: 'No other "member" of our body, perhaps, wreaks so much havoc to a godly life.'[1] James describes the tongue as '*a fire and a world of evil among the parts of the body*' (James 3:6), which shows its immense negative potential to corrupt our whole being. Then, in James 3:8, he describes it as '*a restless evil*', meaning it is 'double-minded, unstable' (as in James 1:8), difficult to control and 'always liable to break out' (JBP). Also, he vividly says it is '*...full of deadly poison*' like the fangs of a snake injecting venom (cf. Psalm 140:3).

There are many ways in which we can use our words destructively: backbiting (Psalm 15:3; Leviticus 19:16; 2 Timothy 3:3); gossiping (Proverbs 11:13); criticizing (Numbers 12:1-2); judging (Matthew 7:1; 1 Corinthians 4:5); boasting (Proverbs 18:12; 2 Timothy 3:3); abusing (2 Timothy 3:3); and lying (Colossians 3:9; Genesis 27:24).

Paul stressed to the Ephesians not to '*...let any unwholesome words come out of your mouths, but only what is* ***helpful*** *for* ***building others up*** *according to* ***their needs****, that it may* ***benefit*** *those who listen*' (Ephesians 4:29, emphasis mine).

Think what enormous, sometimes irreversible, harm has been done because of ignorant, foolish, misinformed,

---

1 Moo, 125.

unsubstantiated, frivolous, or unthoughtful words. Many will know from bitter experience the childhood taunt: 'Sticks and stones will break my bones but names will never hurt me.' The reality is that the wounds of sticks and stones will heal, but the wounds caused by words sometimes take years to heal or don't heal at all.

But we can also use our words for tremendous good. Proverbs 10:11 records that, '*The mouth of the righteous is a fountain of life.*' There are many ways in which we can biblically use our words for good: spiritual gifts (especially prophecy, 1 Corinthians 14:3); encouragement (Romans 14:19; Romans 15:2; Ephesians 4:12; Ephesians 4:29; 1 Thessalonians 5:11); prayer (James 5:13-18); training our children in godly living (Deuteronomy 6:7); praise (Psalm 145:11); witnessing about Jesus (Luke 24:35); preaching (Acts 2:37); and comforting others (1 Thessalonians 5:11).

B. Our words reveal (unmask, unveil) what is within our heart

(Matthew 12:33-35; cf. Matthew 15:17-20; James 3:9-12)

The context in Matthew 12:33-35 is the unforgivable sin. This is a pretty hot topic, so we'll tread carefully. Jesus had just cast an evil spirit out of a man who was blind and dumb (Matthew 12:22). When the Pharisees got wind of this, they attributed this work to the devil (Matthew 12:24). Jesus then responded by speaking about divided kingdoms falling. "*But,*" he continued, "*if I drive out demons by the Spirit of God, then the Kingdom of God has come upon you*" (Matthew 12:28). In saying this, Jesus asserted that the deliverance was *not* a work of Satan, but a work of God evidenced and authenticated by the Spirit's power.

With this setting in mind, Jesus then said that "*...every sin and blasphemy will be forgiven, but the blasphemy against the Spirit will not be forgiven.*" In this light, blasphemy here most probably refers to the Pharisees attributing to the *devil* a work that was clearly a work of the Holy Spirit. Although they should have known better, they were deceived by their evil, unbelieving and jealous hearts.

What was Jesus saying? If these religious leaders charged that Jesus was working as an agent of Satan, and if they consciously rejected him as the Son of God, despite the Spirit giving unmistakable evidence, they were in grave, eternal danger.

Why would God condemn a life to eternal damnation because of mere words? Matthew 12:33-37 provides the answer. Jesus said to the Pharisees, who he called a '*brood of vipers*', that their words were simply the fruit–the *outward* indication–of what they *were* on the inside. For out of the overflow of their hearts, their mouths were speaking (Matthew 12:34). Faces, eyes and moods portrayed little, but their words gave it all away. When they spoke, what was in their hearts was unmasked.

On another occasion, when explaining a parable to the 'dull' disciples, Jesus noted the Pharisees' hypocrisy concerning what was ceremonially 'clean' and 'unclean' and essentially said the same thing:

> *"Don't you see that whatever enters the mouth goes into the stomach and then out of the body? But the things that come out of the mouth come from the heart, and these make a man 'unclean'. For out of the heart come evil thoughts, murder, adultery, sexual immorality, theft, false testimony, slander"* (Matthew 15:17-19).

This is principally the message of James 3:9-12 also. 'As a final, climactic indictment of the tongue', James says the tongue can be double-minded.[2] He finds it deplorable that

2 ibid, 128.

with the same tongue '*we praise our Lord and Father and with it we curse men, who have been made in God's likeness.*' Praising, honoring (or blessing) God '...is the highest, purest, most noble form of speech', but, in contrast, cursing (or speaking against someone or something) is the 'lowest, filthiest, most ignoble form of speech.'[3] In verse 10, he bluntly says, '*Out of the same mouth come praise and cursing. My brothers, this should not be.*'

Why is this so deplorable? Because in verses 11-12 this duplicity and inconsistency of speech means we have duplicity and inconsistency in our heart toward God.[4] James asserts that a pure heart and impure speech are incompatible! To do so, he gives three illustrations. Each is cast in the form of a rhetorical question, expecting the answer, 'No'!

- Can a spring produce both fresh and salt water? No!
- Can a fig tree bear olives, or a grapevine bear figs? No!
- Can a salt spring produce fresh water? No![5]

So, what is James teaching? God the 'Creator has so organized plant life that each plant bears "*fruit...according to its own kind*" (Genesis 1:11-12). The nature of the plant determines the fruit.'[6] The visible (or in this case, audible) fruit indicates the nature of what is within. Jesus said, "*Out of the overflow of his heart his mouth speaks.*" Motyer wrote that: 'A fig must have a fig tree as its source, a grape can only come from a vine and an olive from an olive tree. Salt water has a salt source and [fresh] water has a [fresh] source.'[7]

What is evil at heart will inevitably produce evil. So the heart not right with God cannot help but produce ungodly speech.

---

3 ibid, 128.
4 ibid, 129.
5 ibid, 129.
6 Motyer, 127.
7 ibid, 127.

'Bitter words come from a bitter heart. Critical words from a critical spirit. Defamatory, unloving words from a heart where the love of Jesus is a stranger.'[8] But a good heart must produce good. A heart in tune with God will produce godly speech. Encouragement comes from an encouraged heart. Words of life come from a heart full of life.

Our speech is a barometer of our spirituality because it, above all else, reveals the true state and substance of our heart.

Our speech is a barometer of our spirituality because it, above all else, reveals the true state and substance of our heart.[9] In Moo's words,

> The person who is double and inconsistent with regard to the things of God in his heart (*dippsychos*) will be double and inconsistent in speech… Christians who have been transformed by the Spirit of God should manifest the wholeness and purity of the heart in consistency and purity of speech.[10]

C. Our words will be judged

A number of passages show that each of us is accountable for the words we speak (Matthew 12:36-37; Romans 14:10-12). There is a day of accountability and reckoning when we shall stand before the 'judgment seat of Christ' (Romans 14:12; 2 Corinthians 5:10). On *that* day, we will answer for every unredeemed, careless, thoughtless, meaningless, senseless, worthless and fruitless word we have spoken. According to Jesus' words in Matthew 12:36-37, our words become the

8 ibid, 127.
9 ibid, 129.
10 Moo, 129.

> **If we can control the tongue, we have the potential to control every other passion, desire and drive.**

basis of our own judgment. We set the standard for ourselves. The judgment will reveal the true effect of our tongue.

When I was a child, my parents had a plaque on the wall of our dining room. The plaque was a silhouette of Jesus with the caption, 'Jesus is the silent listener to every conversation.' It was a constant reminder to be careful what I said because Jesus was listening. The fact remains: Jesus *is* the silent listener to every conversation at all times and he's *still* listening. In light of the judgment seat of Christ, let us be self-controlled with our tongue and use our words for incredible good.

D. Scripture is clear in its call to exercise '*self-control*' over our tongues

(James 3:2–4; cf. Colossians 3:8; Proverbs 13:3; James 1:19)

The implication and application of James 3:2–4 is that the degree of self-control we have over our tongue is representative of the degree of self-control we have over all our passions, desires and drives. When the tongue is not restrained, small though it is, the rest of the body is likely to be uncontrolled and undisciplined also. But if we can control the tongue, we have the *potential* to control every other passion, desire and drive.

I'm *not* saying that *if* you control your tongue, every other desire, drive and passion is automatically subdued and controlled. Nor am I saying that we can control our body *by* controlling our tongue. I am saying that *if* we can control our tongue, we will *potentially* be able to control the rest of our body. The control of the tongue is more than an evidence of spiritual maturity; it is a means to it.

Without self-control, says Proverbs 25:28, we are like a city *'whose walls are broken down'*, vulnerable to attack from enemies and wild beasts, defenseless and precarious. Whereas having control of the tongue would defend us from attack and not open us up to vulnerability. Without self-control of our tongue, our words, will be like a horse without a bit (James 3:3)–unrestrained, wild, unruly and potentially dangerous. Whereas controlling our tongue will ensure our words are in check and used for good. If we don't tame the tongue, James' further metaphor of a ship without a rudder (James 3:4) could mean that our words may blow us off course, subject us to the elements and make us directionless. Whereas if we carefully control our tongue, it can be presumed that we can navigate our life in its proper, divinely charted course.

How, then, can we practically exercise self-control over our tongues? Here are some ideas from Scripture:

Repent and reject old ways of speaking (Ephesians 4:22-24; Colossians 3:5, 8-9)

Firstly, we need to identify any pre-Christian habits and patterns of speech; that is, any ways of speaking that are residue from our old life before we knew Jesus. Paul tells us that they are part of our old nature and, as such, need to be *'put off'* (Ephesians 4:22). It is necessary to take full responsibility for these words, and not blame our genes, upbringing or environment. Instead, we should repent from them and ask the Lord to renew our minds and make us new from the inside out (Ephesians 4:23-24).

Yield our tongue to the control of the Holy Spirit (Romans 8:13)

Secondly, the Spirit gives us the power and capacity to tame our tongue, but we must yield to his work in our lives. We must do our part and say 'no' to our natural, selfish impulses, and say 'yes' to the Holy Spirit and his empowering presence.

Be slow to speak (James 1:19)

Thirdly, in his epistle, James instructed us to be '*...quick to listen*' but '*slow to speak...*' In other words, we must think before we speak. Take a moment or two before responding or reacting. Before we speak, think about the words we're about to speak and, if we wouldn't say them in front of Jesus, let's not say them at all. If our words are not edifying, profitable or pleasing to God, let's muzzle our mouths and remain silent. Here are some practical principles from Scripture in this vein:

- Use words with restraint (Proverbs 17:27)
- Guard our lips (Proverbs 13:3; cf. Proverbs 21:23)
- Hold our tongue (Proverbs 10:19)
- Keep a tight rein on our tongue (James 1:26).

Follow Jesus' example (1 Peter 2:21-23)

Fourthly, when Jesus suffered for us, '*...he did not retaliate...he made no threats. Instead he entrusted himself to him who judges justly*' (1 Peter 2:23). Likewise, when we suffer for Christ's sake, or are falsely accused, insulted, or unfairly criticized, we must not take the law into own hands, wallow in self-pity, or yield to natural impulses. Instead, like Jesus, when we are suffering hostility in his name, we commit ourselves to God–the only righteous, unbiased and incorruptible Judge–and let him deal with our persecutors in his perfect justice.

Summary

In this chapter, we've seen that a leader's words are very important, because one of the ways in which we lead people is by our words. Words are powerful and can be used for good or evil. Words unmask what is in our heart; they will be judged by the Lord and are evidence of the level of self-control we have over our lives. We exercise self-control of our tongue: by repenting and jettisoning old pre-Christian patterns of speaking; by yielding control of our tongue to God's Spirit; by thinking before we speak; and by following the example of Jesus.

Self-reflection:

What impacted you the most in reading this chapter?

Why?

What steps will you take to enable yourself to use your words more appropriately?

What specific patterns of speech do you need to work on?

Chapter Eleven

Self-Control of Our Self-Talk

You just never know who is listening.

One time, I was sitting at the Brisbane Cricket Ground, commonly known as the 'Gabba', an abbreviation of the suburb, Woolloongabba, in which the stadium is located. I was spending a leisurely day watching a cricket match. Two men who I didn't know were sitting behind me. As they began to chat, I realized they were talking about someone I knew. They weren't being complimentary, but critical and demeaning. I thought, "If these guys knew that *I* knew who they were talking about, would they be having this conversation in public?" You never know who is listening.

When I was pastoring, I used to come in very early and spend my first hour in prayer before anyone arrived. Normally I'd pray in the church auditorium. However one particular day, I decided to pray in my office with my door locked. One of the cleaning staff, a member of the congregation, came into the general office to empty the bins. Our church maintenance manager was with him. They didn't know, but I could hear their conversation, and they were criticizing me for some recent changes we'd initiated. Do you think they would have had that conversation if they knew I was within earshot? You never know who is listening.

I wonder how differently we would speak if we knew someone was listening. The truth is that Someone *is* listening to *every* word we say, even the words that are not audible.

Flowing on from the previous chapter on the self-control of our tongues, we'll now focus on an area of speech that is often unaddressed; that is, our self-talk. Our self-talk is what we think or say to ourselves, either verbally or in our hearts, about ourselves, others or our circumstances. Self-talk is the voice of our innermost, personal thoughts. Though no-one else may ever hear it (except God), and though it is inaudible or barely audible, we have, nevertheless, still conceived the words.

God responds to self-talk

In Scripture, God heard and responded to people's self-talk, whether it was positive or negative.

A prime example of God responding to self-talk is found in the story of Sarah eavesdropping on Abraham's conversation with the angel of the Lord. Once the angel had declared that a son would be born to Sarah within a year, she '*...laughed to* ***herself*** *as she* ***thought****, "After I am worn out and my master is old, will I now have this pleasure*?"' (Genesis, 18:12, emphasis mine) The Lord heard her inner reaction and asked Abraham, '*Why did Sarah laugh and say, "Will I really have a child, now that I am old"?'* The angel did not let Sarah get away with her inward, disbelieving thought, but challenged her with the question, *"Is anything too hard for the Lord?"* before boldly asserting that he would return *"...at the appointed time..."* the following year and Sarah would, indeed, have a son (Genesis 18:14). At this point, Sarah was afraid and actually lied to the Lord by saying, *"I did not laugh,"* but the angel unflinchingly responded, *"Yes, you did laugh"* (Genesis 18:15).

Sarah thought that no-one else heard or knew her inner thoughts, but the Lord heard and knew. For us, this means that our inward, unspoken words and thoughts, too, are heard and known by the Lord (Psalm 139:2, 4). In Sarah's case, God responded to her private self-talk as if it had been public and audible.

> **Self-talk unmasks what we really think in our hearts. Self-talk has power in our lives.**

Likewise, the Lord is going to respond to *our* self-talk because our self-talk unmasks what we *really* think in our hearts, whether good or evil. Because self-talk reveals the heart, we, as leaders, need to carefully monitor what we say to ourselves through our silent words. Self-talk has power in our lives.

God is examining and probing our hearts (motives, attitudes, desires, and pursuits), he is listening to our meditations and thoughts, and he knows what is in our hearts. He will deal with our hearts because he wants our hearts to be fully devoted to him and purified by the work of his Spirit within us. God desires that our inner talk would be the overflow of his inner work.

A. Self-talk and self-esteem (self-image)

This has application to our self-talk about ourselves. Our self-talk is a reflection of our self-image, which is how we see, feel and value ourselves. As a Christian, we should derive our sense of self, self-esteem, value and worth from who we are 'in Christ'. Basically, an accurate self-image comes from having a right understanding of ourselves in relation to God.

If we don't have a proper, biblical understanding of who we are in Christ, we'll have a distorted view of ourselves and our self-worth. We'll either be looking at ourselves through the eyes of others, the lens of our culture, or the rear vision mirror of past experiences, which all lead to a fractured view of ourselves.

For our self-talk about ourselves to be healthy, we need to align our self-talk with what God says about us

We live in a very image-obsessed culture where many people are consumed by how they are *perceived* (how they look on the outside), rather than by who they *are* (on the inside). Some TV programs portray before-and-after shots of people who've had elective, cosmetic or corrective surgery. Sometimes the results are remarkable. Watching shows like this can form the misconception that, if we could have a few things surgically altered or enhanced, we would feel better about ourselves.

But this is an illusion. The way we look should never become the sole factor in determining our self-esteem. If we form our self-esteem from the perspective of the image-obsessed culture, then we'll never be satisfied or settled in who we are.

True self-esteem has little to do with our external features, our image, others' perception of us, or any external thing for that matter. Is it from being attractive? No, because attractiveness fades and is only the outside–not the real us. Is it from wearing fashionable clothes? No, because fashions change. Is it from having plenty of money? No, because net worth doesn't equal self-worth. Is it from status or success? No, because they are external measures, not an internal indicator. Is it from having profile and popularity? No, because we're looking at ourselves through others' eyes, not our own. Is it from being tough? No, because true strength is inward strength. Is it from the color of our skin or race? No, because all people are created with equal value in God's sight.

For our self-talk about ourselves to be healthy, we need to align our self-talk with what God says about us in his Word. This comes from building our self-image and self-esteem from what the Bible teaches about God our Creator, Jesus our Savior and the Holy Spirit's active work transforming us from the inside out.

Scripture teaches that, because God is our Creator, we are: God's workmanship (Ephesians 2:10); made in his image (Genesis 1:27); *'fearfully and wonderfully made'* (Psalm 139:14); loved with his unfailing, unconditional and selfless love (Jeremiah 31:3; John 3:16; Romans 5:8; 1 John 3:1; 4:9, 4:16).

With Christ as our Savior, we are: redeemed by the blood of Jesus Christ (1 Peter 1:18–19); rescued from the jurisdiction of darkness and brought into *'the kingdom of the Son he loves...'* (Colossians 1:14); cleansed and forgiven from all past sins (Colossians 1:14); baptized into his body so that we are now 'in Christ' (1 Corinthians 12:13; Galatians 3:27); indwelt by God's Holy Spirit so that Christ is now in us (Colossians 1:29; Galatians 2:20); assured of resurrection and eternal life beyond the grave, (Romans 8:11; 1 Corinthians 15:47-51; 1 Thessalonians 4:15–18), where we will be with him eternally in heaven.

With the Spirit living within us we are being: transformed into the likeness of Jesus with ever-increasing glory (2 Corinthians 3:18); transformed by the renewing of our minds (Romans 12:2); and renewed day by day (2 Corinthians 4:16). This means that God *has* changed us, *is* in the process of changing us and will *continue* to change us until *that* day when we *'...he appears'* and *'...we shall be like him, for we shall see him as he is'* (1 John 3:2).

There may be many things we don't like, or maybe have even rejected, about ourselves. Perhaps there are dozens of legitimate reasons why we have hang ups, phobias, fears, inferiorities or insecurities. But, based on the realities that have just been enumerated, we must choose to no longer say or think things that are contrary to God's Word. We mustn't give them power by our self-talk. On the contrary, we need to defeat our negative talk and thinking by speaking the truth of Scripture.

Jeremiah is a case in point. In Jeremiah 1:4–5, the Lord revealed his prophetic destiny for Jeremiah's life: *'Before I formed you in the womb I knew you, before you were born I set you apart; I appointed you as a prophet to the nations.'* Astonishingly, Jeremiah didn't respond enthusiastically at all. We deduce that he must have looked at himself, his limitations and weaknesses, his cultural bias, his perceived appearance in the minds of his potential listeners, and replied, *'I do not know how to speak; I am only a child'* (Jeremiah 1:6).

In essence, Jeremiah responded, 'I don't know if you appreciate this, Sovereign Lord but, in my culture, older people are respected and younger people are tolerated, therefore I can't do what you're calling me to do. I won't be listened to. I'm not mature enough to be taken seriously as a voice to my people. In the eyes of my culture, I'm like a child.'

The Lord, however, wasn't sympathetic with Jeremiah's excuses in the slightest. In fact, he replied, ***'Do not say**, "I am only a child"'* (Jeremiah 1:7, emphasis mine). God commanded him not to use his age, or any other human reason, to legitimize his reluctance to serve the Lord. In saying *'do not say'*, it seems as if the Lord was commanding him not to use the words *'I am only a child'* as an excuse again. God's command could be paraphrased as, 'I never want to hear you say that again!'

Likewise, many of us cite so many similar reasons why we may be insecure, fearful or negative about ourselves. Some blame their upbringing, parents, appearance, impediments, disabilities, education (or lack of it), time constraints, lack of knowledge, inexperience, past failures, introverted personality, what others have said, or what others think, just to name a few. If we have been speaking like this about ourselves, even to ourselves, then we need to listen again to God's loving and living words: '*Do not say*'! Let's be careful and vigilant not to say anything about ourselves that is contrary to how God sees us.

Jeremiah saw himself as a '*child*', whereas God saw him as '*a prophet to the nations*' (Jeremiah 1:4–5). Gideon saw himself as the least in his family, which family was the weakest in the clan (Judges 6:15), whereas God saw him as a '*mighty warrior*' (Judges 6:12). Elijah felt alone, exposed and threatened because he *thought* he was the only prophet left in his nation (1 Kings 19:14), whereas God revealed that there were 7000 who had not compromised their faith (1 Kings 19:18). These examples show us that the way we see and think about ourselves is not how God sees or thinks about us. We need to align our words with his.

Back to Jeremiah. The Lord wasn't finished with him. The Lord continued: *"Do not say, 'I am only a child.' You must go to everyone I send you to and say whatever I command you. Do not be afraid of them, for I am with you and will rescue you," declares the Lord'* (Jeremiah 1:7–8). It seemed that the Lord was indirectly reassuring Jeremiah that it wasn't his appearance or age that qualified or disqualified him; it was God's word in his mouth that would give him authority and credibility. In other words, Jeremiah was being commissioned to get on with what he was called to do, despite what people may think of him. The underlying reason *why* Jeremiah didn't need to fear the people and why he shouldn't speak negatively about himself is captured in God's words: '*Do not be afraid of them, for I am with you and will rescue you...*' (Jeremiah 1:8). God promised his continual, protective and empowering presence.

B. Self-talk about others

While self-talk about ourselves reflects how we feel about ourselves, our self-talk about others reflects our inner thoughts about them.

The four friends who brought their paralyzed friend to Jesus is a great example of this. These four men exercised great initiative by audaciously creating a crude hole in the roof of the home where Jesus was teaching, then lowering their crippled friend right in front of him (Luke 5:17-26). When Jesus saw the faith of the friends, he said to the invalid man, *"Friend, your sins are forgiven"* (Luke 5:20). The religious leaders immediately judged and condemned Jesus for making this declaration of absolution, but not out loud. They *'...began **thinking to themselves**, "Who is this fellow who speaks blasphemy? Who can forgive sins but God alone?"* (Luke 5:21, emphasis mine) It may not have been spoken, but Jesus *'...knew what they were thinking.'* Their inward thoughts exposed their darkened and deceived hearts. Jesus, then, directly confronted their corrupted thoughts by asking a brilliant question (Luke 5:23), then by demonstrating his authority to forgive sin by healing the man (Luke 5:24-25).

The Pharisees were inwardly condemning Jesus, but he knew their inward judgmental attitudes and responded accordingly. Equally, we need to be careful not to judge others in our heart by our inward attitudes. Jesus rightly warned his followers not to *'...judge, or you too will be judged'* (Matthew 7:1). To 'judge' in this context is to draw premature conclusions in our own mind about another person's motives, actions or attitudes without the full knowledge (which God alone has). Paraphrased, it could mean 'not to be judgmental' or have a 'critical spirit' or a 'condemning attitude' toward another.[1] So all Christians, including leaders, need to be very careful about their attitudes and words toward people.

Judging others

The major reason for not judging others, cautioned Jesus, is that *'...in the same way you judge others, you will be judged, and*

1 D.A. Carson, *Jesus' Sermon on the Mount* (Grand Rapids, MI: Baker, 2001), 106.

with the measure you use, it will be measured to you' (Matthew 7:2; cf. Luke 6:37-38). This means that the way a leader (or any Christian) judges others, will become the basis for how God will judge them. In the sobering words of Don Carson, '...we should abolish judgmental attitudes lest we ourselves stand utterly condemned before God. A judgmental attitude excludes us from God's pardon, for it betrays an unbroken spirit.'[2]

The principal problem with judging others is that God alone is Judge.

The principal problem with judging others is that God alone is Judge. Only God knows people's hearts and motives (Proverbs 16:2; 1 Chronicles 28:9). People are not finally accountable to us (or any leader), but to God. Every Christian will be judged by the Lord at the judgment seat of Christ (Romans 14:10-12; 2 Corinthians 5:10). Leaders must, therefore, not pre-judge (even in their hearts) but leave the judgment of others to the Lord (1 Corinthians 4:5). Because of the perfect judgment to come at the *Second Coming* where true justice will be dispensed (2 Thessalonians 1:5-7), leaders must be very careful not to have a judgmental attitude toward anyone (Romans 14:10; James 4:12).

I remember teaching my daughter how to drive. While going along a major motorway, a discourteous driver abruptly and dangerously pulled in front of my daughter at speed. She had to take evasive action. As she skillfully did so, she muttered, 'Idiot!', in reference to the other driver. I immediately reprimanded her, 'Victoria, you shouldn't say that!' Far from being chastized, she turned to me and accusingly said, '...but *you* do!' I suddenly realized that all her life she had been sitting in the back seat hearing me mutter words like, 'moron, idiot and stupid' to other

2 ibid, 107.

drivers. Without knowing it, my self-talk had influenced her. It was like an epiphany. From that day, I have tried very, very hard to stop calling other drivers *idiots*, but it's difficult because there are so many idiots on the road!

As leaders, we need to be careful not to judge others, but instead think and speak well of people.

C. Self-talk about our circumstances

So far, we've covered self-talk about ourselves and self-talk about others, but we also have to monitor our self-talk about our circumstances.

When we pass through times of difficulty, testing, tragedy or adversity, we need to carefully regulate our self-talk, because it will either build or undermine, fortify or putrefy our faith and trust in God. We may not be able to choose what happens to us, but we can choose our attitude toward what happens to us. If we don't adopt a positive attitude, the negative attitude will poison our hearts and inevitably find expression through our inner thoughts and words (self-talk).

Self-talk and expressions of faith

Rather than focus on the negative aspects of our self-talk, let's centre our focus on the link between our self-talk and faith. Self-talk can be used positively and powerfully as an expression of faith, as the following Gospel story reveals.

Mark 5:25–27 introduces us to a lady in a desperate and precarious state. *'And a woman was there who had been subject to bleeding for twelve years. She had suffered a great deal under the care of many doctors and had spent all she had, yet instead of getting better she grew worse'* (Mark 5:25–26).

Three things stand out about this lady and her condition. First, she was a *'woman'*, which immediately meant she was near the bottom or on the edge of the social standings of her day.

Second, she had suffered menstrual hemorrhaging for twelve years; there had been a continual flow. This is significant to the story because, according to the religious laws of her day, she was regarded as unclean and shouldn't have been in public (see Leviticus 15:19, 25-27). Being in public meant she was breaching the purity laws, she was ceremonially unclean, and she was not permitted to take part in any temple worship or the like. If she touched anybody else, *they* would be unclean.

Third, she had spent all she had on doctors, but medical science and the medical profession could do nothing more. Her finances meant she was not in a position to try anything else. Her options were exhausted.

Tying this together, we come to one glaring conclusion: she was excluded! Physically, she was excluded from physical health and wholeness. Medically, she was excluded because there was nothing more anybody could do. Financially, she was excluded because she'd spent all she had on doctors and still had no answers or cure, and now she was broke. Socially, she was excluded from social interaction because of illness. Spiritually, she was excluded from the worship life of the community.

However, '*...when she heard about Jesus, she came up behind him in the crowd and touched his cloak...*' (Mark 5:27). What filled her with such hope, tenacity and boldness, despite her perilous condition and religious exclusion? It was her self-talk! Her self-talk expressed the faith that was in her heart. She thought to herself, *"If I just touch his clothes, I will be healed"* (Mark 5:28). As she reached out and touched his cloak, her bleeding stooped immediately '*...and she felt in her body that she was freed from her suffering*' (Mark 5:29).

What we learn from the lady in this story is that for self-talk to be an authentic expression of faith, it must come from a heart of faith. Despite all the adverse circumstances of her exclusion, she *believed* that if she could just touch Jesus' clothes, she would be healed. Moreover, she *acted* upon her faith by pressing through the crowd as unobtrusively and covertly as possible, but with determination and expectation. Her silent words expressed the faith in her heart. Her actions gave expression to her words. The result of her faith and action was an immediate miracle.

I am not implying that self-talk is just the power of positive thinking, though that can be helpful. The substance of self-talk I am referring to is self-talk impregnated by faith in God and based on the Word of God. The Word of God is the source of true faith. Therefore, may we align our self-talk, prayers of faith and declarations of faith with the Word of God.

Respond to whatever you may be going through with words of affirmation in God's sovereignty, his perfect wisdom, his unfailing love and his immeasurable power, knowing *'...that in all things God works for the good of those who love him...'* (Romans 8:28).

Above all else, this chapter has taught us to regulate what we think in our heart, what we say in our heart and what we say to ourselves. The reason being that God knows, hears and will respond to our self-talk.

To conclude this chapter, may we be able to say and pray the words of Psalm 19:14: *'May the **words of my mouth** and the **meditation of my heart** be pleasing in your sight, O Lord, my Rock and my Redeemer'* (emphasis mine).

Self-reflection:

What area of self-talk do you struggle with the most?

What are you taking from this chapter to apply to your life?

How will you speak differently to yourself about

(a) yourself?

(b) others?

(c) your circumstances?

Chapter Twelve

Self-Control of Our Thought-Life (meditations)

'...*brothers, whatever is true, whatever is noble, whatever is right, whatever is pure, whatever is lovely, whatever is admirable–if anything is excellent or praiseworthy–think about such things*' (Philippians 4:8).

Briefly recall some of the thoughts you've had in the last 2 to 3 days. Thoughts about those you are attracted to, thoughts about other people, thoughts about yourself and maybe thoughts about life and death. Imagine if those thoughts were uploaded to social media or the internet so that any of your followers could *see* who and what you had been thinking about. How would you feel? Embarrassed? Ashamed? Humiliated? Mercifully, no other human knows our thoughts, but the fact remains that we were thinking them.

If we are to lead inside out, then it is imperative to exercise self-control over this vital area of our life: our thought-life. J Oswald Sanders (1902–1992) wrote that, 'The mind of man is the battlefield on which every moral and spiritual battle is fought.'[1] Defeat or victory, conforming or transforming begins with what we think! Who or whatever has the greatest influence in our thought-life has the greatest influence in shaping who we are and what we are becoming.

1 J Oswald Sanders, *A Spiritual Clinic* (Chicago: Moody Press, 1961), 20.

How, then, can we exercise rigorous and righteous self-control over our thoughts, meditations and fantasies?

Romans 12:2

> **Defeat or victory, conforming or transforming begins with what we think!**

To answer this compelling question, we're going to unpack one of the best-known and pivotal verses in the New Testament in relation to our thought-life to discover what Paul was teaching about *how* we can prevail in the battle. It is Romans 12:2, which reads:

> *'Do not conform any longer to the pattern of this world, but be transformed by the renewing of your mind. Then you will be able to test and approve what God's will is–his good, pleasing and perfect will.'*
>
> The Message paraphrase of this verse reads:
>
> *'Don't become some well-adjusted to your culture that you fit into it without even thinking. Instead, fix your attention on God. You'll be changed from the inside out. Readily recognize what he wants from you, and quickly respond to it.'*

Two key aspects of Romans 12:2

In this verse, there are two fundamental applications that are foundational in understanding how we exercise self-control over our thought-life:

- *Do not* conform
- *Be* transformed.

There is something *we* must do (human responsibility), and something only *God* can do (God's prerogative). *Our* responsibility is not to '... *conform to the pattern of this world'. God's* work is the transformation of our lives by renewing our mind. It is not totally up to us, nor is it totally up to God. It is not one without the other–not all us and not all God, but us *and* God.

We are called to non-conformity, to a radically different life than the prevailing culture.

Let's examine both of these aspects.

A. Do not conform to the pattern of this world

This is *our* responsibility, something we alone can do. We are required not to '*...conform any longer...*' We are called to non-conformity, to a radically different life than the prevailing culture which, in other places in Scripture, refers to the '*spirit of the age*' (cf. 2 Corinthians 4:4). The language speaks of choice and human responsibility. We can either conform (fit in) or not conform (not mindlessly fit in).

What does it mean to conform? Here are a number of statements that describe what it may mean to '*conform to the pattern of this world*':

- Mindlessly imitate the prevailing culture
- Think like everybody else thinks
- Do what everybody else does
- Do what we feel like despite the consequences
- Gratify and satisfy every desire and craving we have
- Do our own will
- Be like everybody else.

Therefore, what does it mean not to conform? John Stott gives a number for examples from Scripture of what non-conformity looks like. Firstly, he quotes God's word to Israel through Moses: *"You must not do as they do...in the land of Canaan where I am bringing you. Do not follow their practices. You must obey my laws"* (Leviticus 18:3; cf. 2 Kings 17:15; Ezekiel 11:12). Poised to enter and possess the Promised Land, the people were warned by God not to live like those who currently lived there. They weren't to become like the resident nations, nor adopt their practices. Instead, they were to live as the exclusive people of God by living as the law of God prescribed. Another example is found in the Sermon on the Mount where, in contrast to the hypocritical religiosity of the Pharisees and pagans, Jesus said to his disciples: *"Do not be like them"* (Matthew 6:8). Stott quotes Barclay in saying, 'We are not to be like a chameleon which takes its colors from its surroundings.'[2] In short, the people of God are not to be conformed to the prevailing culture, but rather to be transformed.

The tense of the verse speaks of maintaining a continual attitude of refusing to mindlessly conform to the world's ways, but consciously allowing ourselves to be transformed. Or, as JB Phillips, paraphrases this verse: *'Don't let the world around you squeeze you into its own mould, but let God remold your minds from within.'*

Stott insightfully points out that:

> We human beings seem to imitate by nature. We need a model to copy, and ultimately there are only two. There is *this world*, literally 'this age', which is passing away, and there is God's will, which is *good, pleasing and perfect*.[3]

We are aligning our life with one of these models of living and thinking: either this world or God's will. So we must make a definitive decision to no longer draw our cue from the prevailing

---

2 John R.W. Stott, *The Message of Romans* (Leicester, England: Inter-Varsity, 1996), 322–323.

3 ibid, 323.

culture, but actively seek fundamental, internal change by the renewing of our minds.

B. Be transformed by the renewal of our mind

This is where God's work and power come into the equation. In the process of the renewing of our minds, there is something *only* God can do: that is, bring ongoing transformation. As we're about to see, this transformation of our lives by the renewal of our thought-life is a work of the Holy Spirit–it is not humanly possible.

After Paul told his Roman readers not to conform to this world, which was their responsibility, he instructed them to '... ***be transformed*** *by the renewing of your mind'* (emphasis mine), something which is God's prerogative.

The English word 'transformed' translates the Greek word *metamorphoo* from which we get the English word 'metamorphosis'. This word (*metamorphoo*) is only used 3 times in the New Testament. In the first instance, we find it in Mark 9:2-3 concerning the transfiguration of Christ, where it records how *'...he was* ***transfigured*** *before them. His clothes became dazzling white, whiter than anyone in the world could bleach them'* (emphasis mine). 'A complete change came over him. His whole body became translucent.'[4] Although there was no transformation of Christ's inner being, his outward appearance was *transformed* by the *glory from within* irradiating his whole body. The glory within became visible and apparent on the outside.

A second reference to *metamorphoo* is found in 2 Corinthians 3:18: *'And we, who with unveiled faces all reflect the Lord's glory, are being* ***transformed*** *into his likeness with ever-increasing glory, which comes from the Lord, who is the Spirit'* (emphasis mine). Christians are being changed from the

4 ibid, 323.

inside out as part of an ongoing process of becoming more like Jesus. This transformation is brought about by the work of the Holy Spirit, who is indwelling and changing us.

Significantly, a third reference of *metamorphoo* is Romans 12:2. The change that 2 Corinthians 3:18 and Romans 12:2 envisage 'is a fundamental transformation of character and conduct away from the standards of the world and into the image of Christ himself.'[5]

Scientifically, metamorphosis describes the process of revolutionary transformation from the inside out. It is a biological process by which an insect, amphibian or crustacean physically develops after birth or hatching. A radical and relatively abrupt change takes place in the creature's body structure and is usually accompanied by a change of habitat or behavior. An example of this is the four stages in the lifecycle of a butterfly: (a) egg; (b) larva–which hatches as a caterpillar; (c) pupa or chrysalis is where the caterpillar forms an outer shell called a cocoon–this is when a fundamental change takes place and the body of the caterpillar is transformed into an adult butterfly; and (d) adult (butterfly) emerges from the cocoon.

This is a picture of the Spirit's work in our lives. The Spirit, as God's indwelling and empowering presence, is changing us–transforming us into the likeness of Christ from the inside out. We are going through a metamorphosis. We're not what we were, but we're not (yet) what we will be. We are in a time of radical change.

In this verse, the words '...***be*** *transformed...*' (emphasis mine) are in the present tense, which means it is a continuous process of renewal, not on-again, off-again. Importantly, Paul does not say that the renewal of our thought life is simply mind over matter, nor a replacement of the old ways of thinking, or even the substitution of bad thoughts with good or godly thoughts;

5 ibid, 323.

on the contrary, he writes that it is a *transformation* on the deepest level. Like the process of metamorphosis, what comes out looks, behaves, lives and *thinks* completely differently than how it started. This transformation is not humanly possible. It is a work of the Holy Spirit. So, the language of the verse flows like, 'stop allowing yourselves to be conformed; continue to *let* yourselves be transformed.'

The renewal of our thought-life not only brings transformation of our life, but the capacity to discern and discover God's will.

Does this mean it is all up to the Holy Spirit? Absolutely not. We are not to be passive. We have a responsibility to *allow* the Holy Spirit to do his work and will within us. We must cooperate, yield and submit.

Summary

Let's conclude our look at self-control of our thought-life by summarizing what we've discovered. As believers we are not to be *conformed* to this world but be *transformed*; not have an outward conformity to the culture, but an inward transformation by the Spirit; not merely a mindless adaptation to the world's way of thinking, but a renewal of our minds to God's way of thinking.

To put this thought into computer terms, it is like a re-programming of our minds. This re-programming can only come about by rejecting and erasing the old software, and by allowing the Holy Spirit–the divine programmer–to download the new software. It does not take place overnight, but is a lifelong process.

Romans 12:2 concludes with something significant: *'Then you will be able to test and approve what God's will is–his good, pleasing and prefect will.'* The renewal of our thought-life not only brings transformation of our life, but the capacity to discern and discover God's will. Approving the will of God means to understand and agree with what God wants us to do, with a view to putting it into practice. All of us want to know and to do God's will, and the renewal of our minds is a key to understanding and discerning it.

'Since, then you have been raised with Christ, set your hearts on things above, where Christ is seated at the right hand of God. (2) Set your ***minds*** *on things* ***above****, not on earthly things'* (Colossians 3:1-2, emphasis mine).

Personal Reflection:

What area of your thought-life do you struggle with the most?

What action will you employ to address this area?

What principle or thought resonated the most in your heart as you read this chapter?

Chapter Thirteen

Self-Control of Sexual Desires

There's a particular look in their eyes, and an expression on their face, that is very hard to describe or convey. It is gut-wrenching to see and I have never got used to it. I'm talking about the look in a spouse's face when they've just found out that their wife or husband has been unfaithful. The look is a combination of betrayal, rejection, grief and intense pain. Some are inconsolable, all are utterly heart-broken, while others are seething with anger. Because of the positions of leadership I've held, I have had to witness this on dozens of occasions.

The fallout is horrendous enough when it happens within a marriage, but it is magnified when the infidelity is committed by a *leader*. The armed forces use the misrepresentative term 'collateral damage' to describe the unintended victims of military action. 'Collateral damage' is not an adequate term to describe the ramifications of a failed or fallen leader. I liken the consequences to the effects of an atomic or nuclear disaster: there is immediate catastrophic damage from the shock of the incident, but the far-reaching effects are much, much worse. It's not just the initial disbelief or sadness, but the long term, cancerous effects of mistrust, distrust and disenchantment in leaders.

I have wrestled with whether to include this chapter, but it is such a *huge* issue that I feel it would be negligent to leave it out. I have lost count of the number of good men and women I've seen forfeit their ministries, disillusion their followers and bring disrepute to the reputation of Christian leaders because of an inappropriate sexual liaison. Therefore, my main motivation in writing this chapter is to ask you to be vigilant in this important area, because the stakes are incredibly high.

The Scripture which has threaded its way through this section continues, '*...set an example for the believers in... purity*' (1 Timothy 4:12). One of the foremost areas of purity is that of sexual purity. In our highly sexualized culture, this requires extraordinary and vigilant inside out self-control.

Next to self-preservation, sexual desires are the strongest drives we have as human beings, but Scripture teaches that these desires must be controlled (1 Thessalonians 4:3-6). Exercising self-control over our sexual passions is the way by which we maintain sexual purity. In fact, Paul wrote that believers must 'abstain' and 'flee' from sexual immorality in all its forms (1 Corinthians 6:18-20).

Sex is a good gift from God the Creator. We have been created as sexual beings. It belongs to the essential human makeup, an expression of the whole person. As an old Baptist theologian pointed out to me, according to Genesis 1:28 ('*be fruitful and increase in number*'), the first command God gave the first married couple was to go and have sex!

Purpose of sex

If we are to exercise self-control over improper sexual desires, we firstly need to know the Creator's designed purposes for sex. So, why did God create sex? Firstly, there is the *procreative* (generative) or reproductive aspect of sex. It is the created way to reproduce offspring. Secondly, it has been created to be an intimate *pleasure* within the marriage relationship. The book of Song of Songs depicts this sexual arousal, desire and consummation (Song of Songs 7:1-8:4). Foster writes that: 'If Genesis affirms our sexuality, the Song of Songs celebrates it. Karl Barth has called the Song of Songs an expanded commentary upon Genesis 2:25...'[1] But, thirdly, and importantly, it signifies and seals a personal life-long union to monogamous marriage, being the ultimate *physical* expression of intimacy.

The Fall and its distortions on sexuality

Tragically, the Fall distorted and twisted human sexuality. Rather than just having the potential of sexual *fulfillment* through the intimacy of marriage, the Fall brought the potential for sexual *perversion* and problems through immorality. Any breach of God's original intention brings inescapable consequences. Therefore, human sexual energies need to be rightly channeled and carefully controlled.

The interphase of sexual choices with Scripture

To biblically reflect on sexual self-control, we will centre our discussion on 1 Thessalonians 4:3-8. In this passage, Paul's language is very direct and no holds barred, primarily because promiscuity was rife in the Greco-Roman world of Paul's day. He is writing from Corinth to Thessalonica; both cities were infamous for immorality. So he writes plainly and practically to spell out Christian sexual ethics.

Paul begins his discourse on sexuality by linking sexual purity with the will of God. The will of God is what God wants to do with our life and how he wants us to live our life. His will is clearly written in Scripture and is applicable to *all* believers. In case we miss it, Paul says, *'It is God's will that you should be sanctified...'* (1 Thessalonians 4:3). What is sanctification? In Scripture, the word sanctification can mean 'set apart, holy, separated, or

1 Richard Foster, *Money, Sex & Power* (London, England: Hodder and Stoughton, 1990, Third impression), 95.

purified'. In the Old Testament, it was a *ritual* consecration–a 'cleansing' to signify separation from the unclean in preparation for religious observance. Consecration was attained by following prescribed regulations for ritual purification. In the New Testament, through our union with Jesus, we have been sanctified–that is, set apart for him, made holy through him, and cleansed in every way by him. But sanctification must also have a practical outworking in our everyday lives. The concept of sanctification, then, is the idea of progressively becoming more holy, or being in the *process* of character transformation into the likeness of Jesus.

The word sanctification covers every area of our lives, but Paul singles out one area that was obviously troubling him about the church in Thessalonica: sexual immorality. *'It is God's will that you should be sanctified: that you should avoid **sexual immorality**...'* (1 Thessalonians 4:3, emphasis mine; cf. 2 Timothy 2:22; 1 Corinthians 6:18 and Genesis 39:15).[2] The term sexual immorality (*porneia*) covers every kind of sexual intercourse and, by implication, sexual activity: fornication (sex before marriage); adultery (sex outside of marriage); and homosexuality (sex with someone of the same gender). So Paul is clear: If you want to do God's will, then abstain from *all* sexual immorality.

Continuing his theme, Paul then mentions another aspect of sanctification. Not only must we abstain from sexual immorality, but we must exercise self-control over our bodies. More specifically, we must exercise self-control over our sexual desires because, if left unchecked and not channeled correctly, they may lead to sexual immorality.

Paul wants his readers to take *personal* responsibility for this area of their lives. He urges his readers not to be negligent or haphazard, but to take responsibility before God to do what

2 Also see 2 Timothy 2:22; 1 Corinthians 6:18 and Genesis 39:15.

they need to do to abstain from sexual immorality. This exercise of self-control is a process, in many cases a life-long process, to '...***learn*** *to control* [our] *own body...'* (emphasis mine).

In fleshing out the whole area of controlling our *body*, we need to consider 1 Corinthians 6:18–20. Corinth was the centre of the worship of Aphrodite–the Greek goddess of sex and beauty. This cult sent prostitutes out to roam the streets at night. So Paul has to write in stark and blunt terms to get the message through.

With that background in mind, in 1 Corinthians 6:18–20, Paul implores his Corinthian readers to *'flee'* from sexual immorality. What reason does Paul give for fleeing immorality? There is one very confronting reason: *'All other sins a man commits are outside his body, but he who sins sexually sins against his own body'* (1 Corinthians 6:18b). What does *'sin against his own body'* mean? Paul goes on to help us to understand: *'Do you not know that your body is a temple of the Holy Spirit, who is in you, whom you have received from God? You are not your own; you were bought at a price...'* (1 Corinthians 6:19–20).

In essence, the flow of thought of 1 Corinthians 6:19–20 runs along the following lines: The blood of Jesus was the ransom price to purchase our life from slavery to sin and Satan; we were ransomed from a life of idolatry and immorality; when we surrendered our life to Jesus, he made his home within us by the person of the Holy Spirit; the Spirit now lives within us as God's indwelling presence empowering us to live the Christian life; he was given to us as the seal of our salvation; his presence within us is the guarantee of the coming resurrection; because he lives within us, we know that our mortal body will be raised up again incorruptible; and because our body will be resurrected in this way, our bodies are part of the redemption. Therefore, Paul says, *'You are not your own...'* The body is God's temple in which the Holy Spirit dwells, therefore it is not our own but

If we use our body for immorality it defiles God's redemptive and holy purpose for our lives.

God's. God purchased it by the blood of the cross – '*...you were bought at a price*' (1 Corinthians 6:20). The implication is that our bodies are not our own to do with as we wish in the matter of sexuality.

Paul's discussion on this ends with the sentence, '*Therefore honor God with your body*' (1 Corinthians 6:20). Part of the reason we must flee sexual immorality is because our bodies belong to God through the redemption of the cross. Our bodies are destined for resurrection. We honor God when we choose to use our bodies for right living. So if we use our body for immorality it defiles God's redemptive and holy purpose for our lives. In this sense, '*...he who sins sexually sins against his own body*' (1 Corinthians 6:18).

Having made that little excursion into 1 Corinthians 6, let's come back to our study passage in 1 Thessalonians 4:4 where Paul continues, '*...each one should learn to control his own body in a way that is holy and honorable...*'

He goes on to say that this sexual self-control must be in stark contrast to the prevailing culture: '*...learn to control his body in a way that is holy and honorable,* ***not in passionate lust like the heathen, who do not know God****...*' (1 Thessalonians 4:4–5, emphasis mine). We must not live our lives in complete gratification like the world around us which has no understanding of God's ways, God's word and God's sexual ethics. We do not draw our standards from the prevailing culture. We are not called to be people who reflect the culture; we are called to live by the Christian counter-culture. We are not people of the culture; we are people of the Kingdom. We are not to be like the world around us. We are to be different. We are to live by the highest sexual ethics–the ethics of the kingdom.

Practical suggestions for *how* to control our bodies

How can we control our bodies in a holy and honorable way? Here are a few practical suggestions:

A. Exercise self-control in our thought-life (what we think about)

Sexual self-control begins with regulating what we're thinking about in our minds. In Matthew 5:27-30, Jesus taught that the true meaning of God's command not to commit adultery was much wider than just abstaining from acts of sexual immorality.[3] He clarified and qualified it by adding that not committing adultery also included avoiding the lustful look or imagination. He said that '...*everyone who looks at a woman lustfully has already committed adultery with her* ***in his heart***' (Matthew 5:28, emphasis mine). His point was that immoral thoughts are also sin, not just the acts themselves. If we have fantasized about it in our mind, we have committed the act in our hearts. So, one of the keys to controlling our body is to control our thought life.

B. Exercise self-control in our eyes (what we look at)

In this same passage (Matthew 5:27-30), Jesus went on to give a powerful key in how to control our thoughts. He said that we must be ruthless in what we look at and how we look at people we are attracted to. '*If your right eye causes you to sin, gouge it out and throw it away. It is better for you to lose one part of your body than for your whole body to be thrown into hell*' (Matthew 5:29). In simple terms this means that if temptation comes to us through what we look at or how we look at someone, either don't look or stop looking inappropriately or lustfully. We must exercise self-censorship over what we look at. We all know the difference between looking and lusting. Heart adultery is the

3 Stott, *The Message of The Sermon on the Mount* (Leicester, England: Inter-Varsity, 1996), 87.

Self-control involves exercising rigorous censorship over what a leader feeds their mind on.

result of eye adultery.[4] So the best place to begin controlling our bodies is by controlling our eyes. Job claimed he had learned this: '*I made a covenant with my eyes not to look lustfully at a girl*' (Job 31:1). Self-control requires us to monitor how we look and what we look at.

Let's introduce the topic of pornography at this point. 'Pornography', wrote Stott, 'is offensive to Christians (and indeed to all healthy-minded people) first and foremost because it degrades women [and men] from being human beings into sex objects, but also because it presents the eye of the beholder with unnatural sexual stimulation.'[5] Self-control involves exercising rigorous censorship over what a leader feeds their mind on. Therefore, pornographic movies, pictures, websites or explicit reading should be strenuously avoided.

C. Exercise self-control over our hands (what and where we touch)

Referring back to Matthew 5:27-30, we note in verse 30 that Jesus said, '*And if your right hand causes you to sin, cut it off and throw it away. It is better for you to lose one part of your body than for your whole body to go into hell.*' Jesus' point about hands is very much the logical application of his point about eyes, namely that if temptation comes to you through what you touch–don't touch! Don't touch anything or anywhere that is inappropriate or immoral.

D. Minimize places of temptation (what and where we go)

In a cross reference to Matthew 5:27-30, Mark's gospel records that Jesus also said, '*If your foot causes you to sin, cut it off. It*

4 ibid, 88.
5 ibid, 90.

is better for you to enter life crippled than to have two feet and be thrown into hell' (Mark 9:45). In a similar vein to the other references to eyes and hands, this means that if temptation comes to you from places you go (*'if your foot causes you to sin'*)–don't go there! It is better to amputate some places from our life than open ourselves to temptation and the possibility of judgment. No one can dehumanize their sexuality, but they can minimize the places of temptation.

As Stott notes, Jesus' command to amputate 'troublesome eyes, hands and feet…' is not advocating '…literal physical self-maiming, but a ruthless moral self-denial.'[6]

E. Normal, healthy sexual relations in marriage

For married people, part of controlling one's own body is normal, regular love making within the marriage.

Back to our text in 1 Thessalonians 4:3-8

1 Thessalonians 4:6 contains a sobering warning: *'…and that in this matter no one should wrong his brother or take advantage of him.'* Immorality means that we have defrauded the other person. Sexual immorality is complete selfishness. It is selfishly using the other person for our own gratification. It is taking advantage of them. There is a consequence of this defrauding: *'The Lord will punish men for all such sins, as we have already told you and warned you'* (1 Thessalonians 4:6). In context, the punishment is not so much for the acts of immorality, but for the complete selfishness and disregard for the other person or people involved. The punishment is not so much for the sex itself, but *using* other people for our gratification.

If we have sinned sexually, we must find a place of repentance and forgiveness, not just for the acts of immorality, but for the use and abuse of people for selfish reasons.

6 ibid, 89.

Our calling is to live clean, which includes being sexually clean.

Importantly, 1 Corinthians 6:11 and other Scriptures underline that forgiveness is available for sexual sinners. For example, the woman caught in adultery and dragged before Jesus found grace and mercy (John 8:1–11), and David found forgiveness after his adultery with Bathsheba (Psalm 51). Further, Luke 7:36–50 records the story of *'...a woman who had lived a sinful life in that town'* seeking Jesus out. She couldn't retrieve her wrong choices up to this point, but she made the all-important choice to take her failures to Jesus where she found forgiveness and wholeness (Luke 7:50).

Then we come to a verse which spells out *why* we should live right: *'For God did not call us to be impure, but to live a* ***holy*** *life'* (1 Thessalonians 4:7, emphasis mine). To live immorally is to live below our calling. Our calling is to live clean, which includes being sexually clean.

The final verse of our study passage (1 Thessalonians 4:8) is a very confronting Scripture: *'Therefore'*, or on the basis of God's call to live a holy life, *'...he who rejects this instruction does not reject man but God, who gives you his Holy Spirit.'* Here is the crucial point of choice. Will we *obey* this instruction to choose sexual purity? Or will we choose to *reject* this instruction and choose sexual impurity?

Let me offer some practical advice to leaders about sexual self-control.

For single leaders:

Make the resolute choice to stay pure in your sexuality. In today's permissive culture, sexual purity (chastity or abstinence) is scorned and ridiculed, but, in the church, it should be celebrated and honored.

Single singles

My colleague, Karen Pack, adds a great perspective by pointing out that, 'Within the church, singleness tends to be defined as a "pre-marriage" state, with the assumption often made that this is a *temporary* lifestyle; but in our society this is often no longer the case.' She goes on to mention how statistics show that there are now more 'single adults than married adults in most western nations.' In churches, she wrote, 'long-term singleness is frequently not one's preferred lifestyle, yet it may be the lived reality.'[7] Very few people who are single have a gift of celibacy. There are now increasing numbers of singles in our churches. Within a call to live counter-culturally, Karen reminds them that '...the Christian life is not about sex, or the absence of sex; it is about discipleship–living a cruciform life in the context of relationship with God and membership of his Body.'[8]

Sexual purity as a single is evidenced by abstinence from sexual activity. This does not just mean abstinence from actual sexual acts, but also from sexual imagination, lustful looks and looking at (or reading) sexually inappropriate material on the web, social or any other media. This will require singles: to keep their hearts, minds and eyes pure before God; to regulate how they look at someone to whom we are attracted; to guard their mind; and to exercise rigorous self-censorship over what they watch, read and listen to.

Singles in a relationship

If, however, you're in a relationship, work hard to keep it pure. Let me repeat, we *can't* dehumanize our sexuality or sexual desire, but we can minimize the opportunity to get into trouble. Take

7 Karen Pack, *The Single Strife: Nurturing Wholeness in the Lives of Single Christians* (Unpublished essay, Vancouver, BC: Regent College, 2009), 9-10.
8 ibid, 13.

preventative action, like not being alone together in vulnerable places. Establish clear, non-negotiable boundaries in the relationship, and build in accountability measures with other single people or an older couple. Guys, show leadership and don't let the girl be the moral conscience of the relationship. Pray together. Surrender your lives and relationship to the Lordship of Jesus.

For married leaders:

Part of controlling one's sexual desires is, as mentioned, normal, regular love making (1 Corinthians 7:3–5). Married people should make sex a priority and seek to satisfy their partner, not just gratify themselves.

Sexual purity in marriage is evidenced by absolute fidelity, which is complete faithfulness. Faithfulness is not just the absence of adultery; it is fidelity of heart, mind and eyes (Matthew 5:27–30). As we've seen, Jesus spoke about eye-adultery and sexual fantasy in our minds being evidence of adultery in one's heart (Matthew 5:27–30; cf. Hebrews 13:4).

Adultery is destructive and there are strong warnings in Scripture against it (Proverbs 2:19; 6:32; 1 Corinthians 6:9; Hebrews 13:4). At the end of an extended warning against adultery (Proverbs 6:20–29), Solomon concluded with: '*So is he who sleeps with another man's wife; no one who touches her will go unpunished*' (Proverbs 6:29).

There are always consequences for adultery. In Scripture, for example, Reuben forfeited his rights as the firstborn because he slept with his father Jacob's concubine, Bilhah (Genesis 49:3–4, 35:22). David displeased the Lord through his adultery with Bathsheba, and also suffered the death of the infant son born out of the elicit liaison (2 Samuel 11:27, 12:14–18). The people of Israel committed spiritual adultery against the Lord through their union with idols and gods of the surrounding nations, and were punished through judgment and exile (Judges 2:16-19; Jeremiah 3:6-10; Ezekiel 6:9).

On a lesser scale, a married leader should never flirt, make subtle overtures, or inappropriately touch someone to whom they are not married.

Faithfulness requires that we not covet our neighbor's wife or husband (Exodus 20:17), but be wholeheartedly captivated by our spouse (Proverbs 5:18-19). Let's not wish that our spouse looked like some film star. May we do all within our power to foster romance, build relationship and work on healthy communication.[9]

For single-again leaders or those from a sexually active background:

Find a place of repentance and forgiveness with God over past sins or mistakes. Guard the entrances of sin by knowing your vulnerabilities, so you can guard against temptation. If there has been some spiritual residue from people you've been involved with, then go to some mature people and be prayed over in Jesus' name.

I strongly urge you to not, under any circumstances, get romantically involved with an unbeliever. Dating is not a form of evangelism. As a Pastor, I've heard people say to me: 'He treats me better than any Christian ever has.' 'I'm so lonely... she's shown me interest... I need companionship.' 'There are *no* eligible women in church.' 'He says that he doesn't mind me going to church after we're married.' I completely understand these sentiments and often they are true, but if there is no spiritual compatibility, there is no true oneness in spirit. Remember the Scripture in 2 Corinthians 6:14 about not being '*...unequally yoked with unbelievers.*' One of the strongest reasons why believers should not marry unbelievers is that

9 For practical advice on how to develop in your marriage, see chapter 17, point F.

there will never be that one-spirit connection. A believer's body is destined for resurrection; an unbeliever's is not. Normally, if there is a Christian/non-Christian relationship, someone will have to compromise, and, sadly, from my observation, it is often the Christian. You may be attracted to each other, there may be a palpable chemistry, and he or she may be the nicest person you've ever met, but there needs to be *spiritual* compatibility for the future relationship to work.

Before you marry again, deal with the fallout from previous relationships. Forgive those who have hurt you. Seek professional counseling if you feel that the 'baggage' from past relationships is going to be an impediment for the future. Be honest with your new potential spouse about your past–not the lurid graphic details, but enough for them to know where you've come from.

Summary:

In this chapter, we've seen that sex is a wonderful gift from our Creator that has been designed to be enjoyed within the sanctity and intimacy of marriage. In our highly sexualized world, leaders must exercise self-control to maintain sexual purity. Based on 1 Thessalonians 4:3–8, we examined Paul's teaching on sexual ethics, before providing some practical applications like exercising self-control over our thought-life, eyes and hearts. The chapter concluded with down-to-earth advice to single leaders, married leaders and single-again leaders.

Self-reflection:

What is your biggest area of temptation or struggle in this area?

What will you put into practice as a result of reading this chapter?

What one thing, in particular, had the greatest impact from what you've just read?

Chapter Fourteen

Self-Control in Living Above Reproach

Sometimes good people, including leaders, are accused of bad things. Often, an accused leader's only defense is the quality of being 'above reproach.' What does it mean to be 'above reproach'? This chapter will attempt to answer this question.

At the top of the list of qualifications for church leaders in 1 Timothy 3:1–10 (cf. Titus 1:5–9) is to be *'above reproach'* (1 Timothy 3:2). The words *'above reproach'* have '...in mind mainly aspects of behavior (inward and outward) that have observable results, and as a measurement it signifies that no grounds for reproach or blame have been found.'[1] Other versions of Scripture render or paraphrase *'above reproach'* as *'well-thought-of'* (MSG), a person whose *'life cannot be spoken against'* (NLT), someone who *'must not give people a reason to criticize him'* (NCV), *'blameless'* (KJV), *'blameless reputation'* (JBP). Towner summarizes it by writing, 'The leader's reputation must be able to withstand assaults from opponents inside or outside the church (v. 7).'[2]

In other places in Timothy and Titus, the Greek word translated as *'above reproach'* is rendered *'blameless'* (2 Timothy 3:10; Titus 1:6–7; cf. 1 Timothy 5:7). Being 'blameless' does not mean

1 Towner, 249-250.
2 ibid, 250.

> **Leaders are not perfect, but they must conduct their leadership free from duplicity, inconsistency and incongruity.**

'faultless' or 'sinless', otherwise there'd be no-one qualified to be in leadership–we'd all fall short. Rather, 'blameless' has to do with a leader's reputation within the church and broader community being beyond substantive accusation.

Nor does 'above reproach' or 'blameless' mean the leader will never be criticized or accused of wrongdoing. If a leader hasn't ever been criticized, they haven't been a leader. Even Jesus was falsely accused and spoken against (Matthew 27:12; Mark 14:56; Luke 6:7). Being above reproach means that there will be no substance or foundation to the criticism or accusation. In this sense, the leader is 'blameless'.

Leaders are not perfect, but they must live their lives and conduct their leadership in a manner that is free from duplicity, inconsistency and incongruity.

To understand what is required to live above reproach, we will now explore three key ingredients.

A. Integrity

Being a leader who is above reproach requires, firstly, impeccable personal integrity. When Paul counseled Timothy to '*set an example for the believers*', he explicitly outlined a wide range of areas in which he was to do so: '*...in speech, in life, in love, in faith and in purity.*' Timothy was to demonstrate exemplary and transparent integrity in all parts of his life.

The English word *integrity* comes from a French word (*integrité*) with Latin roots and has a range of meanings such as, 'soundness, wholeness, innocence, blamelessness; chastity, purity.'[3] Webster's dictionary defines integrity as 'the quality of being honest and having strong moral principles; moral uprightness.'[4] For example, we speak of a person's integrity to describe their adherence to a moral or legal code.

Not only is the word *integrity* used of people, it is also used in the construction industry and the engineering profession to describe the structural soundness of a building. After earthquakes, for instance, engineers have to check the integrity of structures to ensure that there are no compromises or breaches in the sturdiness and strength of the structure, so that it can support a designed load without collapsing, breaking or bending.[5]

Contemporary culture would regard a person of integrity as someone who fulfils their stated code of ethics, principles or standards in their profession, industry or partnership. Integrity, in Christian leadership, is not just displayed by our public or professional life, but in *every* area of our lives. This encompasses both public *and* private, professional *and* personal, seen *and* unseen. Christian leaders must beware of the subtlety and hypocrisy of selective integrity, which is only displaying integrity in *selected* areas of our lives.

Some years ago, a newspaper published the following story. One night a couple were going through the drive-through of a fast food restaurant. They ordered and paid for their food. A young employee busily organized their meals and put them into a take-out bag. He momentarily went away from the bag to pour the drinks. Meantime, the duty manager was taking the cash proceeds for the day and was preparing to take them to the night safe at the nearby bank. To disguise the money, he put it into an identical take-out bag. When the young person returned, he inadvertently picked up the wrong bag. Instead of

3 https://en.wikipedia.org/wiki/Integrity.
4 http://www.merriam-webster.com/dictionary.
5 https://en.wikipedia.org/wiki/Structural_integrity_and_failure.

picking up the bag with the food, he picked up the bag with the money. He innocently gave the couple the bag with the money, which they thought was their meal. They drove to a nearby park where they opened the bag ready to eat. To their surprise, all they found was money carefully folded and coins carefully bagged. Realizing what had happened, they immediately drove back to the fast food outlet. The male driver went inside and asked for the manager. He discreetly told the manager what had happened and handed back the bag.

Before I conclude the story, let me ask a question, 'Did the people in this story have integrity?' Keep your answer in mind as I finish the story.

The relieved manager expressed his profuse thanks and asked him to wait while he called media outlets. He wanted people to know that there were honest people in the world. The man resisted his request. His motive for not wanting publicity wasn't humility; it was something far more deceptive. The woman in the car with him was not his wife; she was another man's wife. They were having an adulterous affair.

Let me ask my previous question again, 'Did the people in this story have integrity?' The answer is 'yes' and 'no'. They had what I referred to previously as selective integrity. This couple expressed integrity in regard to financial honesty, but they did not have integrity in regard to sexual morality or fidelity.

In Christian leadership, selective integrity is duplicitous, hypocritical and deceitful. It undermines our credibility and tarnishes the potential influence of our leadership.

Defining integrity

A definition of integrity in Christian leadership could therefore be: the intentional and conscientious commitment to be principled, ethical, honest, trustworthy and authentic in *every* area of one's life.

Examples of integrity

By way of application, a Christian leader should show integrity in the following illustrative areas:

Truthfulness

Being a person of integrity requires that a leader is truthful. Naturally, this means that we do not lie (Proverbs 12:22; Colossians 3:9), not only because lying is a sin, but that lying is the *devil's* native language (John 8:44). More subtly, being truthful also means that we do not fabricate or embellish a story to aggrandize ourselves (Ephesians 4:25; Proverbs 12:19). Further, truthfulness necessitates that we do not abdicate personal responsibility, or apportion blame to someone else, to avoid incrimination (Genesis 3:12–13) or confrontation.

Integrity requires truthfulness in official documents, application forms, employment interviews, our curriculum vitae and in bearing witness.

Trustworthiness

One of the measurements of a leader's integrity is the quality of trustworthiness. A trustworthy leader is one who can be relied on to be honest, truthful and dependable with a promise, commitment or responsibility. It means that others, both those leading us and being led by us, find us deserving of trust or confidence.

As an employee, for example, a trustworthy leader would work industriously (Colossians 3:23–24; Ephesians 6:7), ethically (Titus 2:9–10), respectfully (Ephesians 6:5–9), conscientiously and wholeheartedly (Colossians 3:22–24).

Financial scrupulousness

Leaders of integrity are completely upright in their stewardship of their *personal* finances, the administration and reporting of *church* finances, and the paying of appropriate fees, dues and taxes to the *governing authorities*. Without integrity in all these *three* spheres (personal, church and government), a leader is vulnerable to attacks of financial impropriety and the potential tarnishing of their credibility.

Genuineness

To be known as a leader of integrity demands that we are transparent and sincere, and not living with hidden falseness, duplicity or deceit. Genuineness requires that there is no hypocrisy, double standards or pretence in our lives. In practice, this means that we do not have a secret life, a double life or proverbial 'skeletons in the closet'. Our motives must be pure and our dealings with people must be free of exploitation or dishonesty.

In the early days of personal computers, I remember learning the acronym, WYSIWYG, which stands for 'What You See Is What You Get'. It is an operating system in which what is displayed on the screen will closely resemble what is printed or exhibited in the end result. We need to be WYSIWYG leaders–people must see what they get and get what they see!

Steadiness

If a leader is to exhibit integrity, it is important that they are consistent and stable, not up and down, emotionally erratic or volatile. If their demeanor, leadership style or interaction with people is inconsistent or unstable, their leadership may destabilize, and people's trust in them may be eroded.

Integrity is based on the consistency of our character. Integrity is a choice.

This representative list is not comprehensive because we could add many more examples, such as sexual purity, but Chuck Swindoll (1934-) suggests a helpful list of statements as an integrity test:

You have integrity:

- When you complete a job when no-one is looking
- When you keep your word and no-one checks on you
- When you keep your promises
- When you do what you say
- When you have financial accountability, personal reliability and private purity
- When you do not manipulate others
- When you are not arrogant or full of self-praise
- When you tell the truth even though it hurts to do so (go against you)
- When you stand for God when others around you aren't
- When you do the right thing because it is the right thing to do or not popular.[6]

Integrity is based on the consistency of our character. Living a life of integrity is to live morally, ethically, transparently, appropriately, biblically or, in a word, Christianly. Integrity is a choice. Integrity is inwardly regulated, which means it is initiated from *within*.

Alan K. Simpson (1931-), who served as a US Senator from 1979-1997, famously said, 'If you have integrity, nothing else matters. If you don't have integrity, nothing else matters.'[7] A breach of our integrity in any part of our life will undermine being 'above reproach'.

6 http://www.crosswalk.com/church/pastors-or-leadership/a-battle-for-integrity.
7 http://www.brainyquote.com/quotes/authors.

B. Good reputation in the general community

To be above reproach, I would suggest that a leader, secondly, '*...must also have a good reputation with outsiders, so that he will not fall into disgrace and into the devil's trap*' (1 Timothy 3:7). Leaders are required to have a good reputation with 'outsiders', which is another term for the 'non-Christian public' (NEB) or the broader community. To use some of Paul's other words, leaders are to '*be wise in the way [they] act toward outsiders*' (Colossians 4:5), leading a '*quiet life*', minding their '*own business*', working hard '*...so that [their] daily life may win the respect of outsiders...*' (1 Thessalonians 4:11–12). The reason Paul insists on leaders having a good reputation is to avoid the hazard of potentially being discredited or disgraced. This, he argues, is the devil's principal stratagem against leaders–discredit the gospel by discrediting Christian leaders.

Some years ago, the Australian government initiated a 'Royal Commission' into child abuse in institutions, such as churches, schools and foster homes.[8] The revelations were chilling and harrowing for all involved–the victims, the office holders representing the institutions and the public. The sheer number of clergy involved in abusing children was alarming and deeply disturbing. The unfortunate perception that formed in the minds of many Australians was that the church covered over a lot of criminal acts and didn't refer the perpetrators to the appropriate investigative and judicial authority and processes. Consequently, the church has lost a lot of credibility and moral authority in the minds of the general public. In the aftermath, it is imperative that now, more than ever, Australian Christian leaders do all within their power to gain, retain and sustain a good reputation with their communities.

---

8 A 'Royal Commission' is a type of 'public inquiry'. Public inquiries are temporary ad hoc bodies appointed by executive government to provide advice or to investigate some issue; whose members are drawn from outside government; have public processes; seek community input and release their reports. (Source: http://theconversation.com/royal-commissions-how-do-they-work-10668).

The mission agency in which I serve has a senior couple who have built a ministry training college in central Java, the heavily populated main island of Indonesia. After some time, a group of militants moved into their area and influenced a number of the locals who, until that point, had been peaceful and well-inclined toward the Christians. In fact, Jemaah Islamiyah, which is an Indonesian affiliate of Al Qaeda, had a training camp in the forest nearby, until the locals drove them away.[9] Due to the dedication of this couple over many decades, the local civic Muslim leaders actively seek their help in community events. Such is their credibility and rapport that, when there were threats of violence toward Christians and minorities, the local community rallied to protect the college.

Due to the civil war in Syria and the rise of ISIS (also known as ISIL or DAESH), millions of refugees from both Syria and Iraq have poured into neighboring Lebanon and Jordan. The United Nations and other Aid organizations have done an admirable job, but so have the local Lebanese and Jordanian churches, in caring for these displaced people. While the United Nations forbids aid workers of any faith to proselytize, literally thousands of Syrians have come to faith in Jesus because of the *love* shown by the Christians. One Pastor, who works in the refugee camps, told me that other Aid organizations would bring food, clothing and shelter just as they did, but the refugees would comment, 'You're not like the others, you *love* us. What is it about you?' The Christians were then able to share about Jesus. This was the first time the Syrians had ever heard the gospel. This opportunity came because the Christians gained an excellent reputation among the refugees because of care, compassion and mercy.

9 Jemaah Islamiyah is responsible for many atrocities, including the 2002 bombing of nightclubs in Bali that claimed the lives of 202 people, including 87 Australians.

To be above reproach, a leader must not stay in the insulated, isolated immunity of their church building, but become immersed and active in their community and its needs.

C. Practical holiness

A third ingredient for leaders to be above reproach is found in Peter's exhortation in his first epistle to '*...be holy in all you do*' (1 Peter 1:13–16). We are made holy through Jesus' work on the cross and our subsequent status and standing 'in Christ', but the words '*in all you* ***do***', imply that holiness has a practical expression. To put it succinctly: We are made holy (positionally) through Christ, but we now must live a holy life (practically) by the Holy Spirit.

According to Peter, the holiness we are to demonstrate through our lives is grounded and modeled on God's holiness. This is underlined by Peter's words in 1 Peter 1:15–16, '*But just as he who called you is holy, so be holy in all you do; for it is written: "Be holy, because I am holy."*'

What is God's attribute of holiness? God's holiness is his absolute uniqueness and distinctiveness from all others in the sense of being 'set apart'. There is nothing impure, unrighteous or wrong in him—he cannot be contaminated. God is morally pure, absolutely upright and utterly true. He is the holy one.

Through Jesus, his holy nature resides within us through the indwelling of the *Holy* Spirit. This means that we have the power to live a holy life.

That said, practical holiness is not an outward, illusory show of piety. Holiness isn't rule keeping; that is, if we observe a man-made set of rules (things which Scripture doesn't prescribe), or a list of do nots, we shall be deemed holy. A holy life is not rule keeping, primarily because we can outwardly comply, but inwardly rebel. Far from being authentic holiness, it is a façade and a pretense. If we lived like this, we would be no different than the Pharisees of Jesus' day who, although outwardly adhering to Old Testament law, were inwardly compromising and living hypocritical lives (Matthew 15:1-20; Matthew 23:2-36). As long as others thought they were adhering to the Law, they thought they were holy, righteous and pure. The truth was that they were unholy, unrighteous and impure.

Holiness is a response to God's gracious work of making us holy. It is a lifestyle that God's holy nature reproduces in us.

This reminds me of my first visit to the Baltic nation of Estonia in 1993. I visited there a few years after communism collapsed and the Soviets had left. Under the Soviets, behavior was carefully regulated. *If something wasn't explicitly allowed, it was forbidden*. Some church leaders adopt the same method to control the behavior of their parishioners. If something is not allowed by them, it is forbidden. If you want acceptance, then you must fit in with their rules. This is not holiness, it is legalism and control.

Far from being rule keeping, holiness is a response to God's gracious work of making us holy. It is a *lifestyle* that God's holy nature reproduces in us, which is evidenced by our behavior, words, actions, responses and relationships. Everything about our life should be consistent with the holiness of God; that is, it is pure and pleasing to him.

Summary

If this chapter were boiled down to a mathematical formula, then I'd propose that: integrity + good reputation with the non-Christian public + practical holiness = above reproach.

Self-reflection:

Out of the three ingredients of integrity outlined in this chapter, what one do you need give greater attention?

What actions will you adopt to become increasingly 'above reproach'?

Identify any areas of integrity that you need to work on.

Chapter Fifteen

Self-Control in Managing Stress

The flight schedule had changed. I hadn't been informed. My connecting international flight was leaving in just four hours. I had ministry booked the following day in a significant Malaysian church. I made frantic calls to my travel agent for help, but I was completely powerless. To say I felt stressed would be an understatement. Here's what happened.

I was flying from the city of Nepalgunj, located on Nepal's southern border, to the capital Kathmandu. As I was checking in, I was informed that a month ago the local airline's flight departure time for my flight had been changed to an hour later. My indignant question, "Why wasn't I notified in advance?" was met with polite indifference, but he did organize to put my bag into the aircraft last, so it would be retrieved first. This one hour delay, however, would jeopardize my capacity to catch the connecting international flight I was currently booked on. I immediately rang my Melbourne-based travel agent, who admirably and efficiently rang the office of the international carrier in Kathmandu airport to explain my predicament. They helpfully said that they'd look out for me and keep a check-in person on-site until the last minute. Somewhat relieved, I waited anxiously (not patiently or happily) for the inbound flight to arrive so we could begin the journey.

That's when some more problems began. The flight from Kathmandu arrived late into Nepalgunj. It took longer than expected to board and depart. Unknown to me at the time, when we arrived at Kathmandu, the baggage handlers didn't read the note on my bag. It did indeed come off first, but was loaded first into the bottom of the trailer that transports the bags to the collection area. After the short bus ride to the arrivals area, I waited a seemingly interminable time for the baggage cart to arrive. (There are no carousels at the Kathmandu domestic terminal.) It was only then I realized what they'd done with my bag. I was the *last* person to collect my bag! With 40 minutes until my international flight departed, I tried to run the 1 kilometer road between the domestic and international terminals, but I hadn't factored in Kathmandu's altitude. After 100 meters, I was heaving for breath and realized I couldn't run after all. I eventually made it to the terminal where I hurriedly explained to a security officer what had happened. He escorted me past the long queue through to the check-in counter, which was great because I have an aversion to queues. But it was too late. The flight had closed. I had missed it by minutes. I was despondent.

After a further saga in the downtown ticket office, I was eventually rescheduled on a flight 24 hours later. There was a major festival in Kathmandu that week, so it was difficult to find affordable and comfortable accommodation. Hours later, a suitable hotel was located, and I was driven there by taxi. I was not happy. I was disappointed not be able to speak at the church the next day. I was hungry and thirsty. The sum total of all this was that my stress levels were very high.

Then a thought struck me. I've always wanted to do a scenic flight of Mt Everest. Those flights leave around dawn each day, depending on the weather. I'd have time to do this flight, have breakfast back at the hotel, and get to the airport to catch my international flight. My attitude immediately changed. I made the arrangements, then decided to take a leisurely walk to the tourist precinct of Kathmandu, which I'd never explored before. I thoroughly enjoyed the sights and smells. I had a very enjoyable Italian meal and an excellent sleep. Next morning, I did the flight to Everest, which flies back parallel with the stunning Himalayas. Without equal, it was the most breathtaking and awe-inspiring flight I've ever taken. As I disembarked, my stress levels hardly registered.

Stress is how our physiology reacts to the demands placed upon it.

I had been so annoyed and stressed just fifteen hours before. It's amazing what a shift in attitude and perspective can do to your stress levels. In this chapter, we're going to look at a leader's capacity to manage their stress and its effects.

Contemporary leaders are living and working at a much faster pace than the generation before. The acceleration of changes, complexities and pressures are becoming increasingly stressful. The reality is that stress is not going to decrease; it will only increase. Therefore, leaders must develop a greater capacity for handling stress.

Defining 'stress'

By way of definition, stress has been described as 'nervous tension that results from internal conflicts from a wide range of external situations.'[1] Taylor and Goldsworthy add that 'Stress is tension inside that results from pressure either from our social environment, our physical environment, or our own experiences.'[2] The external pressures are called 'stressors' and the internal result is 'stress'.

1 Anthony D'Souza, *Leadership* (Nagasandra, India: Better Yourself Books, 1985), 494.
2 Cedric Taylor & Graeme Goldsworthy, *Battle Guide for Christian Leaders–An Endangered Species* (Cudgen, NSW: Wellcare, 1981), 26.

Stress is how our physiology reacts to the demands placed upon it. Stress generally begins by being anxious about something. The physical reaction of stress takes place because of the mental and psychological state of being anxious or tense.

Here are some examples of 'stressors':

- Financial pressure
- Work pressures
- Losing our job
- Shifting homes, cities, states or nations
- Illness (or death) of a loved one
- Conflict with people close to us (family, spouse, partner, friend)
- Wayward child
- Discrepancy between expected and actual performance.

Here is a list of some of the mental, physical and emotional symptoms of stress:

- Mind racing
- Stomach churning
- Difficulty in sleeping
- Heart beating rapidly (or hypertension)
- Body tense
- Hands clammy
- Light headed
- Pain in the chest, head or joints
- Uncharacteristically irritable, unmotivated or impatient.

Stress can be any or all of these conditions, emotions or feelings. While some personality types are more prone to stress, today's leaders face pressures that can produce wear and tear on even the most dependable and adaptable person.

How to develop a greater capacity to manage stress?

The underlying question, then, becomes: 'How can a leader handle the stresses of a busy and pressured life and ministry?' Scripture teaches a number of practical ways to develop a greater capacity for handling stress.

A. Live by right priorities by choosing to put God first

In Matthew 6:25 Jesus said, *'Therefore I tell you, do not worry about your life...'* Jesus clearly taught his followers that they didn't need to be crippled by 'worry'. The all-important word to understand the meaning of this verse is *'therefore'*. His exhortation *'not to worry'* is the conclusion of the teaching he had just brought in Matthew 6:19-24. In short, he had just taught, firstly, on having treasures in heaven rather than treasures on earth; that is, live for the eternal, not the temporal, the incorruptible rather than the corruptible (Matthew 6:19-21). Then, secondly, centering our lives on light and not darkness (Matthew 6:22-23). Thirdly, came the challenge of who or what we serve: God or money (Matthew 6:24). Only on the condition that we live for eternal treasure, light and God alone, can we fully apply Jesus' teaching: *'do not worry about your life.'*[3]

Stress is reduced when our life has settled on the right priorities of God and his Kingdom.

There are rhetorical questions implied in this passage:

- Am I living for worldly values or heavenly values?
- Am I living selfishly or unselfishly?
- Am I living for money or God?
- What is my secret inner motivation?

3 Some thoughts in this paragraph adapted from John Stott, *The Message of the Sermon on the Mount*, Bible Speaks Today (Leicester, England: Inter-Varsity, 1996), 159-163.

In summarizing Jesus' words, if we live by right priorities (heavenly treasure, light, God) we will be positioned to live a life that is not preoccupied with worry. Stress is reduced when our life has settled on the right priorities of God and his Kingdom.

B. Don't worry about what you don't have to worry about

Jesus said *'do not worry'* three times in a short but rich teaching found in Matthew 6:25-34 (note vv. 25, 31, 34). He explicitly taught his followers not to worry about three specific things: food, drink and clothes. There is nothing wrong with these three essential things at all, but Jesus was warning them to avoid being preoccupied with material comforts as the be-all and end-all of existence. Humans shouldn't just live to live. They live to love and serve God, to love and serve others, and to fulfill their God-given purpose.

In essence, Jesus told his listeners not to worry about these things because life is so much more than physical existence. In addition, he told them not to worry because the *'...heavenly Father knows that you need them'* (Matthew 6:8, 32). To drive his point home, Jesus referred them to how the Father 'feeds' the birds (Matthew 6:26) and 'clothes' the flowers (Matthew 6:28-30) as evidence that God can take care of his children.

The unmissable implication is: God can take care of us, so why worry? We don't need to worry about what we don't need to worry about. Worry is a failure to trust God. In fact, 'worry is incompatible with trust in God.'[4] There is a Swedish proverb that says, 'Why worry when you can trust. Worry is like a rocking chair; it gives you something to do but doesn't get you anywhere.'

C. Live one day at a time

'Therefore do not worry about tomorrow, for tomorrow will worry about itself. Each day has enough trouble of its own' (Matthew 6:34).

4 ibid, 163.

Jesus mentioned both today and tomorrow. 'All worry is about *tomorrow*, but all worry is experienced *today*.'[5] Jesus, however, told his listeners not to worry about tomorrow, but to live one day at a time.

The lesson here for leaders is to live as if today was the most important day of our lives. Tackle what we can today. Deal with today's challenges and pressures without being strangled by the prospect of what might be tomorrow. Don't allow the problem at hand to become exaggerated in our mind, imagination or fear. Worry is a waste of time, thought and nervous energy. Of course, this doesn't mean we shouldn't *plan* for the future; it *does* mean that we shouldn't *worry* about the future.[6]

D. Be specific and thankful in prayer

'***Do not be anxious about anything***, *but in everything, by prayer and petition, with thanksgiving, present your requests to God. And the peace of God, which transcends all understanding, will guard your hearts and minds in Christ Jesus*' (Philippians 4:6-7, emphasis mine).

Paul urged his Philippian readers not to worry, stress or fret about '*anything*'. 'Anything' is an all-encompassing word–it includes every part of our life. The antidote Paul suggests for worry and anxiety is prayer. Importantly, the type of prayer Paul envisages is thoughtful and detailed. From this verse, there are some key words to describe the nature of prayer that Paul encourages his readers to adopt:

- Pray *comprehensively* ('but in *everything*') – pray about every aspect of our life
- Pray *specifically* ('...by prayer and *petition*...') – be very specific in our prayer as if we were presenting a case before a court of law;

5 ibid, 168.
6 ibid, 168-169.

- Pray *thankfully* ('with *thanksgiving...*') – thoughtfully recall what God has done in our life and verbally express gratitude and thankfulness (cf. 1 Thessalonians 5:18)
- Pray *constantly* ('present your *requests*') – pray regularly for the things for which we're asking and believing God.

The peace of God is a deep-seated confidence and assurance, untroubled by the tests, trials or uncertainties of life.

Paul's exhortation in verse 6 on how to pray is followed by the promise of verse 7 that detailed, thankful and constant prayer will result in the '*peace of God*' guarding our hearts and minds. The peace of God is a peace that originates and emanates from God. It is the peace *of* God because it is *from* God. He is the God of peace (cf. Philippians 4:9; Hebrews 13:20; Romans 16:20). The God who dwells in *shalom* (wholeness, well-being), gives *shalom* to his people. He is the provider of peace. He did so through his own love and initiative by sending Jesus to pay the once-for-all and eternal sacrifice for our sins (Colossians 1:20). This peace is established by God himself now that we are in Christ. This is not only in our status or position of being in Christ, but we can experience this peace in our everyday world by the indwelling presence of the Holy Spirit.

In Paul's mind, peace is one of the fruit of the Holy Spirit. It is an inner assurance, confidence, calm, ease and serenity of heart brought about by the Spirit's presence in our life. The peace of God is irrespective and independent of all earthly experiences. It is a deep-seated confidence and assurance, unruffled and untroubled by the tests, trials or uncertainties of life. Likewise, Jesus said that the peace he would give would not be as the world gives peace (John 14:27). It is not an artificial peace from some substance, relaxant or tranquil environment. It is *his* peace. On this basis, he said, '*Do not let your hearts be troubled and do not be afraid*' (John 14:27; cf. 16:33).

This verse (Philippians 4:7 NLT) goes on to say that the peace of God '*...transcends all human understanding*' or is '*...far more wonderful than the human mind can understand.*' This peace is beyond the range of human comprehension. It is supernatural. It cannot be explained and cannot be explained away.

How does the incomprehensible peace of God help us in our fight against anxiety? Philippians 4:7 continues that the '*peace of God...will guard your hearts and minds in Christ Jesus.*' 'Guarding', in this verse, is a military metaphor. 'The Roman army, when encamped, took great care in setting the watch. Sentries were posted within the camp and on its perimeter. The sentries themselves were kept under surveillance by regular patrols throughout the night.'[7] The Greek verb translated 'to guard' conveys the sense of 'keeping the enemy at bay'. In the specific case of the Philippians, their enemy was *anxiety*, which appears to have been making some serious inroads into their general well-being.[8]

But Paul emphasized that *if* the Philippians would pray specifically, thankfully and constantly, the peace of God would be like an impregnable garrison of soldiers around the vulnerable areas of their lives, which were producing stress in both their hearts and minds. They would experience the peace of God in the everyday reality of their lives, despite their external circumstances. The peace of God, which comes from the 'God of peace', neutralizes the incapacitating effects of anxiety and enables us to endure the stresses of life.

7 Williams, 218.
8 ibid, 219.

E. Cast our care upon the Lord

'Humble yourselves, therefore, under God's mighty hand, that he may lift you up in due time. ***Cast all your anxiety*** *on him because he cares for you'* (1 Peter 5:6-7, emphasis mine).

The context is that Peter had made a call for humility in people's attitudes to one another. A proud person sets themselves up against God, and God, in turn, sets himself against the proud. Then in verse 6, Peter calls his readers to humble themselves under God's mighty hand. This humility is attained, wrote Peter, by *'casting our cares on him.'* Peter adopts a quote from Psalm 55:22, *'Cast your cares on the Lord and he will sustain you; he will never let the righteous fall.'* The word *'cast'* means to throw something upon someone else. In this case it is casting our cares, concerns and anxieties upon the Lord. The main reason we should do so is because *'...he cares for us.'* God cares about every part of our life, therefore we don't have to be riddled by cares.

The application for stressed leaders is to cultivate a daily dependent unburdening of our life and its circumstances to God.

F. Wait upon God for strength

Isaiah prophesied some words of astounding comfort to Judah who, because of their rebellion, were exiled in Babylon. Wholly undeserving, God nevertheless reassured them of his unfailing love and restorative plans. There are a few verses that particularly stand out as being relevant for stressed people.

> *He gives strength to the weary and increases the power of the weak. Even youths grow tired and weary, and young men stumble and fall; but those who* ***hope in the Lord*** *will* ***renew their strength****. They will soar on wings like eagles; they will run and not grow weary, they will walk and not be faint* (Isaiah 40:29-31, emphasis mine).

Like the people of Judah, leaders often experience times of weariness, fatigue and disillusionment. God has revealed himself as a God who strengthens those who place their hope in him. What does it mean to 'hope in the Lord'? The verb translated 'hope' can also mean 'wait' in the sense of 'waiting in confident expectation' (cf. Lamentations 3:25-26; Isaiah 30:18; Psalm 37:7). The expression 'waiting upon the Lord', writes Oswalt,

> '...implies two things: complete dependence on God and a willingness to allow him to decide the terms. To wait on him is to admit that we have no other help, either in ourselves or in another. Therefore we are helpless until he acts. By the same token, to wait on him is to declare our confidence in his eventual action on our behalf.'[9]

In applying this to leaders, the primary lesson from this passage is that those who confidently wait, who trust, who depend, who draw strength from, who are intertwined with God like a vine growing on a wall, will experience an inward renewal in which their weakness will be exchanged for strength, their weariness for energy, and their worrying for trust. When life or leadership is stressing us to breaking point, and there is no-one and nothing else to turn to, we must make time to go to the Lord in confident expectation.

G. Receive strength from the Lord

Toward the end of his second letter to Timothy, Paul wrote some very moving words that revealed the pressure he was under. He urged Timothy to join him as soon as possible:

> *Do your best to come to me quickly, for Demas, because he has loved this world, has deserted me and has gone to Thessalonica. Crescens has gone to Galatia, and Titus to Dalmatia. Only Luke is with me... Alexander the*

---

9 John N. Oswalt, *The Book of Isaiah Chapters 40-66*, The New International Commentary of the Old Testament (Grand Rapids, MI: Eerdmans, 1998), 74.

> *metalworker did me a great deal of harm* (2 Timothy 4:9-14).

The emotion in these words comes from some of the deepest and most sensitive veins of human pain. Paul wrote of rejection, desertion, incarceration, isolation, persecution and opposition. Amazingly, there is no detection of bitterness, self-pity, regret or anger. Paul obviously was managing the stresses he had endured and was experiencing.

He then wrote, in 2 Timothy 4:16, of his isolation and loneliness at facing the Roman judicial process without any support. Everyone had deserted him. His next few words, however, recorded in verses 2 Timothy 4:17-18, reveal how Paul coped with stress and pressure on an unimaginable scale:

> *'But the Lord stood at my side and gave me strength...I was delivered from the lion's mouth. The Lord will rescue me from every evil attack and will bring me safely to his heavenly kingdom.'*

At the time of his greatest need, the Lord's presence surrounded and empowered him to go on. The lesson from this passage for every anxious leader is to remember that we are never alone–the Lord is always with us. His power and strength are available. He will rescue us. He will bring us through. The application for leaders is to receive strength from the Lord.

Practical suggestions for managing stress

Aside from the Scriptural principles that have been articulated in this chapter, here are some practical suggestions for how a leader can manage their stress levels:

1. Take control of your time. Manage your schedule. Work and stick to a plan. Prioritize your time for the things that really matter.

2. Learn to pace your life and leadership to be ordered and live within your physical and emotional limits.
3. Make time for fun, leisure and relaxation. Regularly do things that are enjoyable and rejuvenating, such as walking on a beach, riding motorbikes, crocheting or playing music.
4. Socially engage with people you enjoy being with. Wherever possible, find people with whom you can share your heart, especially about things that are causing stress. Be with people that make you feel 'safe'.
5. Maintain a healthy lifestyle by watching your diet, exercising regularly, reducing caffeine, and going for regular medical check-ups.
6. Get adequate sleep by remembering the old proverb: 'You can't burn a candle at both ends.'
7. Reduce the number of 'stressors' in your life by avoiding unnecessary stress, by learning to say 'no' to some people and tasks, and by minimizing your contact with, and keeping a right heart toward, people who stress you.
8. Plan holidays, take regular days off and avoid doing work on days off or when you get home from work.
9. Talk to the appropriate people for perspective and wisdom when things are getting on top of you.
10. Seek professional help if you're unable to cope or continually feel overwhelmed, drained (emotionally bereft) or depressed.

Summary:

In summary, leadership and ministry are stressful. Stressors are not going to decrease, so leaders must develop their capacity for handling stress. Jesus taught practical advice for handling anxiety (stress). Namely, right priorities, not worrying senselessly and living one day at a time. Paul taught his readers that thoughtful, specific prayer is the antidote to worry. Peter wrote that we must learn to cast our care upon the Lord. God gives strength to people who feel drained by their prevailing circumstances. The chapter concluded by listing some practical measures every leader can adopt for managing stress.

Self-reflection:

What causes you stress?

What symptoms do you display when you feel stressed?

From this chapter, what have you learnt about how to handle stress?

What's been the biggest lesson?

CONCLUSION TO SECTION THREE

In this section, we have focused on a leader's self-control. We defined self-control as exercising self-restraint, personal discipline and control *in* and *over* our lives, especially our natural impulses. Importantly, we noted that the goal of self-control was to have our lives voluntarily under the control of the Holy Spirit. It is by the Spirit's power that we have the divine capacity to have our life in check.

In Section 4 we're going to explore how we can develop ourselves and our leadership. It will be the most practical section to date.

SECTION FOUR

Self-Development

A fourth category of self-leadership is self-development. Self-development occurs when a leader thoughtfully and intentionally works on their personal life and functional growth in leadership.

OVERVIEW OF SECTION FOUR – SELF-DEVELOPMENT

In his first letter to Timothy, Paul instructed him to '*be* ***diligent*** *in these matters;* ***give yourself wholly*** *to them, so that everyone may see your progress.* ***Watch*** *your* ***life*** *and* ***doctrine*** *closely. Persevere in them…*' (1 Timothy 4:15–16). Added to this are his words in his second epistle: '***do your best*** *to present yourself to God as one approved…*' (2 Timothy 2:15, emphases mine).

Language such as '*diligence*', '*give yourself*', '*progress*', '*watch*', '*persevere*' and '*do your best*' suggests that Paul was challenging Timothy to develop himself. Growth as a leader is a personal *choice*. The only person responsible for your growth is *you*.

Growth as a leader is *intentional*. Leaders don't grow by accident; leaders grow on purpose. They grow because they give proactive attention and intention to their personal growth.

The following four chapters will outline a list of practical suggestions for how to maintain a pathway of growth and development in life and leadership. Chapters 16–18 will centre on ten areas of our *personal* development, while chapter 19 will focus on how we can develop our *leadership*.

As you work through these areas, you'll notice that some of the ideas I propose have either been covered in previous chapters or will be repeated in the other areas. This is because they have multiple, relevant applications. If they have been covered in detail, I will only mention them briefly, but a few will require further elaboration.

Because the substance and tone of this section is predominantly practical instruction, I have intentionally changed the personal pronouns from 'us' and 'we' to 'you' or 'your'. Since I'll be offering a lot of suggestions and practical advice, it makes it a lot easier grammatically for me to speak *to* you, than to stick with the more inclusive 'we' I've used in the former sections.

Chapter Sixteen

Personal Development—How to Develop Ourselves (part one)

'Watch your life...closely. Persevere...' (1 Timothy 4:16).

Life is so much more than leadership. Life does not equal leadership, nor does leadership equal life. Leadership is an *expression* of our life, but not the sum total of our life.

Life is about loving, glorifying, worshiping, serving and living for Jesus with every fiber of our being. As we fully integrate our life around this purpose, we will experience what it is to really live.

Therefore, we have the potential of living life to the full. The way we live a full life is by becoming everything God has intended and purposed us to be. This is a day by day process in which we grow to become more and more like Jesus.

Personal development is a partnership

When I use the term 'personal development' in this chapter, I am not suggesting that this is achieved by personal effort alone. Our development results from a *partnership* between us and the Holy Spirit. Our growth as a person is a work of the Holy Spirit, but we have a responsibility to cooperate with him and proactively work on our lives. God's Holy Spirit will do his work and we have to do our work in developing ourselves.

This ongoing, inward transformation of character, conduct, thought processes, ambitions and motivations should have an effect across the whole spectrum of our life.

Life is about loving, glorifying, worshiping, serving and living for Jesus with every fiber of our being.

Lifelong process

I need to emphasize that personal development takes a lifetime. It is a process with ups and downs, progress and regress, successes and failures, joy and tears. But, hopefully, as each year passes, the overall trajectory of our life will be one of holistic growth.

Daily process

Aside from being a *lifelong* process, our development requires *daily* attention. I have a few friends who do body-building. None of them look like Arnold Schwarzenegger, but they work hard to stay in shape (unlike me). The process of developing their bodies is time-consuming and requires a great deal of daily discipline and effort. It's the same with our personal development. It is a day by day venture that involves deliberate, sometimes difficult, daily choices and actions.

Ten areas of personal development

In this and the next two chapters, we'll look at ten areas that characterize and symbolize the spectrum of a leader's holistic, personal development.[1] The following diagram illustrates these ten areas:

1 Some of the practical ideas in 6 of these categories are adapted from the personal notes of Stephen Beaumont PhD, who did some background research for me on a presentation addressing 'wellbeing', and from Dr Johan Roux's 'Seven Dimensions' Model. Both are used with permission.

Diagram 3 - Interphase of the 10 areas of personal development

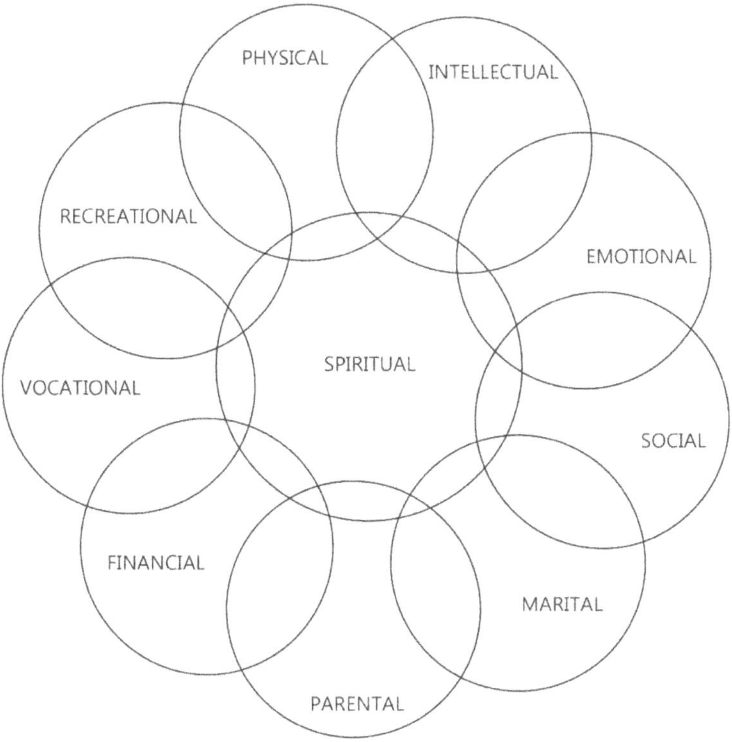

In the diagram above, please note that the spiritual is at the centre of all ten. Our spiritual life should be at the core of who we are, how we live and why we live the way we live. Ideally, the spiritual should inform and influence every other area; in other words, the vibrancy and authenticity of our relationship with God, and the work of God's Word and Spirit in our lives, should be the 'source' from which all the other areas derive.

By way of analogy, a tree has many parts, but it is still one organism.[2] A tree is made up of leaves, twigs, branches, a trunk (that contains outer bark, inner bark, cambium cell layer, sapwood and heartwood) and the roots. The root system, which is generally unseen, is where the process of growth begins. The roots not only anchor the tree to the ground and store food reserves for the winter, they absorb water and minerals from the soil through osmosis. The water is then distributed upward into the leaves where, through photosynthesis, a chemical process takes place in which the sun's light helps the leaves to blend the water from the roots with the carbon dioxide from the air to create food in the form of sugar. These sugars are then 'stored' by the tree in its leaves, branches and roots. It is the sugar which makes the tree grow.

Our spiritual life, by way of parallel, is like the root system of a tree. It not only anchors us, but is the source for the process of growth. In the same way that a branch or leaf cannot grow unless it is joined to the tree, so these areas of our lives will not develop unless they stem and flow from the 'spiritual'.

In addition to these areas being interconnected with the spiritual, it is important to realize that they are also interrelated with one another. I personally think it is dangerous to rigidly compartmentalize or categorize our life into clinical segments. They each have a bearing on the other. For example, if I am physically unwell, it may affect my work (vocationally). If I have problems in my marriage, it will more than likely have a negative influence on our children (parentally). If I am financially under pressure, I am more than likely to be stressed (emotionally). If we do pigeon-hole the various areas of our lives, we are in danger of living disassociated lives, which, as I wrote about in an earlier chapter, may result in people being one thing at home,

---

2 Some basic information for this paragraph was sourced from: http://arborday.org/trees/treeGuide/anatomy.cfm, http://forestry.about.com/od/Treebiology/g/Trees-And-The-Process-Of-Photosynthesis.htm, http://afterschool.smarttutor.com/how-plants-feed-themselves-photosynthesis.

Diagram 4 - Interaction of the 10 areas with each other

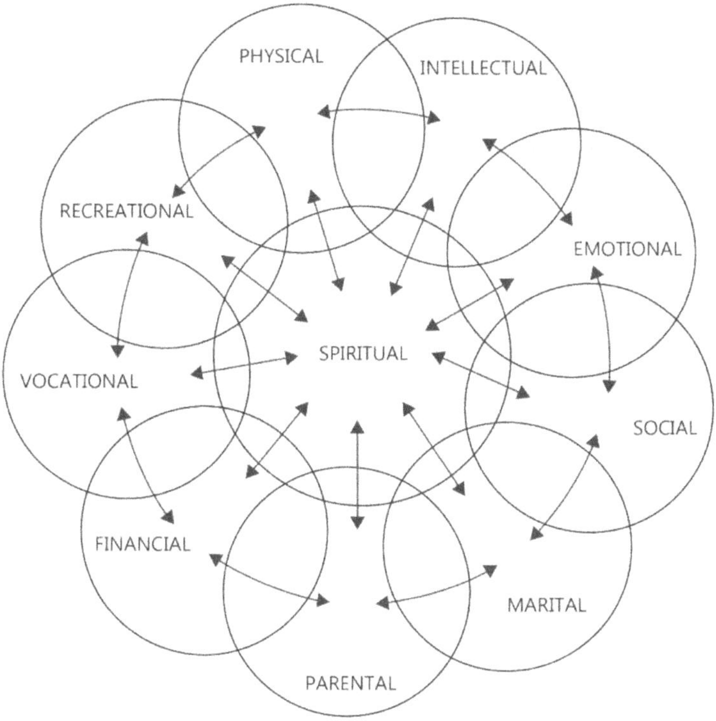

but quite another at work, or one thing in public, but radically different in private. It's far wiser to live a fully integrated life with the spiritual at the core.

Having seen that our personal growth is a process, a daily and lifelong process, and that the spiritual should be at the core of our lives, let's now explore these ten areas that we need to develop. In each one, we'll look at practical ways in which we can develop in the particular area.

A. Spiritually

As we have seen, our spiritual life is the central and pre-eminent wellspring which flows into all other expressions of our life.

If our spiritual life was developing, it would generally be evidenced by the following qualities and characteristics:

- Greater intimacy in our relationship with God
- Heightened sensitivity to the voice of God
- A life of worship
- Christ-likeness in character and conduct, bearing the fruit of the Holy Spirit, and a measurable transformation of our hearts and minds
- Consecrated (sanctified, holy) life, discerning good from evil, pure from impure, righteous from unrighteous
- Disciplined commitment to daily prayer and engagement with Scripture
- Increased effectiveness and empowerment in our personal witnessing
- Displaying a good reputation with our family, work/study colleagues, neighbors and the broader community by the conduct of our life
- Active participation in our local church and its mission through the exercise of our God-given gifts.

But the question most inquiring readers will be asking is: 'How does a leader develop their spiritual life?'[3] Here are some practical ideas:

- Meaningfully engage with God on a daily basis through prayer and interacting with Scripture
- Listen to and for the voice of God
- Foster a relationship with the Person of the Spirit and seek to experience his presence
- Exercise an active life of trust and faith
- Maintain a worshiping heart
- Obey the promptings of the Holy Spirit.

3 See Chapter 7 on being disciplined in our 'Personal Spiritual Practices'.

Self-reflection:

Identify the *one* particular thing you need to work on to develop spiritually.

Leaders need to maintain an adequate level of physical wellbeing to sustain them in their diverse roles and responsibilities.

B. Physically

Paul wrote to Timothy that '... *physical training is of some value*' (1 Timothy 4:8), though he emphasized the more important value of training oneself to be godly (1 Timothy 4:7-8). Leaders need to maintain an adequate level of physical wellbeing to sustain them in their diverse roles and responsibilities.

Listed below are some practical ideas for how we can develop our general physical health and wellbeing:

- **Exercise regularly**. Exercise doesn't have to be a rigorous workout at a local gym, though this is encouraged, but it could be a regular routine or regime of exercises. To maintain a degree of fitness, when I am home from my travel and speaking schedule, I walk every day, unless it is a rare torrential downpour. Having a very cute Cavoodle helps because she requires a good walk every day.[4]
- **Eat a well-balanced diet**. A friend of mine once quipped that a balanced diet consists of half junk food and half healthy food. Eating nutritiously is my biggest personal challenge. The only thing in which I am above average is my weight! This is because I love naughty food, like hot chips.
- **Drink loads of water** and cut down on caffeine and soft drinks.

4 A Cavoodle is a breed of dog that is a cross between a Cavalier King Charles Spaniel and a Miniature Poodle.

- **Get adequate sleep**. Sleep not only makes you feel better, but helps our brains to work properly, and protects our mental and physical health. Doctors recommend that adults sleep 7–8 hours a day with the hours before midnight being the most valuable. Sleep deprivation or deficiencies can cause a lack of concentration, reduce our cognitive skills, increase the risk of chronic disease (such as heart or kidney disease, high blood pressure and stroke), and heighten our risk of obesity.[5]
- **Make informed choices about our medical care** and consult a medical practitioner on a regular basis for preventive checks.
- **Maintain a positive health-promoting lifestyle**. Don't smoke and exercise moderation in the consumption of alcohol or adopt voluntary abstinence.
- **Practice basic hygiene** in things like: showering or bathing regularly, washing your hands after going to the toilet or before handling food.
- **Plan regular, annual vacations**. Take a sustained break. Please don't check emails or do work on your holiday, otherwise you won't fully relax.
- Wherever possible, **have a day off a week** to rest. Do the things you enjoy doing. Maybe do things *outdoors* like a barbeque, picnic, hiking, walking on the beach, sightseeing and, basically, enjoying yourself. More about this soon under 'recreational'.
- **Monitor your stress levels** and maintain balance in your lifestyle.

Self-reflection:

What actions or changes do you need to make to develop physically?

---

5 http://www.nhlbi.nih.gov/health/health-topics/topics/sdd/howmuch http://www.apa.org/topics/sleep/why.aspx.

C. Intellectually

In some of Paul's final words to Timothy, he requested his *'son in the faith'* to bring his *'scrolls, especially the parchments'* that he'd left with *Carpus* (2 Timothy 4:13). It is speculated that the word 'scrolls' refers to portions of the Old Testament or contemporary writings from the early church, and that 'parchments' refer to Paul's own notebooks.[6] The point is that, even in the isolation, restriction and deprivation of his immediate environment, Paul sought for reading and reference material. His precarious circumstances did not deter or discourage him from seeking to keep his mind active. Likewise, if we are to maintain intellectual growth, we need to adopt a similar attitude.

Your 'intellectual development' would be evidenced by being able:

- to keep mentally active, agile and aware
- to develop your capacity to think things through
- to be inquisitive by asking and seeking to answer difficult questions
- to communicate clearly both verbally, non-verbally and in writing
- to have an open, objective mind to different perspectives, new ideas and new ways of doing things.

The following points will enumerate practical ways to develop ourselves intellectually.

- **Reading**. Reading exposes us to ideas, thoughts and scholarship that may inform, challenge, enhance, change or trigger our thinking. As we'll see in the next chapter, leaders are readers (or listeners if they have learning or reading difficulties). I personally enjoy reading biographies, history as narrative and topics relevant to my current work or study.

6 Towner, 629.

- **Physical practices** of regular sleeping patterns, balanced diet and regular exercise. These three things help us to be mentally fresh and require a minimal amount of exertion.
- **Maintain an inquisitive mind**. Keep asking questions–hard questions, probing questions and better questions. Keep curious. In addition, seek to find answers for the questions you're asking. Search, research, enquire, consult and read. Process information and think things through until you form a view, perspective or conclusion, albeit a provisional one.
- **Maintain an open mind**. Closed minds limit your intellectual development. As a leader, you need to be objective and open to appreciate and understand another point of view. There is always more than one side to an issue. It'd be wise to understand the debates that are relevant to you and those you lead, and to clarify the issues. It's important to know what you're talking about and not be naively and ignorantly uninformed. Seek to know *why* you stand for or *against* a particular issue. You don't have to agree with another person's viewpoint or worldview, but you should endeavor to understand it and *why* they're holding or arguing for their position. Don't react ignorantly, but intelligently and compassionately. At all times, prayerfully refer back to Scripture as the basis for your position.
- **Avoid being stuck in ruts**, by being open to new ideas and ways of doing things. Some people categorically reject new ideas or new approaches. I once heard an Afro-American preacher say, 'If I always do what I've always done, I'll always get what I've always got.' Paraphrased this means that if you keep on doing the same old thing, the same old way, you'll keep getting the same old result. A new way of doing something is not necessarily a wrong way.

- **Keep abreast of local, national and global issues**. What's happening in the world? What are the underlying causes? What's happening in your own culture and country? It's important to be conversant with these issues, so you can apply Scripture to the contemporary culture. Or, as someone said, have your Bible and newspaper open at the same time.
- **Learn something new and interesting**. A key to intellectual growth is to discover something new that is outside your current base of knowledge or experience. In my own life, I have done courses on workplace accident investigation, advanced driving and coaching, all of which I found stimulating and challenging.
- **Create something new and interesting**. Another way to keep mentally nimble is to stimulate your creative side. There are many different ways this could be done: carpentry, writing, painting, music, sculpture, crocheting or building models, just to mention a few as examples. Some years ago, I discovered that I thoroughly enjoy photography. I have embraced it as a hobby and, because of the many countries I visit in my role, I have been able to capture some amazing shots of places and people. Photography not only relaxes my mind, but it sharpens me as I endeavor (painfully and slowly) to improve my photographic skill.
- **Stretch yourself by embracing new experiences and opportunities**. In life, there are times when you'll be offered new opportunities, such as, to serve in church, to become a leader, to take a promotion at work or to commit to a new level of study. At these critical moments, you can often withdraw because of a sense of inadequacy, time constraints or a perceived lack of capacity. I encourage you to embrace these new experiences and opportunities because they afford you the prospect of personal growth.

- **Mix with wise, mature and experienced people**. As a leader, you need to be careful who you listen to and who you mix with. I would caution you to minimize contact with negative, critical or small-thinking people. A South African preacher I heard once joked that 'some people are so narrow-minded, they can look through a keyhole with both eyes!' Instead, mix with wise, mature and experienced people who will sharpen, challenge and stimulate you. It will expose you to different ways of thinking, alternate arguments, varied approaches and the wisdom of experience.

Self-reflection:

What stood out to you as something you could apply to your intellectual development?

Record what action steps you'll take.

Chapter Seventeen

Personal Development— How to Develop Ourselves (part two)

In the previous chapter, we began a look at ten areas of our *personal* development. So far, we covered: (a) spiritual, (b) physical and (c) intellectual. This chapter will cover four additional areas, with the final three being addressed in the next chapter.

D. Emotionally (emotional health)

Your wellbeing extends further than merely being *physically* healthy or reasonably fit. According to the World Health Organization, 'health' is defined as: '...A state of complete physical, mental and social well-being and not merely the absence of disease or infirmity.'[1] Your emotional health is often an underrated and undervalued aspect of your overall development, but it is a critical area if you are to develop holistically.

As a leader, you'll be faced with many demands, stresses and disappointments. Added to these are the pressures you face from your everyday life, such as relationships, health, finances and balancing time. The only way you can cope with these multi-faceted challenges is to be emotionally strong.

1 Preamble to the Constitution of the World Health Organization as adopted by the International Health Conference, New York, 19-22 June, 1946.

Emotional strength will help you:

- to cope and adjust to the unexpected traumas, adversities and tragedies of life
- to read, monitor and manage our feelings
- to endure the rigors of leadership
- to help meet the emotional needs of others
- to respond in a measured , mature way when you're under pressure
- to relax and replenish.

The big question, therefore, is how, in practical terms, you can become stronger emotionally? Here are a number of ideas. Some of these have been covered in earlier chapters, but are briefly summarized because they are relevant for this topic.

- **Deal with the residue of past negative experiences** so that it has a diminishing impact. Identify what happened and how it affected you.
- **Learn from your past**. What would you have done differently? Or how should you have responded at the time? Listen to people who've had similar experiences and learn how they coped and overcame their experience. Apply the Scriptures to your experiences. Rather than brood over negative things that have happened, process them thoughtfully and prayerfully.
- **Maintain your sense of humor**. Smile a lot. Laugh at yourself.
- **Meet the emotional needs of others**. Helping others gives perspective to your own problems, as well as building empathy and compassion.
- **Find trustworthy and experienced people to talk to**. Be around people who replenish you. If necessary, please see a Christian counselor or psychologist. There's nothing unspiritual about seeking help.

- **Pray in detail about everything** (Philippians 4:6-7), especially your current circumstances. Ask the Lord to strengthen you emotionally by fortifying your inner person (Ephesians 3:16). Pour out your heart to God (Psalm 62:8).
- **Learn to relax**. Do things you enjoy doing, pursue your passions, and rest your mind until you find a place of peace and rest.
- **Monitor how stress is affecting you**, and take preventative action when you are stressed.[2]
- **Stay on top of your emotional state**: by being conscious of what makes you anxious; by recognizing your feelings and appropriately expressing them to the right people at the right time; by controlling your emotions, such as your temper or tears, wherever possible.
- **Help the poor, disadvantaged or someone in need** in a practical and tangible way. This takes the focus off you and onto someone who may be less fortunate. Doing so may give you a different outlook on your own circumstances and feelings.

Self-reflection:

Which of these ideas is most relevant to your current emotional state?

Which one do you need to give attention?

E. Socially (relationally)

A socially developing leader will display the following attributes: foster healthy friendships, including intimate friends with whom they can share their heart; cultivate people skills, especially conversational and listening skills, and empathy; be respectful of all people; show an authentic interest in others

2 See Chapter 15 for recognizing the symptoms of stress and practical tips on how to manage stress.

and be warm and welcoming; behave and dress appropriately to the social context; maintain a healthy social calendar.

Friendships come in four different, concentric circles:[3]

- **Acquaintances**. These are people you may know in passing, know by name or sight, or maybe have brief interaction with, but there's no relationship other than superficialities.
- **Casual** friendships. These are people you may see from time to time at an activity or social event, whose company you may enjoy, but there isn't a developed relationship, just shared interests, life stage, humor or friends.
- **Close** friendships. These are people who know you well, who understand you, with whom you share time, experiences, thoughts and heart. They'll support you in good times *and* bad, they may sometimes say things that hurt you, but only for your good or to protect you (Proverbs 27:6).
- **Intimate** friends. Generally, most people will only have two or three intimate friends. These are people with whom you share the secrets of your heart, your struggles and pain, your inner thoughts and inner-self. It takes a long time to develop intimate friendships, but the value is incalculable.

It is my observation that the closeness of a relationship is normally governed by your level of disclosure. How much you share about your secret, inner thoughts is a reflection of how close the friendship really is.

The basis of all our friendships and social interactions should be our relationship with God.

3 The four levels of friendship are adapted from http://iblp.org/questions/what-are-four-levels-friendship.

The basis of all our friendships and social interactions should be our relationship with God. Our friendship with God through Christ Jesus is the core of all true friendships (John 15:13–15). Jesus himself had an intimate friendship with John, known as the '*disciple whom Jesus loved*' (John 13:23; 21:7, 20), and a close friendship with a broader group of three comprised of Peter, James and John (Mark 14:33; Matthew 26:37), aside from his relationship with the remaining disciples.

Here is a list of practical suggestions for how a leader can grow socially.

- **Work at developing your social skills** such as: conversational skills; listening skills; showing an interest in others; finding common ground or shared life experiences; being warm; making people feel comfortable with you; accepted and respected by you.
- **Be respectful of all people**, irrespective of their temperament, personality, flaws, age, gender, race, theology, religion, lifestyle, choices or past sins. Treat everyone with dignity and respect.
- **Use manners** such as saying 'please', 'thank you' or 'excuse me', as well as being conscious of social and cultural etiquette.
- **Display the appropriate body language**. Our non-verbal language can speak just as loudly as our words. Often it's not what you say, but how you say it that causes miscommunication and misunderstanding.
- **Develop a social calendar**. Regularly plan to spend time with friends for relaxation, interaction and enjoyment. Engage with people face to face, not simply through social networking.
- **Exercise basic personal-management skills** such as: brushing your teeth after meals or eating a mint before

speaking with people, using deodorant to avoid body odor, and brushing or combing your hair.

- **Watch how others interact**, and learn what to do and what not to do. Learn from your friends about how to be a great friend.
- **Resolve conflicts quickly and biblically**. Because this is such a critical issue, this sub-point will be enlarged.

According to Matthew 18:15, if you are aware of any friction, conflict or hurt with anyone, *you* (the offended person) must take the initiative and *go* to the (offending) person. Jesus did *not* tell his disciples to find sympathetic ears or wait for the offending person to come to them first. On the contrary, he strongly instructed them to have the maturity to *go* themselves. Jesus also said that the motive in seeing the person to discuss the offence must be to reconcile. If you miss this crucial motivation, you've missed the heartbeat of what conflict resolution is about.

Many people carry a 'win/lose' attitude into conflict resolution. If you have a 'win/lose' mindset, the usual result is 'no win', because you're locked into your set positions ('I'm right, you're wrong') and your goal is to win only.[4] You must be prepared to listen objectively and make compromises and concessions for the sake of the relationship.

I will now suggest a step by step way to resolve conflict: Make contact with the offending person to ask for a face-to-face meeting. If a face-to-face meeting is not practical, then set up a phone call. Don't get into the details of why you want to meet with them in the initial contact. It's best to wait until you meet face to face. Carefully choose the time and place you'll meet with them. Be sensitive to the other person's circumstances. Avoid meeting at the end of a hard day or if the other person is under

4 Neil Flanagan & Jarvis Finger, *Just About Everything A Manager Needs To Know* (Brisbane, QLD: Plum, 1998), 233.

pressure.[5] This is critical in conflict resolution. Approach the meeting with a positive attitude. The conflict resolution could be very constructive *if* the other person's behavior changes as a result, and your relationship remains intact or is restored. Above all, initiating contact to resolve a conflict is pleasing to God, and it will keep your life free from offence and bitterness. Pray a lot about the forthcoming meeting. Ask God for his peace. Ask for a good outcome. Ask for a preserved or restored relationship. Rehearse what you're going to say, how you're going to say it and anticipate their possible responses. This will help you think more clearly and respond in measured tones.

Ensure the environment for the meeting between you and the other person is conducive for a conversation of this nature. Avoid places where there are lots of distractions. When you first meet, welcome the other person and thank them for coming. Once you get through the pleasantries, get straight to the issue. If you're feeling anxious or it is a tense atmosphere, have a drink of water, otherwise your mouth may go dry, or silently take some deep breaths to lower your emotional temperature. Begin by saying *why* you called the meeting. 'I have certain feelings about what you said or did yesterday. Could you please help me to understand why? This is how I interpreted what you said.' Explain *why* you're upset and why you feel the way you do. Then listen objectively. There are always two sides to a story. Some say there are actually three sides: theirs, mine and the truth.

At the outset of the conversation, state that your goal is to sort things out and move on in the relationship. 'I don't want anything between us. I don't want any negative feelings. I don't want there to be any misunderstandings.' Keep your cool and listen to everything they say without interruption or judgment. Control your tone of voice, tempo, volume and, importantly, your *non-verbals*, such as your facial expression and body

5 ibid, 232.

language.[6] Don't accuse with your voice or eyes, but show that you're listening by maintaining eye contact. Keep talking through the issues until you feel you have peace and some sense of resolution. Say whatever apologies are appropriate. Determine how it can be avoided in the future. Maybe work out some action steps. Pray for one another. Affirm each other and the relationship. Conclude the discussion.

If, however, you're not getting anywhere, maybe postpone the encounter, go for a short walk, or consider getting another person as a mediator. If it still deteriorates and there's no resolution or reconciliation, senior church leaders will have to be involved (Matthew 18:16-20).

Self-reflection:

Which of these ideas is most relevant to you in the development of friendships and your social life?

In regard to 'conflict resolution', what particular action will you apply from this point?

F. Maritally

One of the qualities Paul singles out for leaders is to have their marriage and family life in appropriate order. He wrote of leaders being the *'husband of one wife'* (1 Timothy 3:2). This has been interpreted in many ways, but generally speaks of being committed and faithful to one's spouse in a loving, monogamous and lifelong marriage.

A healthy, happy marriage generally means a healthy, happy ministry. Marriage and family are our primary ministry. We lead ourselves, then our families, then the church/ministry. Ministry should never come first. Marriage and family must be first.

How then, in practical terms, can we develop healthy, growing marriages?

6 ibid, 233.

- **Put God at the centre of your marriage**. For a marriage to be lifelong, loving and satisfying, there must be *three* people in the marriage. The third person I'm referring to is a *divine* person–God Himself. He created marriage, so he has the best idea of how to give and get the most out of it. The Bible is full of practical wisdom for how to foster your marriage. Pray together. Worship God together. Go to church together. Read the Bible together. Above all, invite the Lord God to be the centre of your marriage. A great picture of this is a triangle. The closer you get to God (as apex), the closer you'll become to each other.

- **Give your best to your marriage**. Make a decision to be totally in love with your spouse. Be unshakably committed to each other. Make sacrifices for each other. Charles Shedd (1915-2004) is attributed as saying, 'Marriage is not finding the right person; it is being the right person.' Eradicate the notion of 'divorce' from your vocabulary–don't even consider it as an option. Make the choice to work at your marriage all the days of your lives together, remembering your vow 'til death do us part'. Aim for the best marriage possible. Endeavor to keep your marriage fresh.

- **Be affectionate toward each other**. Hold hands, hug, kiss, but be spontaneous and natural. Enjoy each other's company and say so. Buy unexpected gifts or cards. My wife's 'love language' is words of affirmation, so thoughtful words in a nice card are like gold.[7] Maintain your joint sense of humor. Laugh at each other's idiosyncrasies. Fiona and I regularly dissolve into laughter, sometimes

7 The term 'love language' comes from Gary Chapman's bestselling 1995 book, *The Five Love Languages: How to Express Heartfelt Commitment to Your Mate* (Grand Rapids, MI: Zondervan, 1995). In it, Chapman outlines five ways to express and experience love, which he proposes as: gifts, quality time, words of affirmation, acts of service (devotion), and physical touch (intimacy). His hypothesis is that one of these five will be your spouse's dominant 'language' in which love is felt and expressed.

uncontrollably, about little things. Fun and laughter are like oil which lubricate the marriage. One note of caution: please don't embarrass your spouse publicly, but only say kind, affirming and loving words.

- **Prioritize time to connect on a meaningful level**. Coordinate your diaries to schedule date nights, day trips, romantic weekends and chats over coffees. The purpose of planning time like this is to connect on a deeper level than the routine of daily living. It's investing time to listen to each other's thoughts, ideas and feelings, and to discuss some of the more important areas of your life together.
- **Communicate openly and honestly**. Make time every day to communicate. Part of communication is active listening. Listen until you have heard and understood what your spouse is saying. Don't shut each other out or shut down the communication because it gets difficult. Talk things through. Nineteenth century fiction author, Charles Dickens (1812-1870), is reported to have said, 'Never close your lips to those for whom you have opened your heart.'[8] If you drift apart *verbally*, you'll drift apart *emotionally*, then you'll inevitably drift apart *physically*.
- **Resolve arguments quickly**. Accept the fact that growing relationships will have conflict. Try and understand each other's points of view and feelings. Be willing to forgive quickly. Don't go to bed with unresolved anger. Avoid allowing things to foment or simmer. Rather than be proud or stubborn, be willing to say, 'I am sorry.' Take 100% responsibility for your share of the problem. Famous Hollywood actor of the 50s and 60s, Charlton Heston (1923-2008), was once asked how he maintained

8 http://www.goodreads.com/quotes.

such a long and successful marriage.[9] His answer was that he often used three little words–not the ones you're probably thinking of, but... 'I was wrong'.[10] Talk things through instead of withdrawing or sulking. Learn from past mistakes and conflicts. Approach confrontation with an attitude of reconciliation: 'Let's sort this out'. If your problems seem irreconcilable, then please seek help quickly from an experienced counselor.

- **Say 'thank you', express gratitude and be appreciative** for the little things and the big things your spouse does. Fiona constantly says 'thank you' for all the things I do, even the mundane things like changing a light bulb. Saying a sincere 'thank you' to your spouse on a regular basis is a way by which you acknowledge all that they do and all that they are, otherwise they may feel that they're just taken for granted or undervalued.

- **Don't allow the pressures of leadership to encroach on your marriage and family**. Your home needs to be a place of safety and refuge from the rigors and weight of leadership. In times of pressure, don't take leadership problems into your bedroom. Keep pillow talk free of any negative church talk. Steer the discussion around the meal table clear of anything remotely to do with tension or contention in your leadership.

- **Celebrate the milestones**. Make any special occasions, like anniversaries, big birthdays or achievements, as memorable as possible. Seek to cultivate and capture a sense of occasion. Take photos. Share the moment with those who are close to you. Create a memory.

---

9 Charlton Heston is most famous for his roles in '*The Ten Commandments*', '*Ben Hur*' and the '*Planet of the Apes*'. After acting, he was the five-time president of the controversial National Rifle association (NRA) in the United States.

10 http://www.spokesman.com/stories/1997/feb/14/celebrity-pairs-share-secrets-to-long-marriages/.

By way of example, on our 20th wedding anniversary, we flew to Hawaii and, as part of our time there, had dinner at a restaurant on the famous Waikiki Beach at sunset. It was *very* romantic. A few days later, we flew to Las Vegas for a concert and shopping. On our 25th anniversary we did back-to-back cruises of the eastern and western Mediterranean respectively. Then on our 30th anniversary we did another cruise, this time of south-eastern Australia, though I was a bit seasick for the first two days. Often on our regular anniversaries we'll each write five personal highlights of the past year and share them through dinner. These special events have become milestones for us that we remember fondly and regularly.

- **Keep romance blossoming**. Romance is not something that comes naturally to me (probably like most men), so I really have to work at it, but here are some ideas for how to stoke the fire of romance. Write thoughtful notes or cards. Buy an unexpected gift at an unexpected time. Spontaneously text with a short loving message. Say 'I love you' or 'You're handsome' or 'You're beautiful' often. Men, buy flowers for your wife. Hold hands when you're walking together, or walk arm in arm. Hug a lot. Enjoy a meal out together in an environment that is conducive for conversation and has a great view. Look into each other's eyes. Compliment your spouse on how fabulous they look with their new hairstyle or clothes. Consciously think of proactive ways to foster romance.

Self-reflection:

If you're married, it may be wise to ask your spouse to reflect with you. Which one of these sub-points is most relevant to your marriage at the moment?

What will you do to improve or develop in that area?

G. Parentally

When kids come along, your life will radically change. Parenthood is a brand new stage of life which adds a fresh dimension. As the kids grow, there will continually be many stages of life, depending on the age and needs of your kids. Fiona and I are now in the stage where all three kids have grown and moved out, though our youngest still lives at home; or, I should more accurately say, he sleeps at home.

Family life is challenging as a leader. Finding the balance between ministry and family can be difficult, but not impossible. This point will aim to be as practical as possible in determining how to develop your family life.

Widening his call for leaders to have their marriage in order, Paul also called for them to 'manage' their families well and have their family life in order. Paul wrote how a leader's children must be *'respectful'* (1 Timothy 3:4) and not *'have a reputation for being wild and rebellious'* (Titus 1:6 NLT). In fact, Paul wrote that if a leader *'...does not know how to manage his own family, how can he take care of God's church?'* (1 Timothy 3:5; cf. 3:12)

As a Christian leader, your home and family life is more critical than ever.

In commenting on 1 Timothy 3:4-5, Stott wrote how Paul 'draws an analogy between the pastors' family and God's church. Indeed, he uses the word *oikos (household)* of both (4, 5, 15)', adding that ministry leaders, especially married pastors, therefore, are called 'to leadership in two families, his and God's, and the former is to be the training-ground for the latter.'[11]

11 Stott, *The Message of 1 Timothy & Titus*, 98.

As a Christian leader, your home and family life is more critical than ever. Not only are there great pressures on families, but there is an urgent need for leaders to be examples in their family life. In our post-modern world, families are changing shape. There is no longer a stereo-typical family unit–a traditional or normal model. Instead, there is a kaleidoscope of diversity. The notion of 'family' means different things to different people. For example, we have single parent families, blended families and cross-cultural families. Future projections, based on current Australian trends, suggest that, if you belong to a family with two parents (who have been exclusively married to each other) and three kids, you will be in the minority by 2030.[12]

How, then, can you develop your skills as a parent while maintaining a busy life of leadership?

- **Put God at the center of the home**. Create a godly, loving, safe, home environment by centering your family-life around biblical principles. Teach your children God's word and his ways (2 Timothy 3:15; Deuteronomy 6:7). Tell stories about what God has done in your lives. Pray with and for your kids (Mark 7:26; 2 Samuel 12:16; 1 Chronicles 29:19; Job 1:5; Matthew 17:15). Pray as a family and read the Bible together as a devotion.

- **Set a godly example to your kids**. Remember that our children are watching and listening to everything. In what areas should we specifically set an example? (a) In *conversation*. Always speak well of the church and others in front of the kids, and avoid any negative talk in their hearing. (b) In *adversity*. When you're going through a hard time, keep trusting in God, expressing faith and perseverance. (c) In *conflict resolution*. How you resolve your conflicts is setting them an example for how they will resolve their conflicts. (d) In *integrity and transparency*. Be

12 https://aifs.gov.au/facts-and-figures.

as 'real' at home as behind the microphone or in front of people. Here's a humorous anecdote. After the dedication of her baby brother in church, little Jennifer sobbed all the way home in the back seat of the car. Her father asked her three times what was wrong, but Jennifer was so choked with emotion she couldn't speak. Eventually, she replied, 'The Pastor said he wanted us brought up in a *Christian* home, but I want to stay with you guys!'

Don't sacrifice your marriage or family on the altar of ministry.

- **Encourage your kids to attend children's programs and youth activities.** It's an excellent investment in their future.

The church where I served as a youth pastor was in the inner Melbourne suburb of Richmond. Most of the young people attending our youth ministry came from many miles away and generally had to rely on their parents to drive them to and from the church building. One particular Board member felt it was too far to drive his son every Saturday night. As the young man grew, he didn't have any Christian friends or input and eventually drifted away from church and the Lord. I distinctly remember his father coming to me later in life and expressing his deep regret for not making the investment of driving his son to the youth program. I learnt that lesson and drove my three kids to every meeting they wanted to attend.

- **Prioritize family**. Plan family holidays as a priority in your forward planning. When you're home, don't do work at night, but be available for the family. When planning time with the family, please remember that it is not necessarily quantitative time, but qualitative time. Don't sacrifice your marriage or family on the altar of ministry.

One of my father's good friends, Denis, related the following story. At the time, he held a senior position in his denomination. One day he'd organized to take his son out bowling, something they'd had planned for some time. As they were leaving, the home phone rang. It was another member of the denomination's executive team. There was a major problem that required Denis' attention. Denis said that he couldn't come because he had another commitment. Given the gravity of the circumstances, the other leader couldn't understand why Denis would not drop everything to attend to the matter. Denis gave his colleague his views on how to handle the situation, but concluded the call by reiterating that he had another commitment, without specifying the nature of it. He put the phone down, and stepped around the corner, where he saw his son with tears rolling down his face. Unknown to Denis, his son had been listening to the conversation and when he realized what his dad had done for him, he broke with emotion. He understood that his Dad loved him more than ministry. Sometime later, Denis' son said, "Dad, if ever you do have to break an appointment in the future, I know it will be *really* important!"

- **Be available to your children**. Be committed to the family by being there for significant birthdays, achievements, celebrations and events. Be *physically* available by investing time and resources in family outings and the children's sports and hobbies. Be *emotionally* available to your children by being attentive, engaged in the moment and listening to them. Be *spiritually* available by praying for or with them at key times. Be *relationally* available by working on your relationship. This will require time, attention and communication.

- **Healthy communication**. Often in parent/child relationships, the parent is quick to speak, but not as quick to *listen*. Listening is one of the measures of any healthy relationship. Even if you're a busy person, take time to listen until you really *hear* what they're trying to say. Give undivided and undistracted attention. Respond to what has been said so they know you have *heard* them.

Learn to ask open questions that elicit thoughtful answers, rather than closed questions which often bring monosyllabic grunts or the stock 'yes', 'no' or 'I don't know'. Avoid asking questions like an interrogation; instead, ask with interest.

Wherever possible, eat meals together as a family and *talk*. Welcome their thoughts and discussion by inviting their opinions and perspectives. Attempt to make meal times fun and interesting.

Invest time one-on-one with each of your children. Kids remember personalized attention. My youngest son vividly remembers the hours we spent while he was learning to drive. In our State, learners have to have 120 hours of supervised driving before they can be tested for the license. We decided to make the most of it, so we planned day trips and weekends away. It was great to have time together.

- **Express your love and affection with words and touch**. Embrace, affirm and encourage your kids. Say, 'I love you' often and meaningfully. My brother, David, went off to his end-of-year work celebration in December 1986. As he walked out the door, my parents said, 'We love you.' He never came home. He was tragically killed in a car accident that night.
- **Learn how to be a good (or better) parent**. There are many excellent resources, courses, books and seminars available that can help you to be a better parent. Observe

other good and experienced parents. Speak with them, pepper them with questions, learn from their mistakes and implement their successes.

- **Lovingly discipline your children**. Ephesians 6:4 instructs parents not to '*exasperate*' their children, but to instruct them in God's ways. This requires that we lovingly train them for their good. Training involves discipline. Discipline is helping a child to learn what is right and wrong in terms of their social behavior, speech and attitudes. Often this means affirming what they do right, but reprimanding them when they do wrong. Hebrews 12:7-11 tells us that God, as our loving Father, disciplines us. The book of Proverbs teaches parents to discipline and correct their children (Proverbs 13:24; 19:18; 22:15; 23:13).

  In practical terms, affirm *them* as distinct from their action or behavior. Address the issues clearly. Don't avoid or deny the issues. The purpose of discipline is to help the child become self-disciplined, to know right from wrong for themselves, and to behave appropriately in any given life circumstance or cultural setting.

  However, in disciplining children, please remember that every child is different and will respond to different styles of discipline. Never compare your children to their siblings or to other leaders' kids. This often has a negative effect. Treat them individually.

- **Be a guiding presence as they mature into adulthood**. As much as we wish our kids could stay at an idealized age, they inexorably keep growing. With each new stage of their development and maturity–from infancy through childhood and adolescence into adulthood–the nature and dynamic of your relationship with them will change. Recognize these biological and emotional changes. Adapt your relationship and communication style accordingly.

Let them know that you are there for them and want to listen. When you do listen, seek to understand. Be patient and flexible with their moods.

There will come a time when their friends will have a greater influence on them than you. Provide whatever direction, instruction or advice is needed, especially if they seek it. Sometimes they'll listen, sometimes they won't. Be available for them either way. Welcome their friends, even the weird ones. At times, my kids have brought home some very *interesting* people. I would rather embrace their friends, than have my kids drawn away.

When your children do (and they probably will) make decisions that disappoint you, remember that your relationship with your child is *the* most important thing. Even though your heart may be filled with sadness or pain because of their choices or actions, endeavor to retain and maintain relationship. Let them know that you love and accept *them* unconditionally, regardless of your disapproval of their actions. This doesn't mean that you condone their decisions or behavior, but it does mean you're treating them as God treats us when we fail him. Through Jesus, he continues to love us unconditionally, and by his Spirit he seeks to bring (turn) us back to himself. If you treat your kids like this, they're more likely to come back to you in the future. Remember the 'prodigal son' (Luke 15:11-32), who knew where to go when everything unraveled in his life (Luke 15:18). Just as importantly, his father was waiting, watching and welcoming (Luke 15:20).

Inevitably, they'll move out of home, but, hopefully, your parenting has meant that they feel welcome anytime. Fiona and I love it when our kids come home to visit. They tease us mercilessly and laugh at our idiosyncrasies, but we thoroughly enjoy having them 'home', even if fleetingly.

- **Deal with the residue of any past, personal dysfunction**. Even if your experience or model of family has been traumatic or dysfunctional, you do not have to repeat the mistakes your parents (or maybe even you) have made in the past. Forgive those who have hurt you, or not shown you love. Talk to those who are now close to you about the problems and conflicts that may have occurred. It may help them to understand you. Learn how to show love and affection to your dysfunctional family members. Ask forgiveness from those you may have hurt or disappointed. Get help for any anger or violence that may be damaging others. Wherever appropriate or possible, initiate reconciliation with any estranged family member.

Aside from past trauma, if you're currently in a messy or flawed marriage or family, remember that you serve a God who can put the fragmented pieces of relationships together again. He is a God of love who can heal broken marriages or severed relationships. He can give you a capacity by his grace to forgive and move forward. By his Spirit, he can radically change your life so that you do not have to be a victim or captive of the past. You *can* start new and not repeat your or others' mistakes. He is able to deliver you from the despair of any and every regret.

Even though you may feel riddled and incapacitated by mistakes, by the teaching of his Word, the transforming work of the Holy Spirit, the love and support of your church community, and the example of solid families, you can get your life, marriage and family together. It's not too late. Choose a different tomorrow and a better future for your family. Change in your family starts with change in *you*.

Self-reflection:

Which of these ideas was most pertinent to your parenting?

What will you apply to become a better parent?

Chapter Eighteen

Personal Development—How to Develop Ourselves (part three)

In the previous two chapters, we've been working our way through a look at ten areas of our *personal* development. So far, we covered: (a) spiritual, (b) physical, (c) intellectual, (d) emotional, (e) social, (f) marital and (g) parental. This chapter will cover the remaining three areas.

H. Vocationally

In this point, we're going to address an area of your life that covers a disproportionate amount of your time. It is an area which can either bring amazing joy and fulfillment, or debilitating boredom and frustration. It is the topic of your work life.

Throughout his writings, Paul addressed several important principles of life in the workplace in Colossians 3:22-4:1, Titus 2:9-10 and Ephesians 6:5-9. Peter also wrote some relevant thoughts in 1 Peter 2:18-21. At the time the New Testament was written, it is estimated that one third of the Roman world were slaves. Paul's instructions to slaves and masters are the nearest thing we can find to employers and employees in the workplace.

Some leaders reading this book may not be full or part-time workers. For example, you may be a stay at home mum or dad, a student, a retiree or on disability or unemployment benefits.

The following principles will still be relevant to you to live a meaningful and influential life.

'Work' as part of creation and being made in God's image

According to Scripture, work is a part of the creation and is part of God's intended purpose for people. 'Work', in John Stott's words, '...is a consequence of our creation in God's image.'[1] He then takes his readers back to creation to form a 'Christian mind on work' by writing how:

> 'God himself is represented in Genesis 1 as a worker. Day by day, or stage by stage, his creative plan unfolded... His final act of creation, before resting on the seventh day, was to create human beings, and in doing so to make them workers too. He gave them some of his dominion over the earth and told them to use their creative gifts in subduing it (Genesis 2:8, 15).
>
> Thus God planted the Garden and created the man. Then he put the man he had made into the Garden and told him to cultivate and protect it... Here then is God the worker, together with man the worker, who shares God's image and dominion. Later Adam's descendants built cities, raised livestock, made and played musical instruments and forged tools of bronze and iron (Genesis 4:17).'[2]

Work is something God has created us to do. It is part of what it means to be made in the image of God.

Stott also refers to Jesus as a worker exercising manual labor

1 John Stott, *New Issues Facing Christians Today* (London, England: HarperCollins, 1999), 187.
2 ibid, 187.

as a carpenter in Nazareth.[3] Therefore, we surmise that work is something God has created us to do. It is part of what it means to be made in the image of God.

4 Purposes of 'work'

What are the purposes of work? Why did God create 'work'?

- **To give you a sense of self-fulfillment, achievement, accomplishment and productivity**.[4] An important part of your self-fulfillment as a human being is to be found in your work. If work is part of what you have been created to do, then you must not have the attitude that work is just a means to get money to do what you really want to do. Your work must have meaning in itself. It must be a means of fulfillment. God himself, after seeing what he had made, pronounced it as 'good'. He enjoyed perfect job satisfaction.

- **To serve others**.[5] Your work is a way in which you are benefiting others and contributing to the collective life of the community. Adam did not cultivate the Garden of Eden merely for his own enjoyment, but to feed his family. Please don't just see your work as a place to get enough money to pay the bills, but as a way to make a difference to others. You may feel that you have the most menial job in the world, but if you're doing it with the right attitude, you are contributing to something bigger than just yourself.

- **It is a means by which you bring glory to God**. Work is a means by which you can serve God and bring glory to God. You glorify God when his purpose is revealed and fulfilled. To do so, you must have an attitude toward your work that you are ultimately working for him and his

3 ibid, 187.
4 ibid, adapted from 188-191.
5 ibid, adapted from 191-197.

purposes. In this way, work is a further expression of your worship of God, especially if you see it as contributing '...in however small and indirect a way, to the forwarding of God's purposes for humankind. Then whatever we do can be done for the glory of God' (1 Corinthians 10:31).[6] By having this approach and attitude to your work-life, you do, indeed, give glory to God through your work. You don't just give glory to God through what you do at church, but if you approach your work as if you are working for him, and if you live Christianly and act Christianly in the workplace, you are glorifying God there, too.

- **It is God's means of provision**. Work is the means by which God provides for our daily needs. In 2 Thessalonians 3:6-13, Paul stressed to the Thessalonians that they should work to provide for themselves and their families. Work is also the means, through our tithes and offerings, to provide finance for God's house and Kingdom. Additionally, work is the means, through taxes, by which God provides Governments with the means to facilitate and regulate our civil lives (e.g. providing roads, basic services, law and order, transport and health).

Defining 'work'

What you believe about work will determine your attitude toward it. So, what is 'work'? Having offered these four purposes for work, I'll now propose a definition of work based on John Stott's thoughts:

> Work is the expenditure of energy (manual, mental, creative or all) in the service of others, which brings fulfillment to the worker, benefit to the community and glory to God.[7]

6 ibid, 195.
7 ibid, adapted from 196.

With this longer than normal background in mind, what, then, can you do to develop your life in the workplace?

- **Live by the Christian work ethic.** To me, the Christian work ethic is encapsulated by Colossians 3:23-24: '*Whatever you do, work at it with all your heart, as working for the Lord, not for men, since you know that you will receive an inheritance from the Lord as a reward. It is the Lord Christ you are serving.*' In essence this means that in everything you do at work, you should do it with all of your heart as if you were working for Jesus and doing his work, so that the whole tone and tenor of your life in the workplace is one of service to God. Work as if you're working for Jesus.

- **Work ethically** (Titus 2:9-10 '*...not to steal from them* [their masters], *but to show that they can be fully trusted...*'). Christians must be the most ethical, honest, trustworthy and conscientious people to employ, work for, or contract. There must be integrity in the following: not stealing property; not robbing time; your word is your word and your words are truthful; complete trustworthiness; conscientiously come on time, leave on time and complete assigned tasks.

- **Work with the right attitude.** Choose to have a right and appropriate attitude to your work, your workplace, other staff, the boss, and to change. Attitude is a choice. If you really believe that you are (ultimately) working *for* Jesus, you need to have the right attitude. *If* you are to be a witness of living and working Christianly, and *if* you want to be fulfilled and productive in your workplace, you need to have the right attitude. Aim to be the *best* employee or employer you possibly can.

- **Conscientiously do what you're asked to do** (Colossians 3:22; Ephesians 6:5). These verses call for obedience, which implies that you must do what you're asked, required and expected to do. This obedience, however, is not merely doing what you're asked to do, but doing so with the right attitude, motive and disposition. Your attitude toward your employer (boss, supervisor) should mirror your attitude toward the Lord himself. The only exception would be if they ask you to do something which violates the Word of God, which is the basis of Christian ethics.

- **Be respectful** (Colossians 3:22; cf. Ephesians 6:5; Titus 2:9). Sometimes this can be difficult because of the attitude, actions or approach of our employers or managers. No matter how flawed or imperfect they are, you should honor and recognize the position of leadership they hold, even if you can't respect the person themselves. Respect should also be extended to those you work with. A right attitude could be all the adjustment you need to have a happier workplace.

- **Work hard** (Colossians 3:23; Ephesians 6:7). Christians should be the hardest workers in any workplace. In practical terms, working hard requires that you give your best effort and attitude to your work, employer and tasks. This means you are not only conscientious when the boss is around, but just as conscientious and hardworking when he or she is not around. Be industrious by doing what you're asked to do with the right attitude, whether you're thanked or not, or whether it is seen or not. Even if you're doing the most mundane work in the world (and remember that Paul was writing to slaves), you'll still work with all your heart. In contrast, the Bible speaks about the dangers of laziness (Proverbs 10:4; 14:23; 18:9; Ecclesiastes 10:18; 2 Thessalonians 3:11).

- **Work harmoniously** (Colossians 4:5-6). Working harmoniously means that you'll do whatever is within your power to work in peace with other employees, business associates, bosses, clients, banks or debtors. Jesus called us to be peacemakers (Matthew 5:9; James 3:18). Avoid taking sides in office politics, office gossip or bitchiness. Remember there are always two sides to a story. Show an authentic interest in the lives of the people you work with and genuinely engage in their lives. Treat people with dignity and respect. Help mediate conflicts or disputes.

- **Be an example of Christian conduct** (Titus 2:10 '*...not to steal from them* [their masters], *but to show that they can be fully trusted...*') The implication of this verse is that your example as a godly employee should draw attention to Christ in you. Christian employers or employees should be examples of Christian purity, practice and principles. In practical terms, this may mean not entering into the profanity, coarse language, sexual discrimination, racism, inappropriate joking or derogatory comments that others may engage in. If you go out with your work colleagues, be very careful that you exemplify moderation in everything. You must be different to the world around you. Endeavor to be a wordless witness and seek to influence your colleagues, clients or supervisors by your ethics, attitude, integrity, behavior and the quality of your work.

Before concluding this point on our work life, I shall address those people who haven't yet been covered by the generic term 'workers'.

- **Employers/business owners/senior executives or managers**

  '*Masters, provide your slaves with what is right and fair, because you know you also have a master in heaven*' (Colossians 4:1).

  Here is my paraphrase of this verse:

'Employers, empower your employees with what they need to get the job done, remunerate them fairly, and treat them respectfully. Here is a good reason why: because you yourself have an Employer in heaven to whom you will give an account for *how* you have treated your employees. Your treatment of others will determine how you yourself will be assessed in the true performance of your life on earth.'

Here are some Biblical and practical ideas to be a great employer: ensure appropriate wages and conditions (Colossians 4:1); treat your employees fairly and without favoritism (Colossians 4:1); impartially hold people to account for their work (Ephesians 6:9); treat employees like you want to be treated by the Lord (Colossians 4:1; Ephesians 6:9); and pay bills to debtors and taxes to government as required (Romans 13:7).

- **Stay at home Moms (or Dads)**

Motherhood *is* hard work. Moms or dads who choose to stay at home and invest in the early, critical, irreplaceable years of a child's pre-school formation should be honored.

I *also* fully understand the financial pressures on families these days, so I completely understand that some moms and single dads have to work. It is simply a financial necessity. Please don't feel guilty. God can give you the grace and energy to shape your little ones. It is not always the quantity of the limited time we spend with them, but the *quality* of time.

- **Retirees**

Retirees are an untapped ocean of experience and wisdom, even if that wisdom has been earned through hardship, adversity and possibly failure. There is a French proverb that says, 'When an old person dies, a library burns to the ground.'

My encouragement to retirees is to: keep your mind active; volunteer for community service; volunteer to serve in the church, not just in services but during the week in visitation, practical help or nurturing new believers; and mentor younger people in handling life's challenges and making informed decisions about their future.

- **Students**

  You've got one shot at education before life becomes a little more complicated with marriage, kids, cars, mortgages, and stress, therefore do your best to make it count. Study hard. Don't drop out. Don't give up. Hold your ground when your faith is under fire. Aim high.

  But if you're not naturally studious, please don't be squeezed into the mould that only measures people by their academic performance. Some people are *not* academically wired, but they are suited and skilled for a trade, the arts or to be entrepreneurial.

  If you don't know what to do with your future life, and before you make far-reaching decisions without really knowing what you want to do, surrender your life to Jesus by asking, 'What do you want to do with my life?' Ask some self-evaluating questions like: 'What do I really *want* to do? What *really* interests me? Talk to some wise, experienced and spiritual people who will serve as navigation beacons on your journey.

- **Entrepreneurs (self-employed, business owners)**

  Ask God for creative ideas. He is a God of immense creativity (Genesis 1). Scripture has examples of God giving creative 'business' ideas:

- Jacob had an innovative idea for multiplying his flocks which resulted in him becoming *'exceedingly prosperous'* with *'large flocks'* (Genesis 30:37-43).
- Peter threw his net on the other side of the boat in direct obedience to a specific word from God and, as a result, *'...they caught such a large number of fish that their nets began to break'* (Luke 5:6). He then had to call other boats (small business owners) to come and help them (Luke 5:7).
- Joseph had the divinely given idea to store grain in Egypt for seven years. This not only provided food in the seven years of famine that followed (Genesis 41:47-49), but also elevated his standing and influence in the nation (Genesis 41:57).

Audaciously pray for favor and influence with contacts, contracts or the right person in a government department. Think of how you can use your business to further or finance God's Kingdom.

Self-reflection:

In your current place of employment, what point was most relevant for you to apply?

Please record specific actions or steps you will implement to work on the area you identified.

I. Financially

Pressure on your personal finances will mean pressure on your life. If you can alleviate the pressure by wisely handling your personal finances, you'll not only reduce one of the major sources of stress, but be in a better position to lead (financially) by your example and be set up for your future.

In chapter 6, I looked at the self-discipline of a leader in the area of financial stewardship. While I've addressed a lot of ground, this point will focus on the practicalities of *how* you can *develop* your personal finances.

- **Establish and stick to a budget**. Here are some ideas for how to formulate a budget:
    - List all sources of income (e.g. wages, gifts, government benefits)
    - List all estimated and known expenditure:
        - Food
        - Household expenses such as rent, mortgage and upkeep
        - Utilities such as power, gas, phone and internet
        - Tithes and offerings
        - Savings
    - Draft an annual, monthly and weekly schedule of income and expenditure:
        - List dates when income is paid or received
        - List dates when expenses are due
        - Work out if you have enough each week / month to maintain a surplus
    - Ensure you make adjustments each month to cover all expenses:
        - Obviously, ensure that more is coming in than is going out

- Adjust budget accordingly to ensure there are sufficient funds in the bank to cover expenses
- Save a percentage of your income
- Review regularly, perhaps monthly and annually

Keep a close watch on your bank account. Balance your account and credit card transactions against statements, because even banks make mistakes. Open and maintain a separate account for paying bills than your normal account for savings.

Check if there are ways to reduce expenditure. Even on fixed cost items, such as mortgages, there are options. The mortgage market is highly competitive. Shop around for better deals and repayment schedules. Check financing options for other items you may have purchased as there may be cheaper alternatives.

The important principle is to have a planned budget and conscientiously adhere to it.

- **Use your surplus wisely**. It is what you do with your unallocated and surplus money from your budget that determines if you get ahead. If you're living beyond your means, you'll go backwards.

  The wisest thing to do with any surplus is to save it. As part of your budget set a goal for what percent of your income will be allocated to savings. On average most people save less than 1% of their income, whereas a good rule of thumb is to aim to save between 5-10% of income.

  Another wise way to use any surplus is to repay debt. Where possible, make additional payments on fixed loans, such as mortgage, car repayments or on the credit card.

Also, earmark some of your surplus, however small, to an emergency fund for contingencies or unexpected things in life.

Even if you receive a wages increase, rather than buy new things why not use the additional income to repay debt or invest to generate further income?

- **Invest for the future**

The real goal of creating a surplus is to take some of what you earn and make it work for you. This comes from investment. Through investment we plan and prepare for the future.

The fundamental principle for successful investment is to take the surplus from your budget and invest it over a *long* period of time. Let compound interest work for you. Albert Einstein called compound interest the 8th wonder of the world![8] But you must be patient. When a farmer plants seed, he or she doesn't expect a return overnight–it takes time, attention and patience–but it will come.

Another principle of investment is to diversify. There is no investment without risk, so play it safe and diversify. To diversify means to spread your money over different investment opportunities and not put all of your money into the one investment. Don't become impatient because there are cycles (ups and downs); hang in there.

Beware of the pitfalls of investment such as get-rich-quick schemes that promise a high return for a low investment. They're normally a scam. I've known too many people who've lost a lot of money through scams. The old saying is so true: 'If it sounds too good to be true, it probably is!'

8 http://www.goodreads.com/quotes.

- **Reduce expenditure**

  Don't live beyond your means or seek to live a higher standard of life than you have the income to sustain. Control impulse spending so that you don't buy things on the spur of the moment. Make adjustments where necessary to reduce spending by distinguishing between need and want. Exercise some self-restraint. Soberly avoid being naive enough to believe all the commercials and advertisements. Don't buy luxury goods or expensive brands just to keep up with trends or impress people. Instead, show restraint and purchase what you can afford within the constraints of your budget.

- **Avoid or minimize debt**

  There has been a subtle change in language from the word 'debt' to the word 'credit'. The debt provides you with credit, but credit is not just another form of money–it is debt. We use 'credit' cards, but the reality is that unless we are paying the owed amount in full each month, it is a debt. As we've already seen, unmanageable debt is a burden and a trip. Once we are in debt we have very little control.

  But there is a distinction between good debt and bad debt. A good debt is when you borrow to purchase something that will increase in value or something that will produce an income. It is also good debt if the value of the item equals or exceeds the purchase price. Another indicator of a good debt is that the repayments are manageable and don't put unnecessary strain on the budget.

  A bad debt is when you borrow to purchase something that will not hold its value or actually reduce in value once it is purchased. It is better to save up and pay cash for items that depreciate. It seems that we have become an instant gratification society. We can have what we want now, but at a price; and the price is normally debt. Ask this question before going into debt: 'Do the long term benefits of staying out of debt outweigh the short term benefits of the purchase?'

The cost of debt is interest! The cost of that debt is not just the actual dollar amount, but the opportunity we have forfeited to save and invest those interest repayments for many years.

If you are in debt, here are some quick ideas for getting out of debt:

- consolidate your debts
- don't borrow beyond your means to repay
- avoid the danger of impulsive buying which may provide instant gratification, but can easily spiral your financial position into a dark place
- ask for professional advice and guidance
- record your assets and liabilities to get an accurate picture of your financial position
- make a debt repayment schedule
- pay your smaller debts off first
- use the money you were paying off the first debt and add it to the money you are paying off your next debt and so on
- earn additional income and use the money to pay off debts (rather than to increase your spending), but don't overwork to the detriment of your relationships with family and friends
- don't accumulate new debt, but use cash or a debit card for everything
- avoid dependence on your credit card

- consider a radical change of lifestyle–like maybe moving back in with parents (if you're young enough) until your debts are paid off Please don't stop until you are debt free, and avert future unmanageable debt.

- **Seek financial advice**

  Another wise choice with money is to seek financial advice. Get professional guidance from a reputable and registered financial planner to help you map out your financial future. Seek a financial counselor to help you get back on track if you're in real trouble, especially in reducing or clearing debt.

  Seek advice on investments such as properties, stocks and shares, or international currencies, particularly if you're new to investment or if you're self-managing your superannuation (retirement fund).

  Also, if you're planning major renovations to add value to your own property or an investment property, please seek advice from other developers and experienced builders.

  Sound advice from experienced and qualified people can prevent us going blindly or naively into financial disaster.

Self-reflection:

Out of these practical suggestions, to which one do you need to give priority and attention?

What will you do and when will you do it?

Be specific.

J. Recreationally

This final area of your self-development is often overlooked and under-rated; it is the area of your recreation. Due to the dual pressures of leadership and life, leaders need to relax, be refreshed and thoroughly enjoy their times of leisure. There's nothing unspiritual or unimportant about recreation. If you desire to develop holistically, you need to have fun and do the things you enjoy doing. Recreation needs to be planned into your weekly schedule, otherwise the time you need to unwind and rejuvenate will be high-jacked by busy-ness.

How can you develop your recreational life? Here are a number of ideas I've learned through my observation of other leaders and my personal experience. Not all of these suggestions will suit you, but there may be one (or more) that'll help you to relax and replenish.

- **Hobbies**. I encourage you to pursue and practice a hobby. It may come in many shapes or forms. Different people enjoy different things. Maybe collect something. For example, I collect stamps from all over the world. From time to time, I categorize them, put them in date order and file them away for viewing in their relevant country folder. Maybe use your hands to build or construct something. One senior and prominent pastor I know builds model replica boats. They're magnificent and provide him with hours of relaxing enjoyment. In addition, he is painstakingly restoring a classic car. This man has a thriving church of thousands and is busily developing church planters all over the world, yet he wisely makes time to invest in his leisure. As I wrote earlier, I thoroughly enjoy photography and, due to my travels, I sometimes have a day between meetings. I use this time to photograph people, architecture, animals or scenery. I find it immensely pleasurable.

- **Sports or an exercise regime**. I know a lot of leaders who play amateur sport, such as golf (big yawn), soccer, netball, ten-pin bowling, badminton and table tennis. By the way, in our Mission, I am the current, undefeated and uncrowned 'King Kong of Ping Pong.' Exercise and sport are great ways to release and relieve stress, though please keep in mind that, as you get older, your recovery takes longer and you're more prone to injuries, so pace yourself. A significant number of leaders I know regularly attend a gym as a safe alternative to contact sport.

- **Involvement in the Arts**. Play, practice or listen to music. Enroll in a drama course or join a production company. Take dancing lessons or participate in a dancing troupe. Improve your drawing skills by signing up for an art course, or learn animation.

- **Regularly indulge yourself in your favorite leisure activity**. I have many friends in leadership who enjoy a wide variety of activities for their leisure. For example, some go off-road (4 wheel) driving, others ride motorbikes, whereas others enjoy hiking, camping and canoeing.

  I have a friend who travels extensively around the world investigating accidents and deaths in mine sites. He owned a boat he named, '*Therapy*'. He and a few mates used to go water skiing on a weekly basis, no matter what the weather, temperature or conditions. It was an incredible opportunity to enjoy their water sport and a great opportunity for the men to enjoy their time together as men! In fact, I learned how to water ski off the back of his boat when I was in my late 40s. I wasn't particularly good, but I loved it. To me, it really was *therapy*.

- **Read recreationally**. Aside from the books that I wrote about earlier, which add to or enhance my knowledge, I really enjoy reading recreationally, especially spy novels, legal dramas and whodunits. There's nothing like a great, un-put-down-able book.

- **Regular (weekly) day off**. Wherever practical and possible, structure and schedule your week to have at least one day off from any church-related activity. Try to disengage from your responsibilities by not answering your phone or checking emails. There will always be domestic things you have to do, such as purchasing groceries, cleaning the house, mowing the grass or paying bills, but plan some time for leisure.

- **Take a short break**. Another idea is to schedule a few days to get away and relax. In every year there are peak times and off-peak times in the church calendar. Plan and block out time in the quieter times of church life to get away. If your budget doesn't allow you to travel somewhere, perhaps do day trips or plan some quiet activities at home.

- **Annual holidays**. Throughout this book I have stressed the importance of the annual holiday. When planning any new year, I always plan the holiday before anything else. Why? Because if it's not planned, other things will encroach and devour your time. I work best when I am rested and re-energized from breaks.

- **Travel**. If you're able, travel! Start with your own city, state (province or shire) and nation before heading overseas. There's a big world out there full of wonderful adventures, inspiring views and exotic food. It expands your horizons, gives you a greater appreciation of your own back yard and exposes you to other cultures and food.

- **Spend time with family and friends**. Time spent with family and friends in a relaxed environment is life-giving. Fiona and I have a granddaughter named Aria. Although

> she lives in another Australian city and state, she stays with us every few months. We love every nanosecond we have with her. I get sheer pleasure out of being with her, talking with her, watching her eat, listening to her incessant talking (like her mother), playing games with her, and taking copious amounts of photos of her. We're exhausted by the time she goes home, but she enriches and enlivens our lives.

For your welfare and wellbeing, I cannot over-emphasize the importance of planning your recreation to be a habitual and intentional part of your overall schedule and life.

Self-reflection:

What will you do to relax and replenish yourself?

Which suggestion was of most relevance to you, and why?

Summary

The sum total of working on these ten areas–spiritual, physical, intellectual, emotional, social, marital, parental, financial, vocational and recreational–will be sustained, holistic growth and development.

But what about the development of your **leadership**? That's the topic of the next chapter. Please keep reading…

Chapter Nineteen

Leadership Development—How to Develop Leadership Skills

So far, throughout Section Four of this book, I've been addressing the area of your self-*development*. Ranging across chapters 16-18, I covered ten different areas of your *personal* development. In this chapter, however, I'll examine how you can develop your *leadership skills*.

A. Sustain an attitude of lifelong learning

Leaders never arrive at some optimum level of growth. There is always more to learn. Until the final day, every leader should be in a continual mindset and process of growth.

It is vital that all of us, as leaders, maintain the heart of a learner. Monroe wrote that leaders need to 'create their own learning environment.'[1] Leaders are learners. Leaders are readers (or listeners). Leaders are self-feeders. Leaders are students. Leaders are observers. Leaders are inquisitive. Leaders approach every challenge as a learning experience. Leaders want to grow. Leaders *choose* to grow.

Growth as a leader, and in leadership, requires us to have the right attitude–an attitude of lifelong learning and an attitude of teach-ability.

1 Monroe, 271.

We need to say to ourselves, 'I have not arrived, but I am on the journey. I am not presently all that I will be, but I am in the process of becoming that leader. There is a lot to learn, so I determine to learn.'

Leaders never arrive at some optimum level of growth. There is always more to learn.

Self-reflection:

What specific things can you currently do to maintain your growth as a leader?

B. Conduct an honest self-audit of your current growth (or otherwise) to identify areas that need development

A useful way to identify areas that require personal development is to conduct an honest self-audit, or have someone experienced conduct it on your behalf. This would cover both strengths *and* weaknesses. Here is a cursory list of leadership skills that may be required for leadership:

- Administration
- Chairing meetings
- Communication
- Conflict resolution
- Consensus building
- Decision-making
- Delegation
- Developing leaders
- Discipline, correction and restoration
- Financial management (including budgeting)
- Fund raising
- Managing complexity
- Mediation

- Personal organization
- Planning
- Recruiting and retaining volunteers
- Strategic planning
- Team building
- Team management
- Time management
- Vision casting.

Self-reflection:

Draw up a list of your leadership strengths and weaknesses that require development.

C. Determine the best means to develop the identified areas

Once a leader has identified areas that need development, both strengths and weaknesses, a third sequential step is to determine the most appropriate means to proactively develop the area(s).

Here are some ideas of how you can develop the areas of leadership you identified:

- **Attend *selective* conferences** that directly address the areas you've identified to work on in your leadership. There are numerous conferences throughout the year, many of which provide inspiration and blessing. Some leaders I know are conference-junkies and go from conference to conference, but never really seem to grow or develop their leadership. While I am not trying to discourage you from attending conferences, I am suggesting that you become more selective in the *type* of conference you attend.

  Check the *topics* to see if they are relevant to your plan of growth. Review the credentials of the *speakers* to ascertain whether they are experienced practitioners, or just academic theoreticians. I remember attending a church growth seminar by a well-known Christian scholar. After his excellent exegetical teaching, he moved into the practical application. Within a few minutes, in response to a pointed question, it became evident that he hadn't been effective at implementing the model he was espousing. He then revealed that he was philosophically opposed to, and highly critical of, mega-churches, one of which I was pastoring at the time. I went to the seminar with great expectations, but, aside from his insightful Bible teaching, I left disappointed that I had wasted my time and money.

Personally, I don't attend many conferences at all. I have become far more selective. My encouragement is to choose to attend seminars or conferences which complement your leadership development.

- **Enroll in Bible (theological) college intensives** that teach on applicable subjects. Many ministry training colleges now offer short intensives for professional development of clergy and church leadership. I have attended many such weeks which I have found stimulating, challenging and enlarging for my leadership.
- **Formal academic study** is another way by which you can develop your leadership. I wholeheartedly urge everyone with a ministry call to prepare themselves as thoroughly as possible, to receive the best possible Bible education available and to study conscientiously, but please do so at a college that provides practical ministry training in an environment of academic excellence.
- **Focused reading**. One of the best ways to develop in a particular area of leadership is to source and read books, journals or blogs that cover topics pertinent to our leadership development. It's helpful, too, to choose

reading material from a different, perhaps thought-provoking, perspective than your own entrenched position, tradition or practice.

As I wrote earlier, before I entered my current ministry in a missions' agency, I was pastoring a reasonably large church in the southern suburbs of Brisbane. To be candid, as a Pastor, I never enjoyed raising money, preaching about giving or taking offerings. The irony is that now, in my new role, I am *completely* dependent on raising money for our support (living expenses) and ministry. I initially felt ill-equipped as a fundraiser, so I bought and read every book I could on how to raise funds and stewardship. It took a couple of years of reading, learning and applying what I read to steadily improve my skills. One of the biggest hurdles was actually *asking* people. I was always timid and awkward, but I had to learn that, by asking people to give, I am not imposing on them; instead, I am providing them an opportunity to invest in something eternal.

My basic point, though, is that focused reading helps to inform, instruct or re-evaluate how you do leadership.

- **Expose yourself to different models, methods and ways of leadership thinking and practice** that are outside your past or present paradigm. You may not copy their methods, but you may learn some of the transferable principles which could be applied to your own context.
- **Spend a day 'shadowing' a bigger leader** or, if this is not possible, observe other leaders and how they lead. The old saying is true: 'Some things are *taught*, some things are *caught*.' Spending a day with a more experienced leader would be an invaluable investment of your time.

Self-reflection:

From the list you compiled in the previous point, what specific actions can you apply from this point to the areas that need development?

D. Foster a mentoring relationship

A fourth principle in developing your leadership is to foster a mentoring relationship with someone who exhibits strengths in the area where you need development.

> **Find a mentor for the specific areas in which you have identified your need to grow.**

Interacting with people who are experienced, intelligent, gifted and spiritual will enlarge, empower and energize you. Proverbs 27:17 states, *'As iron sharpens iron, so one man sharpens another'*, and *'he who walks with the wise grows wise'* (cf. Proverbs 13:20).

Therefore, my advice would be to regularly meet with, read, listen to or engage with people who will keep you on a pathway of growth. In leadership, it is important to cultivate and maintain relationships which nurture you, otherwise you may plateau in leadership, becoming introspective and limited in your thinking. A key, then, is to find a mentor for the specific areas in which you have identified your need to grow.

Australian author, John Mallison, defined Christian mentoring as '...a dynamic, intentional relationship of trust in which one person enables another to maximize the grace of God in their life and service.'[2]

Retired leadership professor, Dr Robert Clinton, who co-authored the book *Connecting* with Paul D Stanley, defines

2 John Mallison, *Mentoring: To Develop Disciples & Leaders* (Adelaide, South Australia: Openbook, 1998), 8.

it as '...a relational process in which a mentor, who knows or has experienced something, transfers that something to a mentoree, at an appropriate time and manner, so that it facilitates development or empowerment.'[3]

According to Clinton and Stanley, mentors fall into three basic groupings:[4]

- **Intensive**. The mentor is very hands-on and meets with the mentee regularly. The relationship is strongly relational and has high accountability.
- **Occasional**. The mentor is not as intense or deliberate, and meetings are irregular. The relationship is more generally centered on the mentee's task or their current topic than relationship, and doesn't have much accountability.
- **Passive**. The mentoring takes place through the mentor's model, example or writings rather than by face-to-face contact or communication. With few exceptions, the relationship is not intentional or relational.

There will rarely be one person who perfectly embodies everything you want to be or become. It is more likely that there will be several people who exemplify qualities and skills that you seek to learn from and emulate. For example, one leader you know may be an admirable mother, another might be an effective preacher, while another might be an excellent discipler. The key is to identify one particular area of their life or leadership in which they can mentor you. If it is impractical or impossible to access the person you seek to learn from, you can still be mentored by them through what Clinton and Stanley called 'passive' mentoring. You can read their writings, listen to their recordings or study their lives and ministries.

3 J Robert Clinton & Paul D Stanley, *Connecting* (Colorado Springs, CO: Navpress, 1992), 40. Since Clinton and Stanley's book was written, the term 'mentoree' has been replaced by 'mentee'.

4 ibid, 41-42.

Sometimes when I am faced with a difficult decision I ask the question: 'What would such and such do if she or he were in my shoes now?' That really helps me see a bigger picture and analyze how they may approach the decision process.

Here are some suggestions for how to find a mentor:

- Clarify with specificity the areas of your leadership that need development
- Identify people who model or display skills and strengths in those areas
- Proactively seek them out. Rarely will they come to you. Make the initial approach to share *why* you've sought them out and ask whether they'd be willing to mentor you
- Discuss with them the particular area that needs mentoring
- Determine the type of mentoring relationship (intensive, occasional or passive) that you feel you need and the mentor can provide
- Mutually plan your future meetings together (when, where, how long).

Engaging with your mentor may sometimes make you feel intimidated, inadequate or vulnerable. Often the discussions will highlight your deficiencies. A good mentor will never expose your weakness to embarrass or belittle you; on the contrary, they'll raise issues with the specific objective of helping you to grow in those areas. A healthy mentoring relationship will sharpen you.

Self-reflection:

What will you do to find a mentor or enhance your relationship with your present one?

E. Be involved in leadership

The pre-eminent way of developing as a leader is to actually immerse yourself in the work of leadership. Do what you can. Learn from who you can. Learn from your mistakes and hindsight. Learn from what others do right and wrong. Learn from the way others lead you. Listen. Observe. Do what you're asked to do. Serve in the little things. Be responsible. Be proactive. Be teachable. Learn and apply leadership principles at the nexus of leadership practice.

F. Organize yourself

Another area of leadership development is that of your personal organization. This involves organizing your workspace, time, tasks and responsibilities as a leader. Here is a list of practical ideas for how to become a more organized leader:

- Designate a specific area in which to carry out your leadership either at home or in the church office, and keep work area uncluttered
- Ensure you have adequate office furniture, equipment and stationery
- Plan ahead–daily, weekly, monthly and yearly[5]
- Develop regular daily and weekly patterns to give rhythm and routine to the exercise of your leadership
- Maintain a paper or electronic diary–keep it up to date and adhere to it
- Develop an accurate, accessible and organized paper or electronic filing system
- Communicate clearly and regularly to your various concentric circles of leadership, like your spouse, family, team, leaders, volunteers and congregation. Do so through whatever method or means is most appropriate,

5 See Chapter Five on 'time management' for some practical tips on how to do this.

such as personally, phone, text, web, email, twitter or Facebook
- Delegate wherever necessary–delegation is empowering and equipping others with the necessary gifts, skills and authority to discharge a responsibility under your oversight.

Develop an annual plan for your growth as a leader by producing workable action steps and measurable goals.

Self-reflection:

How would you describe your degree of personal organization?

What practical steps will you take to become more organized?

Which one of these sub-points is most applicable to you, and what will you do to address it?

G. Develop annual growth goals and action plans

One last idea for developing your leadership is to develop an annual plan for your growth as a leader by producing workable action steps and by setting measurable goals.

This point synthesizes many of my previous points in this chapter. Collate your answers to the questions asked at the end of each point. With that material at hand, here are some practical steps for how to create a growth development plan:

- Clarify your current roles and responsibilities
- Write down where you'd like to be in a year's time in terms of:
  - (a) the function of your leadership responsibilities
  - (b) your personal leadership development

- Record the areas that you've identified need attention in your life and/or leadership (chapters 16-18)
- Detail specific actions you'll employ to work on those areas
- Set realistic and achievable goals to measure the implementation and effectiveness of your action steps.

Self-reflection:

Draft up a growth plan for the next twelve months based on the steps above.

Conclusion:

Personal development stems from a leader's personal choices.

A leader must make conscious choices and take decisive steps to grow.

You can choose to foster a real sense of ownership of your growth.

SECTION FIVE

Self-Sacrifice

In this fifth, final and shortest section, we're going to explore the *cost* of self-leadership. There is a price to pay to become a great leader. We are called to surrender our lives, make sacrifices and endure through hardship to effectively lead ourselves and others. This will demand of us great courage and indefatigable discipline. Put succinctly, to lead ourselves demands a great cost –the cost of paying whatever price is necessary to do what God has called us to do.

OVERVIEW OF SECTION FIVE – SELF-SACRIFICE

Paul's second letter to Timothy is generally regarded as Paul's final written words. Some speculate that, given the internal evidence of the letter, it may have been written on the night prior to his execution, but this is debatable. This letter describes some of Paul's most painful emotions and experiences, but also his absolute, unshakable commitment to his Lord and the Gospel.

Paul wrote of his incarceration (2 Timothy 2:9–10), desertion (2 Timothy 1:15; 4:9–10), persecution (2 Timothy 3:11), opposition (2 Timothy 4:14) and affliction (2 Timothy 3:11). Nevertheless, he emphasized it was all for the Gospel (2 Timothy 2:8–10). Also, in the defense of his ministry against the accusations from scurrilous false apostles who'd infiltrated the church in Corinth, he wrote a long list of what he'd suffered (2 Corinthians 11:23-29). Notwithstanding these adversities, he was prepared to suffer whatever was necessary for the Lord, the Church and Gospel.

Timothy was challenged by Paul to be prepared to make sacrifices for the gospel (2 Timothy 1:8, 12), to deal with false teachers (1 Timothy 1:3-7), to preach potentially unpopular truth (1 Timothy 4:6), to warn people against danger, to flee from distractions and the evil passions of youth. Discharging all these duties would come at a cost.

That is what this short section is about–paying the price. What does 'paying the price' look like? In the following chapter, we're going to examine five key actions that, to me, encapsulate what it means to 'pay the price' of being a great leader.

After the largely instructive language in Section Four, the personal pronouns will return to the more inclusive 'we' and 'our' in this final section.

Chapter Twenty

Paying the Price

We all admire great leaders. We see the fruit of their ministry, we are inspired by their example, and seek to learn from them. Often, successful leaders seem to have it all together. What we see, though, is the *product*; what we have not seen is the *process*. Phrased differently, we see the *result* of what they have been through, but we have not seen *what* they have been through.

There is a cost to being a great leader. We have to be prepared to pay the price for effective leadership. It's not an easy road. There are no shortcuts. More will be required of us, as leaders, than of the average congregational member.

We each have a choice to make: to be a mediocre leader or to be an effective leader. The difference is not just skills or capacity, but the price we are prepared to pay to *be* a leader worth following.

This chapter will now suggest five key actions that describe what it means to pay the price.

A. Deny ourselves

The best place to start an examination of 'paying the price' is with the words of the greatest leader–Jesus Christ. One

There is a cost to being a great leader. We have to be prepared to pay the price for effective leadership.

of the pre-eminent places where Jesus outlined the cost of authentic discipleship is in Matthew 16:24-28 (cf. Mark 8:34-38; Luke 14:25-35).

This confronting passage is preceded by the intriguing conversation started when Jesus asked, *'Who do people say the Son of Man is?'* This exchange climaxed with Peter's declaration: *'You are the Christ, the Son of the Living God'* (Matthew 16:16). Jesus then brought private instruction to his disciples to prepare them for his redemptive mission of suffering, death and resurrection (Matthew 16:21). At this point, Peter verbally and emotionally convulsed. The thought of Jesus being crucified contradicted and clashed with his view of 'Messiah'. Peter was horrified and simply couldn't grasp it. These were unacceptable implications not only for Jesus, but for his own future. *'Peter took him aside and began to rebuke him, "Never, Lord!" he said. "This shall never happen to you!"'* (Matthew 16:22) Jesus rebuked Peter (Matthew 16:24; cf. Mark 8:33), then addressed all the disciples to qualify and amplify in graphic and undiluted terms what it would mean to follow him (Matthew 16:24-28). Here it is: *"If anyone would come after me, he must deny himself and take up his cross and follow me"* (Matthew 16:24).

Jesus' first word to those who would follow him was 'if'. *'If'* is a power-packed word. It speaks of making a choice and decision. It was like Jesus was saying, '*If* you are *really* my disciple, *if* you really love me, *if* you really claim to know who I am, *if* you really want to be like me, *if* you really want my life to flow through your life', then make a measured and considered choice. This is not a light decision, but a whole life decision. Our salvation is free, but discipleship will cost us everything.

The challenge continued with the words: *"If anyone **would** come after me..."* (emphasis mine). The word 'would' is a verb of choice and is used in the sense of 'has resolved to'. It implies a definitive attitude toward ourselves; we resolutely commit ourselves to follow Jesus no matter what the course or cost. Jesus then articulated the threefold price: *"deny himself and take up his cross and follow me"* (Matthew 16:24). Let's explore all three.

Deny ourselves

To deny oneself has a range of applications:

- To deliberately and irrevocably decide to renounce one's rights over one's own life
- To abandon the attitude of self-centeredness
- To say 'no' to independence and willfulness
- To relinquish our own ambitions, aspirations and dreams to the greater call and cause of Christ
- To yield our whole self to God's will
- To die to self-interest by putting Christ's interests above our own.

This is very confronting and stands in complete contrast to the prevailing culture which puts 'self' at the centre. Our age is consumed with 'me', 'I' and 'my', where people say 'I need', 'I want' or these are 'my rights'. Against the consumerist, self-indulgent society, the life which boldly follows Jesus stands up and stands out by saying, 'It is not about me; it is about *him*!'

The New Testament implores us to deny our natural, sinful impulses in order to live a holy, self-controlled life (Romans 13:14; Colossians 3:5; 1 Peter 2:11). Our old life is dead in Christ. We must treat it as such. We need to amputate some pleasures from our life so we don't continue to sin (Matthew 5:29; cf. Matthew 18:8).

Take up his cross

'Taking up his cross' referred to the practice of making a condemned prisoner carry the crossbeam upon which he was to be tied or nailed at the place of his crucifixion. A 'cross' in the first century Roman world was a horrendous way to die. Gas chambers, lethal injection, gallows, firing squad or electric chair don't quite convey the horror, in the Jewish mind, of what death on a cross meant. It was reserved for the most reprehensible of criminals, like the seditious, rebellious and subversive. To die on a cross meant you were an enemy of the state. The prisoners condemned for execution by crucifixion were regarded as the vermin of humanity, the lowest of the low and the scum of the earth. It was degrading, humiliating and excruciating.

In a strict sense, 'taking up your cross' meant to be prepared to face martyrdom, to be willing to lose your mortal life for the sake or cause of Christ.

But let's consider the words 'take up his cross' in a broader context. Jesus had just told the disciples what the cross would mean for him–suffering, death and resurrection were the ultimate *purposes* of his life (Matthew 16:21). In essence, Jesus could well be saying, 'This is *why* I have come. This is the purpose of my life. I am going to fulfill it. I will pay the cost and do whatever my Father determines to accomplish his will.' To take up 'our' cross could therefore mean to find out *our* purpose in life and *fulfill* it–no matter what it takes and no matter what it costs.

Follow me

An authentic disciple *follows* Jesus in the sense of using his way of life as the model on which we build our lives. Following him speaks of emulating his example, his words, his approach to life and the way he served his Father. It implies being like him in areas like obedience (John 8:31), servanthood (John 13:15), suffering (1 Peter 2:21) and humility (Philippians 2:5).

Another aspect of following Jesus is that of responding to God's call irrespective of what we have to leave behind. After Jesus called Levi (Matthew) to follow him, he '*...got up, left everything and followed him*' (Luke 5:27–28). There will be a cost to following Jesus, but we must make the resolute decision expressed in the lyrics of the old song, 'I have decided to follow Jesus. No turning back. No turning back.'

A true disciple puts Jesus above their own natural inclinations and interests. This is the place of self-denial.

'*...but whoever loses his life for me will find it...*' In the strict context 'loses his life' means actual martyrdom for Jesus, but in a discipleship context, it means a person voluntarily surrendering and yielding their rights to Jesus, and abandoning their own self-seeking for the sake of Christ. A true disciple puts Jesus above their own natural inclinations and interests. This is where self-leadership begins–the place of self-denial.

B. Wholehearted *surrender* to Jesus, his Cause and his Church

Building on the foundation of denying ourselves, a second action in the language of 'paying the price' as a leader is that of *wholehearted surrender* to Jesus and his purpose for our lives. As we've seen in the anatomy of self-denial, surrender requires us to yield our rights to the will of God. In response to God's grace, we voluntarily submit ourselves to what we know to be his purposes for our lives.

The nature of 'surrender' I am trying to convey is embodied by Jesus in the Garden of Gethsemane. Knowing the horror of what lay ahead of him on the cross by becoming the sin-bearer, Jesus '*...fell with his face to the ground and prayed, "My Father, if it is possible, may this cup be taken from me."*' At this point, the entire redemptive destiny of the human race was hanging in the balance. But then, Jesus uttered the most eternally heroic words of prayer ever spoken: *"Yet not as **I** will, but as **you** will"* (Matthew 26:39, emphases mine). These words capture the essence of the language of surrender. All of us must come to the point where we say with conviction and submission, 'My Father, I embrace the call and will you have for my life in all of its depths and dimensions. Whatever the task and whatever the cost, I'll do it. I surrender.'

Dr Wilbur Chapman (1859-1918), a Presbyterian evangelist in the late 19th Century, had an interview with the founder of the Salvation Army, General William Booth (1829-1912), on one of Booth's last visits to the United States.[1] Chapman made the following observations:

> When I looked into his face and saw him brush back his hair from his brow, and heard him speak of the trials and conflicts and the victories, I said: *"General Booth, tell me what has been the secret of your success all the way through?"*
>
> He hesitated a second, and I saw tears come into his eyes and steal down his cheeks, and then he said: "I will tell you the secret. *God has had all there was of me*. There have been men with greater opportunities; but from the day I got the poor of London on my heart, and a vision of what Jesus Christ could do with the poor of London, *I made up my mind that God would have all of William Booth there was*. And if there is anything of power in The Salvation Army today, it is because *God has all the adoration of my heart, all the power of my will and all the influence of my life*."
>
> And I learned from William Booth that the *greatness of a man's power is the measure of his surrender*. It is

1 The Salvation Army has been expanded to include 124 countries, and the gospel is faithfully preached by its officers and soldiers in 160 languages.

> not a question of who you are or of what you are, but of whether God controls you.[2]

Let's ask ourselves: What is the measure of my surrender? Am I *fully* surrendered to the Lordship of Jesus Christ? Does he have *all* of me?

When I was growing up in church, we used a sing a lot of old hymns before the advent of contemporary worship. One of my favorite hymns, that always moved me, was composed by Jason W. Van de Venter (1855–1939) in 1896, and entitled, *'I surrender all'*. The words are in old English, but are still impacting. Please read the words slowly and ponder their meaning and application.

1.
All to Jesus I surrender,All to him I freely give;
I will ever love and trust him,
In His presence daily live.

Refrain:
I surrender all, I surrender all;
All to thee, my blessed Savior,
I surrender all.

2.
All to Jesus I surrender,
Make me, Savior, wholly thine;
Let me feel Thy Holy Spirit
Truly know that Thou are mine. [refrain]

3.
All to Jesus I surrender,

2 http://ministry127.com/resources/illustration/the-greatness-of-a-man-s-power-is-the-measure-of-his-surrender (emphasis mine).

Lord, I give myself to thee;
Fill me with thy love and power,
Let thy blessing fall on me. [refrain] [3]

Can we say with unquestioning conviction, 'All to Jesus I surrender'?

Surrender is not limitation but liberation.

When I was studying for my post-graduate degree, I was taught *Ethics* by a brilliant theologian who told the following story. He had a friend who was a leading surgeon in Melbourne. Over many years, and through numerous discussions, the doctor came to the cognitive conclusion that Jesus was the Son of God, that salvation was available through him alone, and that Jesus demands our total allegiance. 'But', the physician said to my lecturer, 'I will not surrender my life to Jesus in case he asks me to give up medicine and become a missionary.'

This surgeon understood surrender to Jesus with greater clarity than many Christians, but he was not prepared to do so for fear of what Jesus may require of him. This is so sad, because Jesus will only ever ask us to do something that is for our eternal good and his ultimate glory. As someone has well said, 'Surrender is not limitation but liberation.'

C. Prepared to make sacrifices

To be an effective and fruitful leader, we must be prepared to deny ourselves, fully surrender ourselves to Jesus and, thirdly, be prepared to make sacrifices for the Lord and his purposes. A Scripture that speaks directly about this is Romans 12:1: '*Therefore, I urge you, brothers, in view of God's mercy, to offer*

3 Public domain.

your bodies as living sacrifices, holy and pleasing to God–this is your spiritual act of worship.'

We'll briefly dissect this verse to see its implications for our lives and leadership on the area of sacrifice.

'Therefore, I urge you, brothers, in view of God's mercy...' In the first 11 chapters of Romans, Paul had been writing about the mercy of God (Romans 9:15–16, 23; 11:30–32), but here, in Romans 12:1, his use of the word 'therefore' is a call to *respond* to God's mercy. God's mercy was expressed to us in Christ Jesus in a total and all-encompassing way, therefore our response to his mercy should also be total and all-encompassing.

'...to offer your bodies as living sacrifices...' The way we're asked to respond to God's mercy is by offering our lives to God as sacrifices. Instead of a lamb, goat or pigeon, as in the Old Testament sacrificial system, we offer *ourselves* as a sacrifice, a *living* sacrifice, not some slaughtered animal. The sacrifice of our 'bodies' is a term which probably refers to our whole person. We offer the whole of our life for the rest of our life. It is an all-encompassing sacrifice that says, 'My life is *yours*.'

'...holy and pleasing to God...' The surrendered (sacrificed) life Paul refers to is to be *holy*, a term in Scripture that signifies being 'set part from the unholy' and 'set apart exclusively for God and his sacred service'. Being 'holy' means being 'his'. With such holy sacrifices, God is well pleased.

'... – this is your spiritual act of worship.' The offering of our bodies to God as a living sacrifice, wrote Paul, is a way by which we truly worship God, not just in outward forms or ceremonies (like the Old Testament). Some versions of Scripture render the word 'spiritual' as 'reasonable' service (KJV, NKJV), conveying the idea that the offering of our all to God is the rational,

We will never truly be able to pay the price until we've settled the issue: Are we living for ourselves or living for him?

thoughtful, sensible and logical response of spiritual beings to the mercy of God.[4]

In seeking to apply Romans 12:1, then, we must respond to God's mercy by *offering ourselves* to him wholly and solely, by *living for him* wholly and solely, by *worshipping him* wholly and solely, and by endeavoring to *please him* wholly and solely.

We will never truly be able to pay the price until we've settled the issue: Are we living for ourselves or living for him? Are we offering ourselves as a living sacrifice, or do we just have an outward show of religion or piety?

Types of sacrifices

From a posture of total surrender, there are a number of sacrifices we may be required to make. We've already covered the offering of our bodies as living sacrifices, but what are some of the other sacrifices?

Sacrificial time. In this book, I have underlined the importance of using our time wisely, but that presupposes that we are willing to sacrificially invest time into the things that really matter. In the context of self-leadership, making sacrifices of time will mean sowing qualitative time into our and other's leadership development.

Sacrificial prayer and fasting. At times, we will need to sacrifice time to seek the Lord in a dedicated season of prayer. Perhaps we need specific guidance, a divine intervention in a crisis, a breakthrough, or a miracle. It was during a time of

4 Stott, *The Message of Romans*, 321.

prayer and fasting that the Holy Spirit called Paul and Barnabas to missionary service from Antioch (Acts 13:1-3). I would also hope that there would be times when we would seek him for no other reason than we simply have a passion to know him (Isaiah 55:6–7).

Sacrificial giving. Another sacrifice seen in Scripture is that of sacrificial giving. This is when we give finances, or something of value, above and beyond our regular giving as an offering to the Lord's work or to someone in need. It may also be the giving of possessions for the needy (Acts 2:45). As Jesus said, *'It is more blessed to give than to receive'* (Acts 20:35). The author of Hebrews wrote that sharing with others is seen as a sacrifice which pleases God (Hebrews 13:16). Some examples in Scripture of sacrificial giving are the widow of Zarephath giving her last handful of flour for Elijah (1 Kings 17:12–15), the impoverished Macedonian churches giving *'beyond their ability'* (2 Corinthians 8:2–4) and Israel's tribal and family leaders who *'freely and wholeheartedly'* gave resources for the building of the Temple (1 Chronicles 29:6-9).

Sacrifice of praise and worship. As Christians, we no longer offer literal flesh and blood sacrifices, such as lambs or goats, because Christ has fulfilled and brought the Old Testament sacrificial system to an end by his once-for-all sacrifice on the cross (Colossians 2:13–14). *'Through Jesus'* we now offer the *spiritual* sacrifices of praise and worship (Hebrews 13:15; cf. 1 Peter 2:5) by: thanking God in prayer (Philippians 4:6); singing psalms or spiritual songs (Ephesians 5:19; Psalm 100:4; Colossians 3:16); clapping to God (Psalm 47:1); declaring God's greatness, glory and works (Psalm 96:3; Luke 19:37); and maintaining a heart of reverence (Hebrews 12:28; Psalm 96:9).

Sacrifice of martyrdom. The ultimate sacrifice for some leaders may be martyrdom. In some cultures where this book will be read, being a Christian is a life and death reality. Taking up *our* cross may be a euphemism in western cultures for counting the cost or paying the price, but in Jesus' day it generally referred to a disciples' preparedness to die for their faith (Matthew 16:24). John the Baptist (Mark 6:27), Stephen (Acts 7:58) and James (Acts 12:2) were all martyred for their faith. Paul spoke of his willingness to die for the Lord (Acts 21:13). Throughout the history of the church and missions, there have been millions who have given their life for the Lord and his Cause.

Example of English missionary C.T. Studd

My favorite sport is cricket, followed closely by Australian Football, also known as AFL. To me, cricket is the game above all games. There have been many famous players such as Don Bradman, Sachin Tendulkar and Dennis Lillee. In line with our topic of self-sacrifice, there was an English cricketer who went on to serve God as a missionary at great personal cost. His name was Charles Thomas Studd (1860–1931), commonly known as C.T. Studd.

C.T. Studd was born and raised in a wealthy, aristocratic, English family. He came to faith as a teenager while a student at England's famous Eton College, located near the historic town of Windsor. From Eton, C. T. Studd went to study at Cambridge University where he joined and, at one stage, captained, the cricket team. Because he was a talented all-rounder, he was selected to represent England where he excelled, especially against Australia in two Ashes series both in England and in Australia.[5] He was very popular and well known as a hero of the British sport-loving public.

But the illness of his brother, George, who was thought to be dying, brought him face to face with eternal realities. While sitting by his brother's bedside watching him hover between life and death, C.T. began to wrestle in his mind:

5 The 'Ashes' are a series of cricket games between England and Australia.

> "Now what is all the popularity of the world worth to George? What is all the fame and flattery worth? What is it worth to possess all the riches in the world, when a man comes to face eternity?"[6]

His brother was restored to health and C.T. went to hear American Evangelist, D.L. Moody, where, in his own words, "The Lord met me again and restored me to the joy of his salvation... and set me to work for him."[7]

While studying at Cambridge, he received a strong call to become a missionary to China. Some members of his extended family opposed and resisted him. He had an interview with Hudson Taylor and was accepted to join the China Inland Mission.[8] Along with six other students–some academics, athletes and military officers–he became one of what is known as the 'Cambridge Seven'. In February 1885 they set sail for China.

At age 25, C.T. was eligible to receive a substantial inheritance from his father, but, as Norman Grubb wrote:

> '...the simple reading of the Scriptures had led him to definite and far reaching conclusions on the matter. The words of Christ, "*Sell your possessions, and give to the needy*" (Luke 12:33), and "*Do not lay up for yourselves treasures on earth*" (Matthew 6:19); the example of the early church at Pentecost, of whom it says, "*They were selling their possessions and belongings and distributing the proceeds to all, as any had need*" (Acts 2:45); and finally the story of the rich young man to whom Jesus

6 Norman Grubb, *C.T. Studd: Cricketer & Pioneer* (Fort Washington, PA: CLC Publications), 36.

7 ibid, 36.

8 The *China Inland Mission* (CIM) was founded in Britain by Hudson Taylor on 25 June 1865 to reach the inland provinces of China with the gospel, while seeking to evangelize the whole nation. It was distinctive because of its unorthodox methods, such as missionaries dressing in Chinese clothes, including a pigtail (queue). Today, CIM is known as OMF (Overseas Ministry Fellowship) International.

said, *"You lack one thing: go, sell all that you have and give to the poor, and you will have treasure in heaven and come, follow me"* (Mark 10:21)... Therefore in light of God's word, he decided to give his entire fortune to Christ.'[9]

Faith laughs at impossibilities and cries, It shall be done.

Based on this unshakable decision, in January 1887, C.T. relinquished his wealth, mansion and fame to continue serving God in China. He gave his whole inheritance away to contemporary ministries like D. L. Moody, George Muller[10], William Booth[11] and the China Inland Mission. In a letter to William Booth he wrote, 'Henceforth our bank is in heaven.'[12]

After many years in China, he served God in India. Then, at around 50 years of age, he felt drawn by God to Africa. It was now 1908. Because he'd had 15 years of ill health, his supporting committee asked him to get a certification from a doctor that he was fit enough to go. The doctor adamantly said he should not go, consequently his committee withdrew their funds and their support. Despite having poor health, no money, and no sending agency, he decided to go anyway out of raw obedience to God.

On the first night of his journey, 15 December 1910, he wrote, 'To human reason the thing was ridiculous, but faith laughs at impossibilities and cries, It shall be done.'[13]

9 Grubb, 67.
10 Prussian born, missionary evangelist to the United Kingdom, where, in Bristol, he established orphan houses caring for over 10,000 children in his lifetime and establishing 117 schools in which over 100,000 children were educated.
11 Founder of the Salvation Army.
12 Grubb, 70.
13 ibid, 132.

On the night before he sailed, he was challenged by a young man, "Is it a fact that at age fifty-two you mean to leave your country, your home, your wife and your children?" He replied with words which, to me, embody the spirit of sacrifice, "If Jesus Christ be God and died for me, then no sacrifice can be too great for me to make for Him."[14]

He went on to have 20 of his most fruitful years of missionary service. C.T. Studd passed away in Africa on Thursday 16 July 1931. Surrounded by missionary colleagues and African converts, his final words were 'Hallelujah! Hallelujah!' with every last breath.[15]

D. Endure hardship

So far, we've seen that paying the price involves denying ourselves, wholeheartedly surrendering our lives to the Lord, and being prepared to make sacrifices, but now we come to a fourth action, which is to endure hardship.

This point is taken from 2 Timothy 2:3 (cf. 4:5) where Paul explicitly encouraged Timothy to *'endure hardship'*. Therefore, a fourth way in which we pay the price of self-leadership is to persevere through the challenges, adversities and trials of leadership. The more effective our leadership is, the greater the cost. Leadership consultant and author, Sam Chand, wrote that leaders '...grow only to the threshold of your pain' and goes so far as to assert that '...If you're not hurting, you're not leading.'[16] With a clever play on words, I heard him redefine 'leadership' as 'bleed-ership' and say that, 'If you're leading, you're bleeding.'[17]

---

14 ibid, 144.
15 ibid, 246.
16 Sam Chand, *Leadership Pain* (Nashville, TN: Thomas Nelson, 2015), 15.
17 Personal notes, National Conference of the Australian Christian Churches, Broadbeach, Queensland, May, 2015.

Hardship

Hardship comes in various dimensions. There is (a) hardship that comes from being a human (mortal), flesh and blood person. Hardship may come in the form of a sickness, an accident, a relational breakdown, the ageing process and, inevitably, death. Then there is (b) hardship that comes from being a Christian, which may involve persecution, discrimination, spiritual attack or rejection. In the context of this book, there is also (c) hardship that comes by virtue of being a Christian leader.

Hardship is part of the cost of leadership. Hardship in leadership can come in many forms, depending on our culture and context. From my observation and experiences of pain in leadership, here is a sample list of some of the hardships of leadership. I'm sure you could probably add to the list:

- Appointing the wrong person to the wrong position
- Removing the wrong person from the wrong position
- Betrayal by close friends
- Betrayal by team members
- Broken relationships
- Correcting people who are unteachable
- Correcting people with a bad attitude
- Criticism that is unwarranted
- Criticism that is justified
- Disciplining people
- Disciplining team members
- Errors of judgment
- False accusations
- False and misleading media reports
- Financial pressure in the church or ministry
- Intimidation

- Leaders failing morally
- Leaders stealing or misappropriating money
- Loneliness of having to make some tough decisions
- Loneliness of bearing the responsibility of leadership that no-one else fully comprehends or understands
- Loneliness of being where the buck stops
- Making mistakes
- Mending those mistakes
- Misunderstanding
- Pressure at home
- Taking responsibility for mistakes
- Explaining other peoples' mistakes
- Fixing other peoples' mistakes
- Marriage breakdown of parishioners
- Selecting the wrong team members
- Sacking staff members
- Collateral damage from sacking team members
- Spouse criticized by parishioners
- Spouse unhappy
- Stress
- Team members who can't get on with others
- Team members who are incompetent
- Team members who are lazy
- Tragic death of a parishioner.

No matter what form it may take, leaders are called to one overriding response to any and all of these leadership adversities: endurance!

Endurance

In conventional language, endurance has a range of meanings such as durability, stamina and fortitude. In Scripture, endurance speaks of an inner strength that enables a leader to stay strong in times of persecution and hardship (2 Timothy 2:3, 10; 3:10).

Endurance speaks of an inner strength that enables a leader to stay strong in times of persecution and hardship.

The language of endurance speaks of many things. Here is a list of synonyms for endurance and a brief definition of each one:

- resilience–the capacity to bounce back after difficulty
- steadfastness–being immovable, unshakable or unflappable
- perseverance–displaying persistence, grit and determination
- fortitude–inward resolve, courage and guts based on one's convictions
- stick-ability–the inward power to stay faithful in our responsibilities, even through hard times
- consistency–quality of steadiness, reliability and evenness
- faithfulness–loyalty, fidelity and commitment to God's call, God's people and our God-given vision.

Endurance is a mindset, an inward disposition and attitude. It is a measure of a leader's character and inner life. A mindset of endurance is one of persevering through adversity, of faithfully serving despite the obstacles, of going the distance, and of never giving up or giving in.

Three metaphors of endurance

After his exhortation for Timothy to *'endure hardship'*, Paul brought three metaphors to illustrate how to endure (2 Timothy 2:3–6): a soldier, an athlete and a farmer. We'll unpack these metaphors and draw principles for how we can endure in contemporary ministry leadership.

Soldier (2 Timothy 2:3–4)

The first metaphor Paul employed to illustrate how we endure as leaders is that of a soldier. In 2 Timothy 2:3 he implored Timothy to endure hardship *'like a soldier'*. The term soldier speaks of being disciplined, trained and prepared for action. But Paul didn't say a soldier in general, but a *'soldier of Jesus Christ'*. In this imagery, Jesus is portrayed as the commanding officer, and Timothy as a soldier in active service under the commander's authority, both in an active military campaign. The hardship Timothy is asked to endure in this war seems to be, in context, a willingness to suffer for the gospel (cf. 2 Timothy 1:8), and to *'fight the good fight'* (1 Timothy 1:18).

How does a solider of Jesus endure hardship? Verse 4 gives some explanation: *'No one serving as a soldier gets involved in civilian affairs–he wants to please his commanding officer.'* There are three embedded leadership lessons from soldiers in these verses. Firstly, leaders, like soldiers, are in active service and shouldn't wilt under the hardship that may come from gospel ministry, but rise in the heat of battle with focused resolve and inward determination (cf. Ephesians 6:11–17).

Secondly, like soldiers, leaders must maintain their focus on what our commander (Jesus) has called and commissioned us to do. We must not be entangled by *'the affairs of this life'* (NLT), which, though not sinful in and of themselves, may distract us from our responsibilities. Instead, leaders must exercise 'single-minded devotion to duty'.[18]

---

18 Towner, 492.

Thirdly, in the same way a soldier *'wants to please his commanding officer'*, our motivation in all we do and say in leadership should be to please the Lord, not ourselves. If we are to endure in leadership, all selfish ambition, willful desires and personal agendas must be eliminated. In summary, if leaders are to endure hardship, they must be disciplined, express single-minded commitment to their responsibilities, and be motivated by one consuming passion–to selflessly please the Lord.

Athlete (2 Timothy 2:5)

The second metaphor is found in verse 5: *'Similarly, if anyone competes as an athlete, he does not receive the victor's crown unless he competes according to the rules.' 'Similarly'* marks the link between the thoughts on the soldier and the athlete. In the same way a soldier endures because of his undistracted focus on his commanding officer's orders, so the athlete will win the competition (the *'victor's crown'*) only if they compete *'according to the rules'*. If an athlete does not abide by the rules, they will be disqualified.

What does it mean for a leader to *'compete according to the rules'*? To answer that question, we need to go back to the original metaphor from athletics where, writes Towner, 'the stipulated condition or requirement ("according to the rules") referred either to the rules of the race or to the ten-month period of disciplined training that professional athletes had to complete to qualify for the games.'[19] In other words, the athlete's adherence to the rules was not just measured by how they competed in the arena on race day, but on how they prepared for the competition in their training regime.

The lesson here is that if leaders are to endure, they must ensure that how they conduct themselves in their private world (behind the scenes) is just as important as how they conduct

19 ibid, 494.

themselves in their public world (out front), as 1 Corinthians 9:24-25 implies. Their life and leadership must be in line with the 'rules' of Scripture and Christian ethics. If not, they won't endure to the end and may potentially disqualify themselves. The important thing is not only how a leader starts, but how they finish, *and* how they have 'run their race' in the intervening period.

As with the soldier, there is a key motivation for the athlete to endure–to win *'the victor's crown'* (cf. 1 Corinthians 9:25). For leaders, there is an eternal reward ('crown') for our enduring service. In Scripture, there are a number of references to *'crowns'* a leader will receive as rewards for faithfulness and perseverance in the face of adversity and persecution. For example, there is the crown of life (James 1:12), crown of glory (1 Peter 5:4), and crown of righteousness (2 Timothy 4:8). These are not literal crowns (or wreaths), but are symbols of the rewards which we can't quite comprehend this side of eternity. We don't know what the rewards are in explicit, quantifiable detail, but we are told that the rewards consist of eternal life, entry into the Kingdom of God and membership of God's family (Matthew 5:1-12; Mark 10:29-30; Luke 6:35). When *rewards* are spoken of, they are referred to as 'great' (Matthew 5:12; 24:47; 25:21, 23; Mark. 10:30).

The key words for endurance from an athlete are self-discipline and determination.

Hardworking farmer (2 Timothy 2:6)

Within the same theme of enduring hardship, Paul adds a third metaphor. *'The hardworking farmer should be the first to receive a share of the crops'* (2 Timothy 2:6). Paul's emphasis here is on the *hard work* of the farmer. Aside from climatic events like floods, fires or pests, successful farming depends as much on a farmer's hard work as his agricultural skill. The farmers I know work long and grueling hours, often in difficult and unpredictable conditions. As we labor for the Lord we know that it is never in vain. Our hard work has counted for something. We've played a part in the process of producing new life.

If the farmer has worked hard, presumably by endurance, there will be a result. Paul said, this type of farmer '*...should be the first to receive a share of the crops.*' 'Crops' may refer to two different harvests we see in Scripture: There is a harvest of (a) holiness (Galatians 5:16; 6:8) for those who live by the Spirit, and a harvest of (b) converts (Matthew 9:37; cf. John 4:35) for those who labor in the gospel ministry. I want both.

There is an important qualification to make. Hard work doesn't automatically translate into fruitfulness. I know a lot of leaders who diligently and conscientiously work hard, but often they are driven and striving for success. When I refer to hard work, I am not speaking of enduring or laboring in our own strength drawn from our inner reservoirs, but with the strength God provides (1 Peter 4:11).

A vital point is necessary before concluding these thoughts on endurance. There will be times when the hardships of leadership will take their toll on even the most durable and dependable of leaders. For the sake of endurance, it may be necessary to take remedial action such as: seeking medical attention; taking time out from leadership; seeking wholeness; enjoying a sustained holiday; resting until you recuperate; or, if necessary, identifying specialized or professional care.

Tying these metaphors together we see that if we are to endure the hardships of leadership we must: exercise the discipline, dedication and singlemindedness of a good soldier; compete according to the rules like an athlete both on and off the arena; and work hard like a farmer.

E. Exercise Courage

There is a fifth and final element required to pay the price of becoming an extraordinary leader–*courage*. Courage sometimes comes at a cost.

Courage is indispensable for effective Christian leadership.

In everyday language, courage can sometimes be defined as braveness, boldness, confidence, daring, or intrepidness. Wikipedia defines courage as:

> 'The choice and willingness to confront agony, pain, danger, uncertainty or intimidation. Physical courage is courage in the face of physical pain, hardship or threat of death, while moral courage is the ability to act rightly in the face of popular opposition, shame, scandal, discouragement or personal loss.'[20]

Courage for leadership

Courage is indispensable for effective Christian leadership. It takes great courage:

- To boldly assume responsibilities
- To make the tough decisions
- To initiate and implement change
- To talk about what isn't being talked about
- To deal with what is not being dealt with
- To do what is right despite the circumstances
- To be willing to be misunderstood
- To equip and empower people to do leadership for themselves
- To cast a compelling vision for the future

20 http:en.wikipedia.org/wiki/courage.

- To silence the inaudible voices of negativity in our own mind
- To believe God when all the visible evidence says something to the contrary
- To pray audacious prayers.

Biblical courage

The nature of Scriptural courage is best illustrated by some great Bible leaders. We can learn the following lessons of courage from their example:

- Like Abraham, it takes courage to leave the known to go into the unknown in simple obedience (Genesis 12:1; Hebrews 11:8-10)
- Like Joseph, it takes courage to maintain our sexual integrity when it would be so easy to compromise (Genesis 39:11-12)
- Like Moses, it takes courage to face our own inadequacies and insecurities to accept a role or position we feel unqualified, unskilled or unwilling to fulfill (Exodus 4:1-17)
- Like Joshua, it takes courage to take over leadership from a highly experienced and respected leader (Deuteronomy 31:6; Joshua 1:6)
- Like Deborah, it takes courage to show initiative and take the lead when powerful enemies are against you (Judges 4:4, 9)
- Like Jephthah, it takes courage to lead even when our own family rejects us and doesn't believe in us (Judges 11:2; 4)
- Like David, it takes courage to face the giants in our lives and the things that intimidate others (1 Samuel 17:32)

- Like Joab, it takes personal courage to instill courage into our key leaders when they struggle with hesitancy (2 Samuel 10:12; cf. 1 Chronicles 19:13)
- Like Eleazar, one of David's mighty men, it takes courage to hold our ground in difficult times when other people back off in fear (2 Samuel 23:10)
- Like a further three of David's 'chief men', it takes courage and bold action to do something to express honor to our leaders (2 Samuel 23:13–17)
- Like Ezekiel, it takes courage to speak to people who will probably reject us and our message, because we know God has told us to speak to them (Ezekiel 3:10–11)
- Like Shadrach, Meshach and Abednego, it takes courage to stand up against social, moral and political injustice (Daniel 3:16–18)
- Like Daniel, it takes courage to exercise civil disobedience in defiance of ungodly legislation (Daniel 6:10)
- Like Esther, it takes courage to boldly advocate for those who have no voice (Esther 4:15–16)
- Like Nehemiah, it takes courage to keep our focus while adversaries seek to distract and deter us (Nehemiah 6:11)
- Like Jonah, it takes courage to face our past mistakes and do what God has told us to do (Jonah 3:3)
- Like Peter, it takes courage to get out of our comfort zone and rely on nothing else but God's Word to us (Matthew 14:29)
- Like Peter and John, it takes courage to keep preaching the gospel when religious authorities forbid us from doing so (Acts 4:20)
- Like Paul, it takes courage to declare our faith in God when the prevailing circumstances are life-threatening (Acts 27:21–26)

- Like Paul, it takes courage to go against everything we've ever known in pursuit of what we now know to be true about Jesus and his gospel (Philippians 3:4–14).

Three components of courage

Courage in leadership involves three actions. First, courage necessitates that we *subdue fear* (or any negative attitude or feeling) in our life and leadership. Fear is the opposite of courage. Fear stifles and suffocates courage. Someone has well said, 'courage is not the absence of fear, but mastery of it.' Another unknown person said that 'courage is fear that has said its prayers.' So, a first action in becoming courageous is to extinguish all unhealthy or unfounded fears.

To illustrate this point, when the disciples did not recognize Jesus as he walked to them on the water in the pre-dawn light, they cried out in unmitigated terror, *'It's a ghost!'* But Jesus told them to, *'Take courage! It is I. Don't be afraid'* (Matthew 14:27; cf. Mark 6:50). They were urged to master their natural inclination to fear.

As I pointed out in my book *Fearproof*, the command *'do not fear'* is God's most common command in the Bible.[21] Throughout Scripture, the Lord commanded people not to fear, but to respond in faith to his word, character and power (Exodus 14:13–14; 2 Kings 6:16–17; 2 Chronicles 20:15–17).

Secondly, courage requires that we *draw upon an inner strength*. Courage comes from within. Before we ever do or say anything courageous, it begins as an inward attitude. We are to *be* courageous. Moses commanded Joshua to *be* strong and courageous (Deuteronomy 31:6; Joshua 1:6). In turn, Joshua commanded some of his leaders to do likewise (Joshua 10:25; 23:6), as did David to Solomon (1 Chronicles 22:13; cf. 28:20),

---

21 Bruce Hills, *Fearproof* (Brisbane, QLD: CHI-Books, 2015), 4.

and Hezekiah to his military leaders when surrounded by the Babylonians (2 Chronicles 32:7).

In some versions of Scripture, one of the Greek words sometimes translated as 'courage' is rendered 'take heart'. It is used in the sense of *responding to a given circumstance with an inward attitude of confidence, trust and faith*. For example, the Lord told the woman who'd been hemorrhaging blood for 12 years to *"take heart"* because her faith had brought healing (Luke 8:48). On the night of his betrayal, Jesus warned the disciples of the trouble ahead, but, he said, *"...take heart. I have overcome the world"* (John 16:33). After Paul's encounter with the partisan Sanhedrin, the Lord appeared to him and said, *"Take courage! As you have testified about me in Jerusalem, so you must also testify in Rome"* (Acts 23:11). After receiving an angelic visit and assurance, Paul spoke to the sailors, soldiers and slaves on board his storm-ravaged vessel that they should *"...keep up* [their] *courage"* because none of them would be lost (Acts 27:22).

Because we have the Holy Spirit and God's Word in our hearts, we can draw strength from the Spirit's indwelling presence (Ephesians 3:16) and the power of Scripture (Hebrews 4:12). Added to these two dynamic forces are our own reserves of tenacity, will power and resolve. By the combination of both, we can *'take heart'*, *'take courage'* and *'be strong and courageous'*. With this in mind, we need to remind ourselves of the Lord's words to Gideon to *"...go in the strength you* ***have****..."* (Judges 6:14, emphasis mine).

Thirdly, on the basis of subduing fear, and drawing inward strength from the Lord and within, courage also requires *bold or obedient action*. Moses' parents courageously *hid* him for three months because *'...they were not afraid of the king's edict'* (Hebrews 11:23). As an adult, Moses courageously *led* the Israelites out of Egypt *'...not fearing the king's anger'* (Hebrews

11:27). Caleb courageously declared that, with God's help, he would *drive out* the Anakites from the land allotted to him (Joshua 14:12). Jonathan and his armor-bearer courageously *fought* the Philistines (1 Samuel 14:6; 13-14).[22]

Courage isn't really authenticated until it is demonstrated by courageous actions.

Likewise, there comes a point when every leader needs to boldly step out, step up, speak out and courageously lead–no matter what the cost. Courage isn't really authenticated until it is demonstrated by courageous actions. Subduing fear, inwardly drawing strength, combined with bold or obedient actions equals biblical courage.

The Challenge

If we don't make this choice to pay the price, we have already chosen, by default, to be a mediocre leader. Let's not settle for mediocrity and be an ordinary leader who only does what's expected or required; instead, let's rise to the challenge of extraordinary, visionary, courageous and compelling leadership. This is a choice–a choice to pay the price to be what God has called us to be.

Someone that, to me, embodies the message of this chapter to pay the price is another extraordinary missionary, John Patton (1824-1907). After serving for ten years as a city missionary with the Glasgow City Mission, John Patton heard that the Reformed Presbyterian Church of Scotland had been advertising for two years for missionaries to go to the islands of the New Hebrides–the modern day South Pacific nation of Vanuatu–to join one of their serving missionaries there. No-one responded, mainly because the previous people that were sent had been eaten by cannibals. Compelled by what he called the

22 For other examples of courage see Nehemiah 6:11; Daniel 3:16–17, Acts 4:13; 20.

'wailing of the perishing Heathen in the South Seas'[23], John made himself available and was formally accepted, subject to the normal preparatory processes.

While he was preparing for his mission's service, word began to spread of his decision. John Patton wrote that '...nearly all were dead against the proposal.'[24] One elderly man tried to deter him with the argument, 'The cannibals! You will be eaten by cannibals!' Patton replied, 'Mr Dickson, you are advanced in years now, and your prospect is soon to be laid in the grave, there to be eaten by worms; I confess to you, that if I can live and die serving and honouring the Lord Jesus, it will make no difference to me whether I am eaten by cannibals or by worms; and in the Great Day my resurrection body will arise as yours in the likeness of our risen Redeemer.'[25]

The important thing to John Patton was not how he died, but how he *lived*. Whether he lived or died on the mission field, he was determined to serve and honour Jesus with everything within him. He was prepared to pay the price.

On December 1857, aged just 33, John Patton set sail for the New Hebrides. On 30th August 1858, he came ashore on the island of Aneityum (also known as Anatom or Keamu), the southernmost island, where he began his first years of service. Enduring dangers, death threats, profound personal tragedies and debilitating bouts of sickness, John Patton went on to have decades of effective and fruitful service–at great personal cost.

John Patton, CT Studd, William Booth and thousands of other biblical, historical and contemporary leaders leave us an enduring example of the necessity to pay the price to be a leader worth following.

---

23 John G Paton, '*Missionary to the New Hebrides: An autobiography*' (Fearn, UK: Christian Focus, 2009), 43.
24 ibid, 43
25 ibid, 44

CONCLUSION

Self-leadership is the foundational level of Christian leadership. Before we can effectively lead our families, others, or churches and ministries, we need to be able to lead ourselves.

In this book, self-leadership was defined as 'the intentional practice of disciplining, regulating and developing our lives and leadership so we can effectively lead ourselves and others to fulfill God's ultimate purposes of maturity and mission.'

In the introduction I underlined the importance of our leadership being an expression and extension of all that we are within. Our leadership should flow from the inside out, rather than top down. I warned against the danger of having duplicitous and hypocritical lives in which we are one thing in public, but quite another in private. Any incongruity or disparity between our public and private lives will undermine and discredit our leadership, whereas an eclipse of the two will foster credibility and follow-ability.

To understand self-leadership, I proposed five inter-related and integrated refractions of self-leadership, that each formed the sections of the book.

The first component of self-leadership we explored was *self-awareness*. Using Paul's letters to Timothy, we overviewed twelve areas from Timothy's life in which we need to be self-aware. We underscored the importance of knowing ourselves by reflecting on who has and is shaping us, where we've come from and where we're going, our strengths and weakness, and what the Lord has done and is doing in our lives. Self-awareness is important because it helps us to understand ourselves, who we are, where we're at in our leadership journey, and how we can effectively interact with others.

A second aspect of self-leadership we examined was *self-discipline*. We observed four representative areas in which leaders need personal discipline: pursuing their God-given vision; management of time; stewardship of finances; and the exercise of their spiritual disciplines. The overriding theme of this section was that self-leadership necessitates leaders to be personally disciplined.

Drilling deeper into the topic of self-leadership we covered a third facet of self-leadership, which was being *self-controlled*. We defined this as a leader's capacity for self-regulation. Self-control, we noted, was one of the biblical qualities of leadership and one of the fruit of the Holy Spirit. As such, God's Spirit can empower a leader to *be* self-controlled in and over their lives. Each chapter in this section addressed one specific area in which a leader requires self-control; namely, our temper, responding to criticism, words, self-talk, thought-life, sexual desires, living above reproach and managing stress. This section asked the questions: Who or what is controlling my life? Is it God's Holy Spirit or my own impulses and desires? To lead ourselves requires rigorous self-control that relies on the indispensable combination of the Spirit's power and our will power.

Coming to an intensely practical section, our fourth focus on self-leadership was the all-important area of *self-development*. We explored and applied ten interconnected areas of our lives that require personal development. Flowing from the spiritual, we covered the physical, intellectual, emotional, social, marital, parental, financial, vocational and recreational. In each one, I suggested numerous practical instructions and applications. These chapters emphasized how imperative it is to develop holistically.

Finally, our journey finished with a look at a fifth element of self-leadership, which is *self-sacrifice*. Self-sacrifice is another way of saying 'paying the price'. If we are to be effective leaders, then we must be prepared to pay whatever cost is necessary to be what God has called us to be and do what God has called us to do. I proposed five components of self-sacrifice, which are: self-denial; making sacrifices; total surrender; enduring hardship; and exercising courage. This chapter is the most confronting because it brings us face to face with ourselves and the probing question: 'Am I prepared to count the cost to be a leader worth following?'

Toward the end of his second letter, Paul charged Timothy to be an extraordinary preacher, leader and minister:

> *'...continue in what you have learned and have become convinced of... Preach the word; be prepared in season and out of season; correct, rebuke and encourage–with great patience and careful instruction.... ...keep your head in all situations, endure hardship, do the work of an evangelist, discharge all the duties of your ministry'* (2 Timothy 3:14–4:5).

To me, if I was to paraphrase these words to a new generation of younger leaders, I'd be saying, 'Timothy [insert your name], remember what godly people and great leaders have shown you in the past. Give attention to your growth and development. Never allow fear or intimidation to hold you back from preaching truth. Endeavour to do so persuasively, not brashly, and patiently, not presumptuously. Stay calm, retain your God-given peace and hold your ground in difficult times. Be completely gospel-centered. Preach Jesus! Be diligent, conscientious, dutiful, faithful and thorough in doing what's in your hand to do.'

If I could encapsulate the key themes throughout this book, I'd say this: Work on yourself. Be intentional in everything you do. Get your life together. No-one else can do it for you; it's up to you. Be real, authentic and transparent. Make the right choices and God will strengthen you with his power. Find the right people and they'll help you. Look within and summon the will power and resolve to be a great leader. Make wise and courageous decisions. Love and serve God, love and lead people, and love and embrace life.

Above everything, remember that, in serving God as a leader, it's not about your popularity, power, prominence or position, but who you *are*. Effective and influential leadership flows from within. Therefore, I encourage you with every fiber of my being to lead from the inside out.

BIBLIOGRAPHY

Adamson, James B., *The Epistle of James* (The New International Commentary of the New Testament), Grand Rapids, MI: Eerdmans, 2000.

Banks, Robert, *The Tyranny of Time*, Homebush West, NSW: Lancer, 1983.

Barna, George, *The Power of Vision*, Ventura, CA: Regal, 1992.

Carson, D.A., *Jesus' Sermon on the Mount*, Grand Rapids, MI: Baker, 2001.

Chand, Sam, *Leadership Pain*, Nashville, TN: Thomas Nelson, 2015.

Clinton, Robert J. & Stanley, Paul D., *Connecting: The Mentoring Relationships You Need to Succeed in Life*, Colorado Springs, CO: Navpress, 1992.

Conner, Kevin, *Tithes and Offerings: Christian Stewardship in Old & New Testaments,* Melbourne, Victoria: KJC Publications, 1993.

Conner, Mark, *'Time Management Tips'*, *Leadership Now Magazine*, July, 2000.

D'Souza, Anthony, *Leadership*, Nagasandra, India: Better Yourself Books, 1985.

Flanagan, Neil & Finger, Jarvis, *Just About Everything A Manager Needs To Know*, Brisbane, QLD: Plum, 1998.

Foster, Richard, *Money, Sex & Power*, London, England: Hodder and Stoughton, Third impression, 1990.

Grubb, Norman, *C.T.Studd: Cricketer & Pioneer*, Fort Washington, PA: CLC Publications, 2014.

Haggai, John, *Lead On*, Waco, TX: Word, 1987.

MacDonald, Gordon, *Ordering Your Private World*, Surrey, UK: Highland, 1993.

Mackenzie, Alec, *The Time Trap*, New York, NY: Amacom, 1990.

Mallison, John, *Mentoring to Develop Disciples & Leaders*, Lidcombe, NSW: Scripture Union, 1998.

Malphurs, Aubrey, *Being Leaders*, Grand Rapids, MI: Baker, 2003.

Maxwell, John, *Developing the Leader Within You*, Nashville, TN: Thomas Nelson, 1993.

Monroe, Myles, *The Spirit of Leadership*, New Kensington, PA: Whitaker, 2005.

Moo, Douglas J., *The Letter of James: An Introduction and Commentary,* (Tyndale New Testament Commentaries), Leicester, England: Inter-Varsity, 1993.

Motyer, Alec, *The Message of James*, Bible Speaks Today (New Testament Editor: John R.W. Stott), Leicester, England: Inter-Varsity, 1997.

Oswalt, John N., *The Book of Isaiah Chapters 40-66,* The New International Commentary of the Old Testament. Grand Rapids, MI: Eerdmans, 1998.

Pack, Karen, *The Single Strife: Nurturing Wholeness in the Lives of Single Christians*, Unpublished essay, Vancouver, BC: Regent College, 2009.

Patton, John, *John G. Patton, Missionary to the New Hebrides: An Autobiography*, Fearn, UK: Christian Focus, 2009.

Piper, John, *What Jesus Demands From The World,* Wheaton, IL: Crossway, 2011.

Richards, Lawrence O., *Expository Dictionary of Bible Words*, Grand Rapids, MI: Zondervan, 1990.

Sanders, J Oswald, *A Spiritual Clinic*, Chicago: Moody Press, 1961.

Stanley, Andy, *The Next Generation Leader*, Colorado Springs, CO: Multnomah, 2003.

Stanley, Andy, *Visioneering: God's Blueprint for Developing and Maintaining Vision*, Colorado Springs, CO: Multnomah, 1999.

Stott, John R.W., *New Issues Facing Christians Today*, London, England: HarperCollins, 1999.

Stott, John R.W., *The Message of Romans*, Bible Speaks Today (General Editor NT, John R.W. Stott), Leicester, England: Inter-Varsity, 1996.

Stott, John R.W., *The Message of The Sermon on the Mount*, Bible Speaks Today (General Editor NT, John R.W. Stott), Leicester, England: Inter-Varsity, 1996.

Stott, John R.W., *The Message of 1 Timothy & Titus*, Bible Speaks Today (General Editor NT, John R.W. Stott), Leicester, England: Inter-Varsity, 1996.

Stott, John R.W., *The Message of 2 Timothy*, Bible Speaks Today (General Editor NT, John R.W. Stott), Leicester, England: Inter-Varsity, 1997.

Taylor, Cedric & Goldsworthy, Graeme, *Battle Guide for Christian Leaders–an Endangered Species*, Cudgen, NSW: Wellcare Publications, 1981.

Toon, Peter, *Meditating as a Christian,* London, England: Collins, 1991.

Towner, Philip H., *The Letters to Timothy and Titus,* New International Commentary on the New Testament, Grand Rapids, MI: Eerdmans, 2006.

Warren, Rick, *Purpose Driven Life*, Grand Rapids, MI: Zondervan, 2002.

Williams, David. *Paul's Metaphors*. Peabody, MA: Hendrickson, 1999.

ABOUT THE AUTHOR

Pastor Bruce Hills (B Min, MA Theo)

Bruce has been in Christian ministry since 1984 and brings a wealth of experience and wisdom. He is known and respected around Australia for his prophetic and insightful preaching. One well-known Christian leader in Asia described him as having the 'precision of a teacher, but the fire of a prophet'. Bruce frequently travels to many nations speaking at seminars and conferences. For nine years (2000-2009) Bruce pastored one of Australia's largest Pentecostal churches. He now serves as International Director for World Outreach International, a mission agency with a vision for least reached people groups.

Bruce has authored two books, *Praying with Power - How to Engage in a Deeper Level of Personal Prayer by Praying the Scriptures and Fearproof - How to Overcome the Paralyzing Power of Fear* - exploring the *'do not fear'* statements of the Old Testament. Bruce has been married to Fiona since 1983 and has three grown children and one granddaughter. They live in Melbourne, Australia.

Visit www.world-outreach.com for more information on the author.

www.ingramcontent.com/pod-product-compliance
Lightning Source LLC
Chambersburg PA
CBHW060246100426
42742CB00011B/1658
* 9 7 8 0 6 4 8 0 1 1 6 0 6 *